Windows Server 2012 Automation with PowerShell Cookbook

Over 110 recipes to automate Windows Server
administrative tasks by using PowerShell

Ed Goad

BIRMINGHAM - MUMBAI

Windows Server 2012 Automation with PowerShell Cookbook

First published: March 2013

Production Reference: 1150313

Published by Packt Publishing Ltd.
Livery Place
35 Livery Street
Birmingham B3 2PB, UK.

ISBN 978-1-84968-946-5

www.packtpub.com

Cover Image by Abhishek Pandey (abhishek.pandey1210@gmail.com)

Credits

Author
Ed Goad

Reviewers
Anderson Patricio
Donabel Santos

Acquisition Editor
Kevin Colaco

Commissioning Editor
Shreerang Deshpande

Lead Technical Editor
Azharuddin Sheikh

Technical Editors
Ankita Meshram
Kirti Pujari
Varun Pius Rodrigues

Project Coordinator
Anugya Khurana

Proofreaders
Mario Cecere
Dirk Manuel

Indexer
Hemangini Bari

Graphics
Valentina D'silva

Production Coordinator
Conidon Miranda

Cover Work
Conidon Miranda

About the Author

Ed Goad is a Systems Architect who has been working in various roles in the IT field for 16 years. He first became interested in scripting and automation when presented with the task to uninstall software from over 1,000 systems with limited time and resources. He has worked with scripting and automation on multiple platforms and languages including PowerShell, VBscript, C#, and BASH scripting.

Ed currently holds multiple Microsoft certifications, most recently including the Microsoft Certified IT Professional—Enterprise Administrator. Additional non-Microsoft certifications include VMware Certified Professional (VCP), Red Hat Certified System Administrator (RHCSA), EMC Proven Professional, Brocade Certified Network Engineer (BCNE), and Cisco Certified Network Associate (CCNA).

Ed is currently on sabbatical, and is volunteering full time at the Amor Fe y Esperanza school in Honduras (`http://www.afehonduras.org`). There he is teaching computer and math classes to children who live and work in the garbage dump outside of the capital city of Tegucigalpa.

I would like to thank my parents for always encouraging me when I was younger by telling me that I could be anything that I wanted, as long as I had good math skills. They bought our first computer before I even started school, and then let me break it and repair it over and over, driving my interest in computers.

I want to thank my wife for loving me and encouraging me to grow and be more than I was. Without her love and encouragement my life wouldn't be nearly as full as it is now.

And lastly, I would like to thank God for his blessings and the opportunities he has given me. As much as I have learned and accomplished, it is nothing compared to knowing his love.

About the Reviewers

Anderson Patricio is an Exchange Server MVP and a Messaging consultant based in Toronto, Canada, designing and deploying solutions in clients located in North and South America. He has been working with Exchange since Version 5 and has had the opportunity to use PowerShell since its beta release (code name Monad at that time).

Anderson contributes to the Microsoft communities in several ways. In English, his blog www.andersonpatricio.ca is updated regularly with content for Exchange, PowerShell, and Microsoft in general. In Portuguese, he has an Exchange resource site (www.andersonpatricio.org). He is also a TechEd presenter in South America and also the creator of a couple of Exchange trainings in the Brazilian Microsoft Virtual Academy (MVA).

You can follow him on Twitter at http://twitter.com/apatricio.

He is the reviewer of several books such as *Windows Powershell in Action* by Bruce Payette, *PowerShell in Practice* by Richard Siddaway, and *Microsoft Exchange 2010 PowerShell Cookbook* by Mike Pfeiffer.

Donabel Santos is a SQL Server MVP and is the senior SQL Server Developer/DBA/Trainer at QueryWorks Solutions, a consulting and training company in Vancouver, BC. She has worked with SQL Server since Version 2000 on numerous development, tuning, reporting, and integration projects with ERPs, CRMs, SharePoint, and other custom applications. She holds MCITP certifications for SQL Server 2005/2008, and an MCTS for SharePoint. She is a Microsoft Certified Trainer (MCT), and is also the lead instructor for SQL Server Administration, Development, Tableau, and SSIS courses at the British Columbia Institute of Technology (BCIT). Donabel is a proud member of PASS (Professional Association of SQL Server), and a proud BCIT alumna (CST diploma and degree).

Donabel blogs (www.sqlmusings.com), tweets (@sqlbelle), speaks and presents (SQLSaturday, VANPASS, Vancouver TechFest, and many more), trains (BCIT, QueryWorks Solutions), and writes (Packt, Idera, SSWUG, and so on). She is the author of Packt's SQL Server 2012 with PowerShell V3 Cookbook, and a contributing author of Manning's PowerShell Deep Dives.

Thank you Eric, for all the support and love. Thank you for cooking the delicious dinners that invigorate me after a long day's work. You are my home.

Thank you to my family—Papa, Mama, JR, RR, Lisa—you all give me strength and I am very blessed to have you in my life. Special shout out to my Tito Boy, who proudly told people in his network about my first book – thank you Tito Boy.

Thank you to my BCIT family—Kevin Cudihee, Elsie Au, Joanne Atha, Charlie Blattler, Paul Mills, Bob Langelaan, Benjamin Yu, Brian Pidcock, Albert Wei and so many others—to all of my mentors, colleagues, and students, who never fail to inspire me to do better, be better. It's been a great ten years teaching at BCIT—and I look forward to a lot more wonderful years of learning, inspiring, and sharing.

Special thanks to the Microsoft team and Microsoft communities, especially #sqlfamily. You guys are awesome and so many of you continuously and selflessly share your knowledge and expertise to a lot of people. I've been on the receiving end so many times, and I hope I can continue to pay it forward. I am so proud to be part of this community.

Thank you to the PowerShell community, for the awesome blogs, books, and tweets, which immensely helped folks to learn, understand, and get excited about PowerShell.

Most importantly, thank you Lord, for all the miracles and blessings in my life.

---

www.PacktPub.com

Support files, eBooks, discount offers and more

You might want to visit www.PacktPub.com for support files and downloads related to your book.

Did you know that Packt offers eBook versions of every book published, with PDF and ePub files available? You can upgrade to the eBook version at www.PacktPub.com and as a print book customer, you are entitled to a discount on the eBook copy. Get in touch with us at service@packtpub.com for more details.

At www.PacktPub.com, you can also read a collection of free technical articles, sign up for a range of free newsletters, and receive exclusive discounts and offers on Packt books and eBooks.

http://PacktLib.PacktPub.com

Do you need instant solutions to your IT questions? PacktLib is Packt's online digital book library. Here, you can access, read and search across Packt's entire library of books.

Why Subscribe?

- ▶ Fully searchable across every book published by Packt
- ▶ Copy and paste, print and bookmark content
- ▶ On demand and accessible via web browser

Free Access for Packt account holders

If you have an account with Packt at www.PacktPub.com, you can use this to access PacktLib today and view nine entirely free books. Simply use your login credentials for immediate access.

Instant Updates on New Packt Books

Get notified! Find out when new books are published by following @PacktEnterprise on Twitter, or the *Packt Enterprise* Facebook page.

Table of Contents

Preface

Automating server tasks allows administrators to repeatedly perform the same, or similar, tasks over and over again. With PowerShell scripts, you can automate server tasks and reduce manual input, allowing you to focus on more important tasks.

Windows Server 2012 Automation with PowerShell will show several ways for a Windows administrator to automate and streamline his/her job. Learn how to automate server tasks to ease your day-to-day operations, generate performance and configuration reports, and troubleshoot and resolve critical problems.

Windows Server 2012 Automation with PowerShell will introduce you to the advantages of using Windows Server 2012 and PowerShell. Each recipe is a building block that can easily be combined to provide larger and more useful scripts to automate your systems. The recipes are packed with examples and real world experience to make the job of managing and administrating Windows servers easier.

The book begins with automation of common Windows Networking components such as AD, DHCP, DNS, and PKI, managing Hyper-V, and backing up the server environment. By the end of the book you will be able to use PowerShell scripts to automate tasks such as performance monitoring, reporting, analyzing the environment to match best practices, and troubleshooting.

What this book covers

Chapter 1, Understanding PowerShell Scripting, explains how to use basic PowerShell features such as functions, cmdlets, modules, and loops. These are the basic building blocks of PowerShell that are used repeatedly and in various forms.

Chapter 2, Managing Windows Network Services with PowerShell, covers the installation and configuration of Active Directory, DNS, DHCP, and Certificate Services. This chapter should cover everything necessary to prepare an environment as a fully functioning Active Directory domain for use in labs or new domain build-outs.

Chapter 3, Managing IIS with PowerShell, covers how to install, configure, manage, and maintain IIS websites on Windows Server 8. In addition to basic management of IIS, this will also cover monitoring and reporting of IIS, using NLB for load balancing, and utilizing a dev/staging/prod configuration/promotion scheme. This chapter should cover everything necessary to set up and configure a load-balanced dev/test/prod web environment and automate code promotion.

Chapter 4, Managing Hyper-V with PowerShell, covers installing, configuring, and managing Hyper-V servers and guest OSs. In addition to basic management of Hyper-V, this chapter also covers how to automate the deployment and management of guest VMs, managing VM snapshots, migrate VMs between hosts and prepare a host for maintenance, and how to utilize clustering to make highly-available VMs. This chapter should cover everything necessary to set up and manage an enterprise Hyper-V farm, including reporting, performing maintenance, and monitoring performance.

Chapter 5, Managing Storage with PowerShell, covers how to configure and manage storage using traditional disk, storage pools, reduplication, and SANs.

Chapter 6, Managing Network Shares with PowerShell, covers creating, managing, securing, and using CIFS, NFS, and iSCSI shares. This chapter will also cover how to use server clustering to create highly available network shares, managing replication, and configuring BranchCache.

Chapter 7, Managing Windows Updates with PowerShell, This chapter details the installation and configuration of WSUS as well as the Windows Update client. Additionally, this chapter will include methods to report on installed updates and to automate update installation.

Chapter 8, Managing Printers with PowerShell, covers creation, managing, and updating of printers on print servers. This will also include using PowerShell to map clients to printers and using Windows Clustering to make highly available print servers.

Chapter 9, Troubleshooting Servers with PowerShell, covers utilization of PowerShell troubleshooting packs, Windows Best Practice Analyzers, and using Windows Event Logs. This will also include basic monitoring and configuration of services as well as creating a central Event Log server.

Chapter 10, Managing Performance with PowerShell, shows how to use PowerShell to track and report on historical performance and identify bottlenecks. This chapter will also show how to integrate PowerShell objects with Excel to create usable performance reports and graphs.

Chapter 11, Inventorying Servers with PowerShell, explains how to inventory the hardware and software configurations of Windows 8 servers and create a detailed inventory and configuration report. Additionally, this chapter will cover methods to track configuration changes over time and export the configuration report via Word. This chapter should cover everything necessary to create a centralized hardware and software inventory of all servers in the enterprise.

Chapter 12, Server Backup, covers setting up and scheduling backups on a Windows server. This will include on-demand backups, restoring files, and Windows components, and standardizing the configuration amongst systems.

What you need for this book

To make efficient use of this book, you will need Windows Server 2012 and Microsoft Office to perform code testing and practically implement the recipes mentioned in the book.

Who this book is for

This book is written to assist the daily tasks for systems administrators, engineers, and architects working with Windows Server 2012.

Conventions

In this book, you will find a number of styles of text that distinguish between different kinds of information. Here are some examples of these styles, and an explanation of their meaning.

Code words in text are shown as follows: "The installer is a fairly simple class, similar to the cmdlet class, which inherits the PSSnapin class and contains overrides that return information about the cmdlet."

A block of code is set as follows:

```
Function Multiply-Numbers
{
    Param($FirstNum, $SecNum)
    Try
    {
        Write-Host ($FirstNum * $SecNum)
    }
    Catch
    {
        Write-Host "Error in function, present two numbers to
multiply"
    }
}
```

When we wish to draw your attention to a particular part of a code block, the relevant lines or items are set in bold:

```
Write-Host "Static Size:`t`t" ("{0:0000000000.00}" -f $jenny)
Write-Host "Literal String:`t`t" ("{0:000' Hello '000}" -f $jenny)
Write-Host "Phone Number:`t`t" ("{0:# (###) ### - ####}" -f
($jenny*10000))
```

Any command-line input or output is written as follows:

```
Block-SmbShareAccess -Name Share2 -AccountName CORP\joe.smith `
-Confirm:$false
```

New terms and **important words** are shown in bold. Words that you see on the screen, in menus or dialog boxes for example, appear in the text like this: "clicking the **Next** button moves you to the next screen".

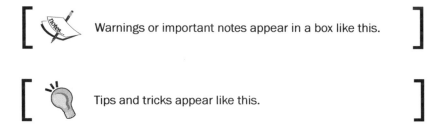

Warnings or important notes appear in a box like this.

Tips and tricks appear like this.

Reader feedback

Feedback from our readers is always welcome. Let us know what you think about this book—what you liked or may have disliked. Reader feedback is important for us to develop titles that you really get the most out of.

To send us general feedback, simply send an e-mail to feedback@packtpub.com, and mention the book title via the subject of your message.

If there is a topic that you have expertise in and you are interested in either writing or contributing to a book, see our author guide on www.packtpub.com/authors.

Customer support

Now that you are the proud owner of a Packt book, we have a number of things to help you to get the most from your purchase.

Errata

Although we have taken every care to ensure the accuracy of our content, mistakes do happen. If you find a mistake in one of our books—maybe a mistake in the text or the code—we would be grateful if you would report this to us. By doing so, you can save other readers from frustration and help us improve subsequent versions of this book. If you find any errata, please report them by visiting http://www.packtpub.com/submit-errata, selecting your book, clicking on the **errata submission form** link, and entering the details of your errata. Once your errata are verified, your submission will be accepted and the errata will be uploaded on our website, or added to any list of existing errata, under the Errata section of that title. Any existing errata can be viewed by selecting your title from http://www.packtpub.com/support.

Piracy

Piracy of copyright material on the Internet is an ongoing problem across all media. At Packt, we take the protection of our copyright and licenses very seriously. If you come across any illegal copies of our works, in any form, on the Internet, please provide us with the location address or website name immediately so that we can pursue a remedy.

Please contact us at copyright@packtpub.com with a link to the suspected pirated material.

We appreciate your help in protecting our authors, and our ability to bring you valuable content.

Questions

You can contact us at questions@packtpub.com if you are having a problem with any aspect of the book, and we will do our best to address it.

1
Understanding PowerShell Scripting

In this chapter we will cover the following recipes:

- ▶ Managing security on PowerShell scripts
- ▶ Creating and using functions
- ▶ Creating and using modules
- ▶ Creating and using PowerShell profiles
- ▶ Passing variables to functions
- ▶ Validating parameters in functions
- ▶ Piping data to functions
- ▶ Recording sessions with transcripts
- ▶ Signing PowerShell scripts
- ▶ Sending e-mail
- ▶ Sorting and filtering
- ▶ Using formatting to export numbers
- ▶ Using formatting to export data views
- ▶ Using jobs
- ▶ Dealing with errors in PowerShell
- ▶ Tuning PowerShell scripts for performance
- ▶ Creating and using Cmdlets

Introduction

This chapter covers the basics related to scripting with PowerShell. PowerShell was released in 2006 and is installed by default starting with Windows 7 and Server 2008R2. PowerShell is also available as a download for Windows XP, Windows Vista, and Server 2003. One of the main differences between PowerShell and VBScript/JScript, the other primary scripting languages for Windows, is that PowerShell provides an interactive runtime. This runtime allows a user to execute commands in real time, and then save these commands as scripts, functions, or modules to be used later.

Since its introduction, support for PowerShell has increased dramatically. In addition to managing Windows environments, Microsoft quickly created snap-ins for additional applications such as Exchange Server, the System Center suite, and clustering. Additional vendors have also created snap-ins for PowerShell, with some of the most popular being VMware and NetApp.

Many of the recipes presented here are the building blocks commonly used in PowerShell such as signing scripts, using parameters, and sorting/filtering data.

Managing security on PowerShell scripts

Due to the powerful capabilities of PowerShell, maintaining a secure environment is important. Executing scripts from untrustworthy sources could damage data on your system and possibly spread viruses or other malicious code. To deal with this threat, Microsoft has implemented **Execution Policies** to limit what scripts can do.

 The execution policies only limit what can be performed by scripts, modules, and profiles, these policies do not limit what commands are executed in the interactive runtime.

How to do it...

In this recipe, we will view the system's current execution policy and change it to suit various needs. To do this, carry out the following steps:

1. To find the system's current execution policy, open PowerShell and execute `Get-ExecutionPolicy`.

```
PS C:\> Get-ExecutionPolicy
Restricted
```

2. To change the system's execution policy, run `Set-ExecutionPolicy <policy name>` command.

```
PS C:\> Set-ExecutionPolicy AllSigned

PS C:\> Get-ExecutionPolicy
AllSigned
```

3. To reset the execution policy to the system default, set the policy to `Undefined`.

```
PS C:\> Set-ExecutionPolicy Undefined

PS C:\> Get-ExecutionPolicy
Restricted
```

4. To change the execution policy for a specific session, go to **Start | Run** and enter `PowerShell.exe -ExecutionPolicy <policy name>`.

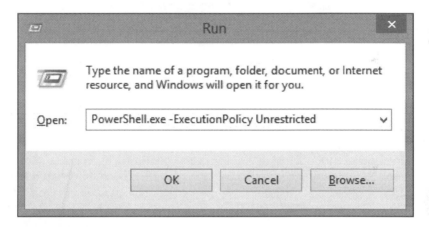

How it works...

When a script is executed, the first thing PowerShell does is, determine the system's execution policy. By default, this is set to **Restricted**, which blocks all the PowerShell scripts from running. If the policy allows signed scripts, it analyzes the script to confirm it is signed and that the signature is from a trusted publisher. If the policy is set to unrestricted, then all the scripts run without performing checking.

Setting the execution policy is simply done via the command. Here we see several examples of viewing and setting the execution policy to various settings. There are six execution policies as follows:

- **Restricted**: No scripts are executed. This is the default setting.
- **AllSigned**: This policy allows scripts signed by a trusted publisher to run.
- **RemoteSigned**: This policy requires remote scripts to be signed by a trusted publisher.
- **Unrestricted**: This policy allows all scripts to run. It will still prompt for confirmation for files downloaded from the internet.
- **Bypass**: This policy allows all scripts to run and will not prompt.
- **Undefined**: This policy resets the policy to the default.

When changing the execution policy, you will be prompted via a command line or pop-up window to confirm the change. This is another level of security, but can be disabled by using the **–Force** switch.

There's more...

- Approving publishers: When running scripts from new publishers, there are two primary methods for approving them. The first method is to open the certificates MMC on the local computer and import the signer's CA into the **Trusted Publishers** store. This can be done manually or via a group policy. The second method is to execute the script, and when prompted, approve the publisher.

- Defining execution policy via GPO: The execution policy for individual computers, groups, or enterprise can be controlled centrally using group policies. The policy is stored under **Computer Configuration | Policies | Administrative Templates | Windows Components | Windows PowerShell**. Note however that this policy only applies to Windows 7/2008 or newer operating systems.

- Permissions to change the execution policy: Changing the execution policy is a system-wide change, and as such requires administrator level permissions. With Windows default access controls in place, this also requires you to start PowerShell as an administrator.

  Changing the execution policy requires elevated permissions to run, so you may need to open PowerShell with **Run as administrator** to set the policy. If you are attempting to change the policy without sufficient permission, an error will be returned.

```
Windows PowerShell                                      –  □  ×

PS C:\> Set-ExecutionPolicy RemoteSigned

Execution Policy Change
The execution policy helps protect you from scripts that you do not trust.
Changing the execution policy might expose you to the security risks described
in the about_Execution_Policies help topic at
http://go.microsoft.com/fwlink/?LinkID=135170. Do you want to change the
execution policy?
[Y] Yes  [N] No  [S] Suspend  [?] Help (default is "Y"): y
Set-ExecutionPolicy : Access to the registry key 'HKEY_LOCAL_MACHINE\SOFTWARE\M
icrosoft\PowerShell\1\ShellIds\Microsoft.PowerShell' is denied.
At line:1 char:1
+ Set-ExecutionPolicy RemoteSigned
+ ~~~~~~~~~~~~~~~~~~~~~~~~~~~~~~~~~~
    + CategoryInfo          : NotSpecified: (:) [Set-ExecutionPolicy], Unautho
   rizedAccessException
    + FullyQualifiedErrorId : System.UnauthorizedAccessException,Microsoft.Pow
   erShell.Commands.SetExecutionPolicyCommand

PS C:\> _
```

 Best practice is to enforce some level of signature checking in most environments. In Dev/Test environments, it may be common to set the policy to **Unrestricted** to expedite testing, but it is always suggested to require fully signed scripts in production environments.

Creating and using functions

Functions could be considered one of the cornerstones of PowerShell scripting. Functions allow for individual commands or groups of commands and variables to be packaged into a single unit. These units are reusable and can then be accessed similar to native commands and Cmdlets, and are used to perform larger and more specific tasks.

Unlike Cmdlets, which are precompiled, functions are interpreted at runtime. This increases the runtime by a small amount (due to the code being interpreted by the runtime when executed), but its performance impact is often outweighed by the flexibility that the scripted language provides. Because of this, functions can be created without any special tools, then debugged, and modified as needed.

Let's say we are preparing for Christmas. We have made a large list of things to complete before the Christmas morning—wrap the presents, decorate the tree, bake cookies, and so on. Now that we have our list, we need to know how long we have until Christmas morning. In this way, we can prioritize the different tasks and know which ones can wait until later.

We could use something simple like a calendar, but being PowerShell experts, we have decided to use PowerShell to tell us how many days there are until Christmas.

How to do it...

Carry out the following steps:

1. We start by identifying the necessary PowerShell commands to determine the number of days until Christmas.

```
PS C:\> $Christmas=Get-Date("12/25/" + (Get-Date).Year.ToString() + " 7:00 AM")

PS C:\> $Today = (Get-Date)

PS C:\> $TimeTilChristmas = $Christmas - $Today

PS C:\> Write-Host $TimeTilChristmas.Days " Days 'til Christmas"
94  Days 'til Christmas

PS C:\> |
```

2. Next, we combine the commands into a function:

```
Function Get-DaysTilChristmas
{
<#
    .Synopsis
    This function calculates the number of days until Christmas
    .Description
    This function calculates the number of days until Christmas
    .Example
    DaysTilChristmas
    .Notes
    Ed is really awesome
    .Link
    Http://blog.edgoad.com
  #>
    $Christmas=Get-Date("25 Dec " + (Get-Date).Year.ToString() + "
7:00 AM")
    $Today = (Get-Date)
    $TimeTilChristmas = $Christmas - $Today
    Write-Host $TimeTilChristmas.Days "Days 'til Christmas"
}
```

3. Once the function is created, we either type it or copy/paste it into a PowerShell console.

4. Finally, we simply call the function by the name, Get-DaysTilChristmas.

```
PS C:\temp> Get-DaysTilChristmas
119 Days 'til Christmas

PS C:\temp>
```

How it works...

In the first step, we are attempting to find out how many days until Christmas using the basic PowerShell commands. We begin by using the Get-Date command to calculate the exact date of Christmas and put this into a variable named $Christmas. Actually, we are calculating the date *and* time until 7 a.m. Christmas morning—in this case, the time I plan to begin opening presents.

Next, we execute the Get-Date function without any parameters to return the current date and time into another variable named $Today. We create a third variable named $TimeTilChristmas, and subtract our two dates from each other. Finally, we write out the number of days remaining.

 Note: This assumes that the script is being executed *before* December 25th in the year. If this script is run after the 25th of December, a negative number of days will be returned.

The second step uses exactly the same commands as the first, except with the commands being included in a function. The Function command bundles the code into a reusable package named Get-DaysTilChristmas.

The function is input into PowerShell manually, via copy/paste or other methods. To use the function once it is created, just call it by its name.

At its simplest, a function is composed of the Function keyword, a function name, and commands encapsulated in curly braces.

```
Function FunctionName{
    # commands go here
}
```

The benefit of packaging the code as a function is that now it can be accessed by a name, without having to retype the original commands. Simply running Get-DaysTilChristmas again and again will continue to run the function and return the results.

There's more...

▶ **Function scope**: Custom functions are traditionally limited to the currently active user session. If you create a function such as Get-DaysTilChristmas, and then open a new PowerShell window, the function will not be available in the new session, even though it is still available in the original session. Additionally, if you close your original session, the function will be removed from the memory and won't be available until it is re-entered.

▶ **Variable types**: It may be interesting to note that the variables $Christmas and $Today are of different types than $TimeTilChristmas. The first two are *date and time* variables which refer to a specific point in history (year, month, day, hour, minute, second, millisecond, ticks). $TimeTilChristmas however is a *time span*; which refers to a length of time (day, hour, minute, second, millisecond, ticks), relative to a specific time. The type of a variable can be viewed by typing $<variableName>.GetType() as shown in the following screenshot:

```
PS C:\temp> $Today.GetType()

IsPublic IsSerial Name                                     BaseType
-------- -------- ----                                     --------
True     True     DateTime                                 System.ValueType


PS C:\temp> $TimeTilChristmas.GetType()

IsPublic IsSerial Name                                     BaseType
-------- -------- ----                                     --------
True     True     TimeSpan                                 System.ValueType
```

▶ **Returning content**: This function in its current form returns the number of days until Christmas, but that is all. Because the function uses *date and time* variables, it can easily include the number of hours, minutes, and seconds as well. See Get-Date | Get-Member for a list of properties that can be accessed.

▶ **Naming of functions and commands in PowerShell**: Commands in PowerShell are traditionally named in a verb-noun pair, and for ease of use, a similar process should be used when naming custom functions. You can see in this example, we named the function Get-DaysTilChristmas, the verb Get, tells us that we are getting something. The noun DaysTilChristmas tells us what object we are working with. There are several common verbs such as Get, Connect, Find, and Save that should be used when possible. The noun in the verb-noun pair is often based on the object you are working with or the task you are doing. A full list of verbs for PowerShell can be found by executing Get-Verb.

Creating and using modules

Modules are a way of grouping functions for similar types of tasks or components into a common module. These modules can then be loaded, used, and unloaded together as needed. Modules are similar in concept to libraries in the Windows world—they are used to contain and organize tasks, while allowing them to be added and removed dynamically.

An example of a module is working with the DNS client. When working with the DNS client, you will have various tasks to perform: get configuration, set configuration, resolve hostname, register client, and so on. Because all of these tasks have to do with a common component, the DNS client, they can be logically grouped together into the DNSClient module. We can then view the commands included in the module using Get-Command -Module DnsClient as shown in the following screenshot:

```
PS C:\> Get-Command -Module DnsClient

CommandType     Name                             ModuleName
-----------     ----                             ----------
Function        Add-DnsClientNrptRule            DnsClient
Function        Clear-DnsClientCache             DnsClient
Function        Get-DnsClient                    DnsClient
Function        Get-DnsClientCache               DnsClient
Function        Get-DnsClientGlobalSetting       DnsClient
Function        Get-DnsClientNrptGlobal          DnsClient
```

Here we will show how to create a module for containing common functions that can be loaded as a unit. Because modules typically group several functions together, we will start off by creating multiple functions.

For our recipe, we will be creating a module named Hello. In this example, we have created two simple "Hello World" type functions. The first simply replies "Hello World!", while the second takes a name as a variable and replies "Hello *name*".

How to do it...

Carry out the following steps:

1. Create several functions that can be logically grouped together.

    ```
    Function Get-Hello
    {
        Write-Host "Hello World!"
    }
    Function Get-Hello2
    {
        Param($name)
        Write-Host "Hello $name"
    }
    ```

2. Using the PowerShell ISE or a text editor, save the functions into a single file name `Hello.PSM1`.

3. If the folder for the module doesn't exist yet, create the folder.

```
$modulePath = "$env:USERPROFILE\Documents\WindowsPowerShell\
Modules\Hello"

if(!(Test-Path $modulePath))
{
    New-Item -Path $modulePath -ItemType Directory
}
```

4. Copy `Hello.PSM1` to the new module folder.

```
$modulePath = "$env:USERPROFILE\Documents\WindowsPowerShell\
Modules\Hello"
Copy-Item -Path Hello.PSM1 -Destination $modulePath
```

5. In a PowerShell console, execute `Get-Module -ListAvailable` to list all the available modules:

```
PS C:\> Get-Module -ListAvailable


    Directory: C:\Users\Ed\Documents\WindowsPowerShell\Modules


ModuleType Name                     ExportedCommands
---------- ----                     ----------------
Script     Hello                    {Get-Hello, Get-Hello2}
```

 A large list of modules will likely be returned. The modules in the current user's profile will be listed first, and you may need to scroll up the PowerShell window to see them listed.

6. Run `Import-Module Hello` to import our new module.

 See the recipes Managing Security on PowerShell Scripts and Signing PowerShell Scripts for information about the security requirements for using modules.

7. Run `Get-Command -Module Hello` to list the functions included in the module:

```
PS C:\> Get-Command -Module Hello

CommandType      Name                                          ModuleName
-----------      ----                                          ----------
Function         Get-Hello                                     Hello
Function         Get-Hello2                                    Hello
```

8. Execute the functions in the module as normal:

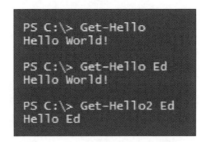

```
PS C:\> Get-Hello
Hello World!

PS C:\> Get-Hello Ed
Hello World!

PS C:\> Get-Hello2 Ed
Hello Ed
```

How it works...

We start off by identifying several functions or commands to group together as a module. These commands do not necessarily have to relate to each other, but it is often best to organize them as well as possible. The commands are then saved into a single file with a `.PSM1` file extension. This file extension indicates to PowerShell that the file is a PowerShell module.

The module is then stored in the user's profile directory. If the folder doesn't already exist, we create a new folder named the same as the module. Once the folder exists, we copy the `.PSM1` file into the folder. PowerShell automatically searches this location for new modules to load.

 There are two locations PowerShell looks for installed modules: `C:\Windows\system32\WindowsPowerShell\v1.0\Modules\` and `%userprofile%\Documents\WindowsPowerShell\Modules`. The first location is used by the entire system and requires administrative permission to access; most third party modules are installed here. The second location is user specific and does not require elevated rights to install scripts.

Once saved, we can load the module to the memory. The command `Import-Module` loads the contents of the module and makes the commands available for use. We can then view the contents of the module using `Get-Command -Module Hello`. This returns all publicly available functions in the module.

Modules are viewed by PowerShell similar to scripts and they rely on the same security requirements as other scripts. Because of these restrictions, it is best practice to sign your modules once they have been created.

Finally, once the module is loaded, we can execute the included commands.

There's more...

▶ Auto-loading of modules: PowerShell 3.0 automatically imports modules as they are needed. While it is best practice to load and unload modules, you do not necessarily have to use `Import-Module` prior to accessing the functions contained within. As you can see in the following screenshot, I listed the currently loaded modules using `Get-Module`. Once I confirmed my new `Hello` module was not loaded, I then execute the `Get-Hello2` function in the module which completed successfully. Executing `Get-Module` again shows the module has been automatically loaded.

```
PS C:\> Get-Module

ModuleType Name                              ExportedCommands
---------- ----                              ----------------
Script     ISE                               {Get-IseSnippet, Import-IseSnippet...
Manifest   Microsoft.PowerShell.Management   {Add-Computer, Add-Content, Checkp...
Manifest   Microsoft.PowerShell.Utility      {Add-Member, Add-Type, Clear-Varia...


PS C:\> Get-Hello2 Ed
Hello Ed

PS C:\> Get-Module

ModuleType Name                              ExportedCommands
---------- ----                              ----------------
Script     Hello                             {Get-Hello, Get-Hello2}
Script     ISE                               {Get-IseSnippet, Import-IseSnippet...
Manifest   Microsoft.PowerShell.Management   {Add-Computer, Add-Content, Checkp...
Manifest   Microsoft.PowerShell.Utility      {Add-Member, Add-Type, Clear-Varia...
```

▶ Module manifest: In addition to the modules themselves, you can also create a module manifest. A module manifest is a file with a `.PSD1` extension that describes the contents of the module. Manifests can be useful because they allow for defining the environment in which a module can be used, its dependencies, additional help information, and even which set of commands to make available. The following code is a basic example of creating a manifest for our `Hello World` module:

```
New-ModuleManifest -Path "$env:USERPROFILE\Documents\
WindowsPowerShell\Modules\Hello\Hello.PSD1" -Author "Ed Goad"
-Description "Hello World examples" -HelpInfoUri "http://blog.
edgoad.com" -NestedModules 'Hello.PSM1'
```

Once the manifest is created, we can view the manifest properties using the following code:

```
Get-Module Hello -ListAvailable | Format-List -Property *
```

See also

More information about creating and using PowerShell modules can be found at:

- http://blogs.technet.com/b/heyscriptingguy/archive/2012/05/24/use-a-module-to-simplify-your-powershell-profile.aspx

- http://msdn.microsoft.com/en-us/library/windows/desktop/dd901839(v=vs.85).aspx

Creating and using PowerShell profiles

User profiles are used to set up user customized PowerShell sessions. These profiles can be blank, contain aliases, custom functions, load modules, or any other PowerShell tasks. When you open a PowerShell session, the contents of the profile are executed the same as executing any other PowerShell script.

How to do it...

In this recipe, we will modify the PowerShell console profile for the current user on the current host. By default the profile file does not exist, so we will create the file, and then configure it to create a transcript of our actions. To do this, carry out the following steps:

1. Open the PowerShell console (not the ISE) and list your current profile locations by executing $PROFILE or $PROFILE | Format-List * -Force|:

```
PS C:\> $PROFILE
C:\Users\Ed\Documents\WindowsPowerShell\Microsoft.PowerShell_profile.ps1
PS C:\> $PROFILE | Format-List * -Force


AllUsersAllHosts        : C:\Windows\System32\WindowsPowerShell\v1.0\profile.ps1
AllUsersCurrentHost     : C:\Windows\System32\WindowsPowerShell\v1.0\Microsoft.P
                          owerShell_profile.ps1
CurrentUserAllHosts     : C:\Users\Ed\Documents\WindowsPowerShell\profile.ps1
CurrentUserCurrentHost  : C:\Users\Ed\Documents\WindowsPowerShell\Microsoft.Powe
                          rShell_profile.ps1
Length                  : 72


PS C:\>
```

2. If the CurrentUserCurrentHost profile file doesn't already exist, create the folder and file structure:

```
$filePath = $PROFILE.CurrentUserCurrentHost
if(!(Test-Path $filePath))
{
    New-Item -Path $filePath -ItemType File
}
```

3. Edit the CurrentUserCurrentHost profile by opening it in a text editor. Make the necessary changes and save the file.

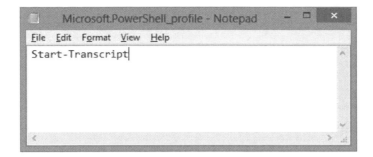

 NOTE: It is best practice to sign your profiles after making changes. This ensures that the profile is secure and hasn't been unintentionally changed.

More information about code signing in PowerShell can be found in the recipe Signing PowerShell scripts

How it works...

When a PowerShell session is started, the profile files are executed before the session is handed over to the user. At that time, any aliases or modules that were loaded will be in effect. Additionally, any background commands, such as `Start-Transcript`, will continue to operate in the background.

We start by opening PowerShell and listing our profile files. By default, `$PROFILE` command only returns the `CurrentUserCurrentHost` profile. By piping the output through `Format-List` with the `-Force` switch, we can see all applicable profile files.

 In this example we are specifically using the PowerShell console, instead of the PowerShell ISE, because the `Start-Transcript` command is only supported in the console.

There's more...

There are six user profile files in total, and they are applied to PowerShell sessions one at a time. First the more general profiles, such as `AllUsersAllHosts` are applied, ending with more specific profiles such as `CurrentUserCurrentHost`. As the individual profiles are applied, any conflicts that arise are simply overwritten by the more specific profile.

Not all six profiles are used at a time, and by default, these profiles are empty. Two of the profiles are specific to the PowerShell console, and two of them are specific to the PowerShell ISE. At the most, you can have four active profiles on a given session.

See also

▸ More information on PowerShell profiles can be found at http://msdn. microsoft.com/en-us/library/windows/desktop/bb613488(v=vs.85). aspx

▸ More information on PowerShell security can be found in the recipes:

□ The *Managing security on PowerShell scripts* recipe

□ The *Signing PowerShell scripts* recipe

Passing variables to functions

One of the most powerful features of PowerShell functions is in using variables to pass data into the function. By passing data into a function, the function can be more generic, and can perform actions on many types of objects.

In this recipe, we will show how to accept variables in functions, and how to report errors if a mandatory variable is not included.

How to do it...

1. For this recipe we will be using the following function.

```
Function Add-Numbers
{
    Param(
    [int]$FirstNum = $(Throw "You must supply at least 1 number")
    , [int]$SecondNum = $FirstNum
    )
    Write-Host ($FirstNum + $SecondNum)
}
```

How it works...

At the beginning of the function we reference the Param() keyword which defines the parameters the function will accept. The first parameter, $FirstNum, we define as being mandatory and of type [int] or integer. We did not have to classify the parameter type, and the function would have worked without this, but it's a good practice to validate the input of your functions.

The second parameter, $SecondNum, is also typed as [int], but also has a default value defined. This way if no value is passed for the second parameter, it will default to the $FirstNum.

When the function runs, it reads in the parameters from the command line and attempts to place them in the variables. The parameters can be assigned based on their position in the command line (that is, the first number is placed into $FirstNum, and the second number is placed into $SecondNum). Additionally, we can call the function using named parameters with the −FirstNum and −SecondNum switches. The following screenshot gives an example of this:

```
PS C:\> Add-Numbers 4 5
9
PS C:\> Add-Numbers -FirstNum 7 -SecondNum 9
16
PS C:\> _
```

If a parameter has a Throw attribute assigned, but the value is not provided, the function will end and return an error. Additionally, if a parameter has a type defined, but the value received is incompatible (such as a string being placed into an integer), the function will end and return an error.

There's more...

Functions are not only capable of receiving input, but also returning output. This ability can come in very handy when trying to return values into other variables instead of simply returning the values to the screen. In our example, we can replace our Write-Host command with a Return command.

```
#Write-Host ($FirstNum + $SecondNum)
Return ($FirstNum + $SecondNum)
```

The output of the function is mostly the same, except now we can assign the output to a variable and use that variable at a later time.

```
PS C:\> Add-Numbers 5 22
27

PS C:\> $foo = Add-Numbers 9 8

PS C:\> $foo
17
```

In addition to returning values from functions, Return also causes the function to exit. The Return command should always be placed at the end of a function, or at a point where processing of the function should stop.

Validating parameters in functions

Whenever a script or program receives data from an unknown source, the general rule is that the data should be validated prior to being used. Validation can take many forms, with simple validations such as confirming the value exists, is of the right type, or fits a predefined format. Validation can also be complex multi-stage events such as ensuring a username exists in a database before prompting for a password.

This section will review several basic validation-testing methods for use in PowerShell.

How to do it...

Here we will discuss creating a function without input validation:

1. Create a basic function with no input validation:

```
Function Hello-World
{
    param($foo)
    "Hello $foo"
}
```

2. Test the function using different input types.

```
PS C:\> Hello-World Ed
Hello Ed

PS C:\> Hello-World 55
Hello 55

PS C:\> Hello-World
Hello
```

Update the function to perform input type validations as discussed in the following steps:

3. Update the function to include the **basic string validation**.

```
Function Hello-WorldString
{
    param([string] $foo)
    "Hello $foo"
}
```

4. Test the function using different input types:

```
PS C:\> Hello-WorldString Ed
Hello Ed

PS C:\> Hello-WorldString 4
Hello 4
```

5. Update the function to perform **basic integer validation**.

```
Function Hello-WorldInt
{
    param([int] $foo)
    "Hello $foo"
}
```

6. Test the function using different input types:

```
PS C:\> Hello-WorldInt 4
Hello 4

PS C:\> Hello-WorldInt 867.5309
Hello 868

PS C:\> Hello-WorldInt r
Hello-WorldInt : Cannot process argument transformation on parameter 'foo'. Cannot
convert value "r" to type "System.Int32". Error: "Input string was not in a correct
format."
At line:1 char:16
+ Hello-WorldInt r
+                ~
    + CategoryInfo          : InvalidData: (:) [Hello-WorldInt], ParameterBindingAr
   gumentTransformationException
    + FullyQualifiedErrorId : ParameterArgumentTransformationError,Hello-WorldInt
```

7. Update the function to perform **basic float validation**.

```
Function Hello-WorldFloat
{
    param([float] $foo)
    "Hello $foo"
}
```

8. Test the function using different input types:

```
PS C:\> Hello-WorldFloat 867.5309
Hello 867.5309
```

9. Update the function to perform basic array validation.

```
Function Hello-WorldStringArray
{
    param([string[]] $foo)
    "Hello " + $foo[0]
}
```

10. Test the function using different input types:

```
PS C:\> Hello-WorldStringArray ("Ed", "Goad")
Hello Ed

PS C:\> Hello-WorldStringArray Ed
Hello Ed
```

Update the functions to perform validation of input values:

1. Create a function to validate the length of a parameter:

```
function Hello-WorldLength{
    param([ValidateLength(4,10)] $foo)
    "Hello $foo"
}
```

2. Test the function using different input types:

```
PS C:\> Hello-WorldLength Ed
Hello-WorldLength : Cannot validate argument on parameter 'foo'. The number of
characters (2) in the argument is too small. Specify an argument whose length
is greater than or equal to "4" and then try the command again.
At line:1 char:19
+ Hello-WorldLength Ed
+                   ~~
    + CategoryInfo          : InvalidData: (:) [Hello-WorldLength], ParameterB
   indingValidationException
    + FullyQualifiedErrorId : ParameterArgumentValidationError,Hello-WorldLeng
   th

PS C:\> Hello-WorldLength "Ed Goad"
Hello Ed Goad
```

3. Create a function to validate a number in a range:

```
function Hello-WorldAge{
    param([ValidateRange(13,99)] $age)
    "Hello, you are $age years old"
}
```

4. Test the function using different input types:

```
PS C:\> Hello-WorldAge 36
Hello, you are 36 years old
PS C:\> Hello-WorldAge 3
Hello-WorldAge : Cannot validate argument on parameter 'age'. The 3 argument
is less than the minimum allowed range of 13. Supply an argument that is
greater than or equal to 13 and then try the command again.
At line:1 char:16
+ Hello-WorldAge 3
+                ~
    + CategoryInfo          : InvalidData: (:) [Hello-WorldAge], ParameterBind
   ingValidationException
    + FullyQualifiedErrorId : ParameterArgumentValidationError,Hello-WorldAge

PS C:\>
```

5. Create a function to validate a set of parameters:

```
function Hello-WorldSize{
    param([ValidateSet("Skinny", "Normal", "Fat")] $size)
    "Hello, you are $size"
}
```

6. Test the function using different input types:

```
PS C:\> Hello-WorldSize normal
Hello, you are normal
PS C:\> Hello-WorldSize average
Hello-WorldSize : Cannot validate argument on parameter 'size'. The argument
"average" does not belong to the set "Skinny,Normal,Fat" specified by the
ValidateSet attribute. Supply an argument that is in the set and then try the
command again.
At line:1 char:17
+ Hello-WorldSize average
+                 ~~~~~~~
    + CategoryInfo          : InvalidData: (:) [Hello-WorldSize], ParameterBin
   dingValidationException
    + FullyQualifiedErrorId : ParameterArgumentValidationError,Hello-WorldSize

PS C:\>
```

7. Create a function that validates against a script:

```
function Hello-WorldAge2{
    param([ValidateScript({$_ -ge 13 -and $_ -lt 99})] $age)
    "Hello, you are $age years old"
}
```

8. Test the function using the different input types:

```
PS C:\> Hello-WorldAge2 36
Hello, you are 36 years old
PS C:\> Hello-WorldAge2 360
Hello-WorldAge2 : Cannot validate argument on parameter 'age'. The "$_ -ge 13
-and $_ -lt 99" validation script for the argument with value "360" did not
return true. Determine why the validation script failed and then try the
command again.
At line:1 char:17
+ Hello-WorldAge2 360
+
    + CategoryInfo          : InvalidData: (:) [Hello-WorldAge2], ParameterBin
   dingValidationException
    + FullyQualifiedErrorId : ParameterArgumentValidationError,Hello-WorldAge2

PS C:\>
```

9. Create a function to validate the input as a phone number:

```
Function Test-PhoneNumber
{
    param([ValidatePattern("\d{3}-\d{4}")] $phoneNumber)
    Write-Host "$phoneNumber is a valid number"
}
```

10. Execute the `Test-PhoneNumber` function using different input types:

```
PS C:\> Test-PhoneNumber 867-5309
867-5309 is a valid number

PS C:\> Test-PhoneNumber 206-867-5309
206-867-5309 is a valid number
```

Use custom validation to test parameters inside our function:

1. Update the function to use custom validation internal to the script with regular expressions:

```
Function Test-PhoneNumberReg
{
    param($phoneNumber)
    $regString=[regex]"^\d{3}-\d{3}-\d{4}$|^\d{3}-\d{4}$"
    if($phoneNumber -match $regString){
        Write-Host "$phoneNumber is a valid number"
    } else {
        Write-Host "$phoneNumber is not a valid number"
    }
}
```

2. Test the function using different input types:

```
PS C:\> Test-PhoneNumberReg 867-5309
867-5309 is not a valid number

PS C:\> Test-PhoneNumberReg 206-867-5309
206-867-5309 is a valid number

PS C:\> Test-PhoneNumberReg 1-206-867-5309
1-206-867-5309 is not a valid number
```

How it works...

We start off with a simple `Hello-World` function with no input validation. Three different calls to the function are performed, one with a username (as the function was designed to work), one with a number, and yet another without any parameters. As you can see, all three commands complete successfully without returning errors.

In the first group of functions in the steps 3 to 10, we see a set of examples using Type Validation to confirm the parameters are of a specific type. There are four iterations of the `Hello-World` example that accept a `string`, `integer`, `float`, and `array` as inputs. As you see from the calls to `Hello-WorldString`, both text and numbers are viewed as strings and return successfully. However, the calls to `Hello-WorldInt` succeed when a number is passed, but fail when text is passed.

 You may notice that the original number 867.5309 passed to the function `Hello-WorldInt` was rounded and truncated when returned. This is because integers are whole numbers—that is, not partial numbers. When the number was cast as an integer, it was rounded to the nearest whole value, which in this case caused it to round up to 868.

In the second set of functions in steps 11 to 20, we see a set of examples using basic input validation. These functions use `ValidateLength`, `ValidateRange`, `ValidateSet`, `ValidateScript`, and `ValidatePattern` attributes of the parameters to validate the input. Additionally, these validation types can be used in conjunction with the basic type validations to further ensure the input is of the correct type and value.

The last set of examples in steps 21 to 24 perform validation internal to the script, instead of relying on the in-built validation. The function named `Test-PhoneNumberReg` uses a regular expression in order to validate the input as part of the script. Instead of relying on validation using types or `ValidatePattern`, this function simply passes the variable to the PowerShell code in order to check the input. By managing the validation as part of the function, we have more flexibility on how we handle and present validation errors to our users, and can return a more user-friendly message to the end user.

There's more...

It is considered a best practice to perform at least basic validation for all inputs. Lack of input validation can result in the function crashing, operating unpredictably, or even resulting in damaging data in your environment. This has been a common method for computer attackers to access secure systems and should be taken diligently.

See also

▶ More information about using regular expressions for validation can be found at `http://technet.microsoft.com/en-us/magazine/2007.11.powershell.aspx`

▶ Additional information about input validation can be found by executing `help about_Functions_Advanced_Parameters`

Piping data to functions

In addition to passing data to functions via parameters, functions can receive data directly from another object or command via a pipe "**|**". Receiving values by piping helps improve scripting by limiting the use of temporary variables, as well as more easily passing complex object types or descriptors.

How to do it...

In this recipe, we will create a simple function that receives input from command line as well as pipe. To do this, carry out the following steps:

1. Create a simple function that accepts a parameter:

```
Function Square-Num
{
    Param([float] $FirstNum)
    Write-Host ($FirstNum * $FirstNum)
}
```

2. Use the `ValueFromPipeline` parameter to enable the script to accept input from the pipeline:

```
Function Square-Num
{
    Param([float]
    [Parameter(ValueFromPipeline = $true)]
    $FirstNum )
    Write-Host ($FirstNum * $FirstNum)
}
```

3. Test the function using parameters and by passing data from the pipeline:

```
PS C:\> Square-Num 9
81

PS C:\> 5 | Square-Num
25
```

How it works...

The script in the first step itself is simple—it creates a variable named $FirstNum, squares it by multiplying the number against itself, and returns the result. In the second step we updated the parameter line with the following code:

```
[Parameter(ValueFromPipeline=$true)]
```

This parameter option allows the function to assign a value to $FirstNum from the command line, as well as from the pipeline. PowerShell will first look for the value on the command line via name or location, and if it isn't listed, it will look for the value from the pipe.

There's more...

PowerShell will attempt to use all arguments provided to a function, and will report errors if there are unknown arguments. For instance, if we try to provide values from the pipeline and command line at the same time as shown in the following screenshot:

```
PS C:\> 8 | Square-Num 7
Square-Num : The input object cannot be bound to any parameters for the command
either because the command does not take pipeline input or the input and its
properties do not match any of the parameters that take pipeline input.
At line:1 char:5
+ 8 | Square-Num 7
+
    + CategoryInfo          : InvalidArgument: (8:Int32) [Square-Num], Parameter
   BindingException
    + FullyQualifiedErrorId : InputObjectNotBound,Square-Num

49
```

As you can see from the example, we attempt to pass both 8 and 7 to the Square-Num function, the first via the pipe and the second via the command line. PowerShell reports an error, and then provides an answer of 49, the result of *7 X 7*.

Recording sessions with transcripts

When working in PowerShell doing various tasks, I find myself doing something that I then want to document or turn into a function and I have to ask myself *What did I just do?*, *Do I know all of the variables I had previously set?*, *Do I know all the objects I am using?*, *What kind of authentication am I using?*, and so on.

The PowerShell console and ISE have some level of in-built history, but if you're doing large tasks across multiple server environments, this history quickly becomes too small.

Enter PowerShell transcripts. Transcripts are a great way of recording everything you do in a PowerShell session and saving it in a text file for later review.

How to do it...

Carry out the following steps:

1. Open the PowerShell console (not the ISE) and begin recording a transcript in the default location by executing Start-Transcript.

```
PS C:\> Start-Transcript
Transcript started, output file is C:\Users\Ed\Documents\PowerShell_transcript.
20121013181446.txt
PS C:\> _
```

2. Stop the recording by executing Stop-Transcript.
3. Begin recording a transcript into a different location by calling Start-Transcript with the -Path switch:

```
PS C:\> Start-Transcript -Path C:\temp\foo.txt -Force
Transcript started, output file is C:\temp\foo.txt
PS C:\>
```

How it works...

In the first step, we execute the command Start-Transcript, which automatically creates transcript under the user's My Documents folder. Each transcript file is named with a unique timestamp that ensures files don't overwrite or conflict with each other. We can stop the recording by then executing Stop-Transcript.

In the third step, we tell PowerShell to save the transcript file to C:\temp\foo.txt. When pointing transcripts to an existing file, PowerShell will attempt to append to the file. If the file is read-only, using the -Force command will instruct PowerShell to attempt to change the permissions on the file, and then append to it.

There's more...

▶ Transcript limitations: Session transcripts only work with the PowerShell console, and not the PowerShell ISE. The ISE helps overcome some of this limitation by providing a larger scroll-back area, but if you want to use transcripts, you have to use the console application.

▶ Fun with transcripts: Also, because transcripts capture anything typed or written to the screen, you need to be careful what you run. For instance, if you run the following commands, you will result in a recursive loop that has to be manually stopped:

```
PS C:\> Start-Transcript -Path c:\temp\foo.txt
Transcript started, output file is c:\temp\foo.txt
PS C:\> Get-Content C:\temp\foo.txt_
```

See also

▶ See the *Creating and using PowerShell profiles* recipe for information on how to automatically start transcripts for your sessions.

Signing PowerShell scripts

When creating PowerShell scripts, modules, and profiles, it is considered best practice to digitally sign them. Signing scripts performs the following two functions:

▶ Ensures the script is from a trusted source

▶ Ensures the script hasn't been altered since it was signed

Getting ready

To sign a PowerShell script, a code-signing certificate will be needed. Normally these certificates will be provided by your enterprise **Private Key Infrastructure** (**PKI**), and the PKI Administrator should be able to help you with the requesting process. Code-signing certificates can also be purchased from third party **Certificate Authorities** (**CA**) which can be helpful if your scripts are being distributed outside of your corporate environment.

Once received, the code-signing cert should be added to your **Current User | Personal | Certificates** certificate store on your computer. Additionally, the root certificate from the Certificate Authority should be added to the **Trusted Publishers** store for all computers that are going to execute the signed scripts.

How to do it...

Carry out the following steps:

1. Create and test a PowerShell script.
2. Sign the script with `Set-AuthenticodeSignature`.

```
$cert = Get-ChildItem Cert:CurrentUser\My\ -CodeSigningCert
Set-AuthenticodeSignature C:\temp\ServerInfo.ps1 $cert
```

How it works...

The signing process is fairly simple, but also extremely powerful. The process starts by searching the `Current User` certificate store for a certificate capable of code signing and is placed into a `$cert` variable. `Set-AuthenticodeSignature` is then called to sign the script with the certificate.

If there is more than one code signing certificate on your system, you need to select which certificate to use. To achieve this, update the first line to include a `where` clause. For example:

```
$cert = Get-ChildItem Cert:CurrentUser\My\ -CodeSigningCert | Where-
Object Subject -eq 'CN=CorpInternal'
```

If you open the script in a text editor after it has been signed, you will notice several lines of content appended to the end. These additional lines are the signature that PowerShell will verify before running the script.

Any change to the script (even adding or removing a space) will invalidate the signature. Once the script has been signed, if you need to make changes, you must repeat the signing process.

There's more...

If you don't have an available PKI to obtain a code-signing certificate, or your PKI Administrator is hesitant to give you one, you can create a self-signed certificate for testing purposes. To do this, you can use the following PowerShell script which is based on the script by Vishal Agarwal at `http://blogs.technet.com/b/vishalagarwal/archive/2009/08/22/generating-a-certificate-self-signed-using-powershell-and-certenroll-interfaces.aspx`:

```
$name = new-object -com "X509Enrollment.CX500DistinguishedName.1"
$name.Encode("CN=TestCode", 0)

$key = new-object -com "X509Enrollment.CX509PrivateKey.1"
$key.ProviderName = "Microsoft RSA SChannel Cryptographic Provider"
$key.KeySpec = 1
$key.Length = 1024
$key.SecurityDescriptor = "D:PAI(A;;0xd01f01ff;;;SY)
(A;;0xd01f01ff;;;BA)(A;;0x80120089;;;NS)"
$key.MachineContext = 1
$key.Create()

$serverauthoid = new-object -com "X509Enrollment.CObjectId.1"
$serverauthoid.InitializeFromValue("1.3.6.1.5.5.7.3.3") # Code Signing
$ekuoids = new-object -com "X509Enrollment.CObjectIds.1"
$ekuoids.add($serverauthoid)
$ekuext = new-object -com "X509Enrollment.
CX509ExtensionEnhancedKeyUsage.1"
$ekuext.InitializeEncode($ekuoids)

$cert = new-object -com "X509Enrollment.
CX509CertificateRequestCertificate.1"
$cert.InitializeFromPrivateKey(2, $key, "")
$cert.Subject = $name
$cert.Issuer = $cert.Subject
$cert.NotBefore = get-date
$cert.NotAfter = $cert.NotBefore.AddDays(90)
$cert.X509Extensions.Add($ekuext)
$cert.Encode()
```

```
$enrollment = new-object -com "X509Enrollment.CX509Enrollment.1"
$enrollment.InitializeFromRequest($cert)
$certdata = $enrollment.CreateRequest(0)
$enrollment.InstallResponse(2, $certdata, 0, "")
```

Executing this script will create the certificate and install it on the local computer as shown in the following screenshot:

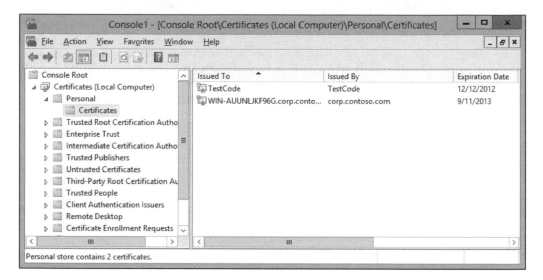

 The self-signed certificate still needs to be added to your Trusted Root Certification Authorities and Trusted Publishers store for the certificate to be considered valid by client computers.

Sending e-mail

Integration with e-mail is a key capability for automating administration tasks. With e-mail, you can run tasks that automatically let you know when they are complete, or e-mail users when information is needed from them, or even send reports to administrators.

This recipe shows different methods of sending e-mail to users.

Getting ready

To send an e-mail using PowerShell, we will need a mail system capable of accepting SMTP mail from your computer. This can be a Microsoft Exchange server, and IIS server, a Linux host, or even a public mail service such as Google Mail. The method we use may change how the e-mail appears to the end recipient and may cause the message to be flagged as spam.

How to do it...

To send e-mail using the traditional .NET method:

1. Open PowerShell and load the following function:

```
function Send-SMTPmail($to, $from, $subject, $smtpServer, $body)
{
        $mailer = new-object Net.Mail.SMTPclient($smtpServer)
        $msg = new-object Net.Mail.MailMessage($from, $to, $subject,
$body)
        $msg.IsBodyHTML = $true
        $mailer.send($msg)
}
```

2. To send the mail message, call the following function:

```
Send-SMTPmail -to "admin@contoso.com" -from "mailer@contoso.com" `
-subject "test email" -smtpserver "mail.contoso.com" -body
"testing"
```

3. To send e-mail using the included PowerShell Cmdlet.

4. Use the Send-MailMessage command as shown:

```
Send-MailMessage -To admin@contoso.com -Subject "test email" `
-Body "this is a test" -SmtpServer mail.contoso.com `
-From mailer@contoso.com
```

How it works...

The first method shown uses a traditional .NET process to create and send the e-mail. If you have experience programming in one of the .NET languages, this process may be familiar. The function starts by creating a Net.Mail.SMTPclient object that allows it to connect to the mail server. Then a Net.Mail.MailMessage object is created and populated with the e-mail content. Lastly, the e-mail is sent to the server.

The second method uses a in-built PowerShell cmdlet named Send-MailMessage. This method simplifies the mailing method into a single command while providing flexibility in the mailing options and methods of connecting to mail servers.

There's more...

Most e-mail functions can be performed by the `Send-MailMessage` command. More information can be found by executing `help Send-MailMessage`. The following additional command switches allow the command to perform most mail functions needed:

- ▶ Attachments
- ▶ CC/BCC
- ▶ SMTP authentication
- ▶ Delivery notification
- ▶ E-mail priority
- ▶ SSL encryption

Sorting and filtering

One of the great features of PowerShell is its ability to sort and filter objects. This filtering can be used to limit a larger result set and reporting only the information necessary.

This section will review several methods of filtering and sorting data.

How to do it...

1. To explore the filtering capabilities of PowerShell, we look at the running processes on our computer. We then use the `Where` clause to filter the results.

   ```
   Get-Process | Where-Object {$_.Name -eq "chrome"}
   Get-Process | Where-Object Name -eq "chrome"
   Get-Process | Where-Object Name -like "*hrom*"
   Get-Process | Where-Object Name -ne "chrome"
   Get-Process | Where-Object Handles -gt 1000
   ```

2. To view sorting in PowerShell, we again view the processes on our computer and use `Sort-Object` to change the default sort order.

   ```
   Get-Process | Sort-Object Handles
   Get-Process | Sort-Object Handles -Descending
   Get-Process | Sort-Object Handles, ID -Descending
   ```

3. To explore the select features of PowerShell, we use `Select-String` and `Select-Object` clause:

   ```
   Select-String -Path C:\Windows\WindowsUpdate.log -Pattern
   "Installing updates"
   Get-Process | Select-Object Name -Unique
   ```

4. To view the grouping capabilities of PowerShell, we use `Format-Table` with the `-GroupBy` command:

```
Get-Process | Format-Table -GroupBy ProcessName
```

How it works...

In the first section, we review various methods of filtering information using the `Where` clause:

▸ The first method uses the PowerShell `Where-Object` clause format. The `$_` identifier represents the object being passed through the pipe, so `$_.Name` refers to the `Name` property of the object. The `-eq` is an equals parameter that instructs `Where-Object` to compare the two values.

▸ The second method performs the same task as the first but uses a parameter format that is new in PowerShell 3.0. In this method the `Where-Object` comparison no longer needs to use `$_` to reference the object being passed, and we no longer need the curly braces { }.

 Even though the second method shown can often be easier to use and easier to understand, it is important to know both methods. The first method is still in use by PowerShell scripters, and there are some situations that work better using this method.

▸ The last three methods perform similar comparisons using different parameter. The `-like` parameter allows for the use of the wildcard character `*` allowing for less exact filtering. The `-ne` parameter means *not equal* and is the exact opposite of the equals parameter. And the `-gt` parameter means *greater than* and compares the attribute value to a known value.

The second section uses the `Sort-Object` command to sort and organize the object attributes. In this section, we show sorting by the `handles` attribute in both ascending (the default method), and descending format. Additionally, we see that multiple attributes can be sorted at the same time.

The third section uses the `Select-String` and `Select-Object` commands to restrict what is returned. The first method searches the `WindowsUpdate.log` for the string `Installing updates` and returns the results. The second method takes the output of `Get-Process` and filters it to only return a unique list of named processes.

The fourth section shows how to perform grouping based on an attribute. The `Format-Table` command includes a property named `-GroupBy` that, instead of returning a single table, will return multiple tables. In this case, for each unique `ProcessName`, a separate table is returned.

Using formatting to export numbers

Numbers in their raw form are useful when you want the most exact calculation, but can become messy when presenting them to users. Because of this PowerShell uses standardized .NET formatting rules to convert and present numbers in different contexts.

In this recipe, we will take a number and use PowerShell to present it in different number formats. This allows us to quickly see the differences between how PowerShell performs number formatting.

How to do it...

Carry out the following steps:

1. Start with a simple PowerShell script to present numbers using different formats:

```
$jenny = 1206867.5309
Write-Host "Original:`t`t`t" $jenny
Write-Host "Whole Number:`t`t" ("{0:N0}" -f $jenny)
Write-Host "3 decimal places:`t" ("{0:N3}" -f $jenny)
Write-Host "Currency:`t`t`t" ("{0:C2}" -f $jenny)
Write-Host "Percentage:`t`t`t" ("{0:P2}" -f $jenny)
Write-Host "Scientific:`t`t`t" ("{0:E2}" -f $jenny)
Write-Host "Fixed Point:`t`t" ("{0:F5}" -f $jenny)
Write-Host "Decimal:`t`t`t" ("{0:D8}" -f [int]$jenny)
Write-Host "HEX:`t`t`t`t" ("{0:X0}" -f [int]$jenny)
```

2. Execute the script and review the results:

```
Original:            1206867.5309
Whole Number:        1,206,868
3 decimal places:    1,206,867.531
Currency:            $1,206,867.53
Percentage:          120,686,753.09 %
Scientific:          1.21E+006
Fixed Point:         1206867.53090
Decimal:             01206868
HEX:                 126A54
```

How it works...

Because PowerShell is based on the .NET framework, it automatically inherits its number formatting capabilities. In this script, we are creating a variable named $jenny and assigning a number to it. Then, several number formatting strings are created (the string in the curly braces { }) and the formatting is applied to $jenny.

In the code shown, we are using `` `t `` (backtick + letter *t*) to make the output easier to read. This causes a tab to be added to the text, which then aligns the output on the right.

The backtick character on most keyboards is the key to the left of the number *1* and also contains the ~ character. In PowerShell this character is occasionally referred to as an *Esc* character and is used to pass special commands such as tabs and new lines.

The formatting strings are composed of three distinct elements, each with a unique role. Inside the curly braces, the first zero (before the colon) refers to the first variable being used. Since we are only using one variable, this number never changes. The letter after the colon defines the format type of number, percentage, decimal, and so on. And the final number defines how many decimal places to include in the results.

One area of special note is when we convert $jenny to a decimal or hexadecimal number. You may have noticed the [int] attribute before the variable. This attribute explicitly casts the variable as an integer prior to applying the formatting. This is necessary because decimal and hexadecimal numbers only work with integers by default. Attempting to pass a complex number like ours natively to these formatting commands will result in an error.

There's more...

In addition to the built in formatting strings shown previously, custom formatting strings can also be created and applied.

```
Write-Host "Static Size:`t`t" ("{0:0000000000.00}" -f $jenny)
Write-Host "Literal String:`t`t" ("{0:000' Hello '000}" -f $jenny)
Write-Host "Phone Number:`t`t" ("{0:# (###) ### - ####}" -f
($jenny*10000))
```

The first custom string creates a number that is composed of 10 digits, a decimal point, and two digits. If the number is not large enough to fill the formatting, zeros are prepended to it.

The second string creates a number with a literal string in the middle of it.

The third string multiplies the variable by 10,000 (to make it an 11 digit integer), and formats it into a phone number. The number is returned complete with county and area codes.

```
Static Size:        0001206867.53
Literal String:     1206 Hello 868
Phone Number:       1 (206) 867 - 5309
```

See also

▶ More information on formatting in `.NET` Framework 4.5 is documented on MSDN at `http://msdn.microsoft.com/en-us/library/26etazsy`

Using formatting to export data views

One of the great things about PowerShell is that it gives you access to lots of information. However, this plethora of information can be a downside of PowerShell if it is not the exact information or type of information you are looking for. In previous chapters, we saw how to filter and format data; in this chapter, we will review different methods to format data to provide the information in a way that is usable to us.

How to do it...

Carry out the following steps:

1. Using `Get-Process` to list all running Chrome processes

   ```
   Get-Process chrome
   ```

2. To list all available attributes for our processes, execute the following code:

   ```
   Get-Process chrome | Select-Object *
   ```

3. To return a select list of attributes, update the following command:

   ```
   Get-Process chrome | `
   Select-Object Name, Handles, Threads, `
   NonpagedSystemMemorySize, PagedMemorySize, `
   VirtualMemorySize, WorkingSet, `
   PrivilegedProcessorTime, UserProcessorTime, `
   TotalProcessorTime
   ```

   > Note the use of the backtick character at the end of all but the last line. This tells PowerShell to include the contents of the lines as a single line. This allows us to more easily format the script for readability.

4. Combine the values of different attributes to provide more usable information

   ```
   Get-Process chrome | `
   Select-Object Name, Handles, Threads, `
   NonpagedSystemMemorySize, PagedMemorySize, `
   VirtualMemorySize, WorkingSet, `
   PrivilegedProcessorTime, UserProcessorTime, `
   ```

```
TotalProcessorTime, `
@{Name="Total Memory";Expression=`
{$_.NonpagedSystemMemorySize + `
$_.PagedMemorySize + $_.VirtualMemorySize + `
$_.WorkingSet}}
```

5. Use formatting to return the values in a human readable format.

```
Get-Process chrome | `
Select-Object Name, Handles, Threads, `
NonpagedSystemMemorySize, PagedMemorySize, `
VirtualMemorySize, WorkingSet, `
PrivilegedProcessorTime, UserProcessorTime, `
TotalProcessorTime, `
@{Name="Total Memory (M)";Expression=`
{"{0:N2}" -f (($_.NonpagedSystemMemorySize + `
$_.PagedMemorySize + $_.VirtualMemorySize + `
$_.WorkingSet)/1MB)}}
```

How it works...

In the first step, we simply execute `Get-Process` to return all running processes named `chrome`. This command returns basic process information such as the number of handles, the amount of memory resources, and the amount of CPU resources used by each process.

In the second step, we do the same as before, but this time telling the command to return all attributes for the processes. Dozens of attributes are returned, including details about the executable, threads, debugging information, and even when the process was started. Most importantly, this returns all available attributes for the process, thus allowing us to determine which attributes we are interested in returning in future queries.

The third step identifies specific attributes to return from the running processes. Any available process attribute can be included here in addition to or instead of the memory related attributes shown here.

The fourth step uses an expression to create a calculated result. In this situation, we create a calculated column named `Total Memory` and add several of the memory related attributes together. Most mathematical functions such as multiplication and subtraction, and most textual commands such as append or replace, can be used as well.

The final step adds numeric formatting to the calculated column to make it more readable to the user. Two types of formatting are performed here:

  ▶ The result is divided by `1 MB` (or `X / 1,048,576`) to present the number in megabytes instead of bytes

  ▶ Formatting is applied to limit the resulting number to two decimal places

Using jobs

Many of the PowerShell scripts we will create will execute in a serial fashion, that is, A starts before B which starts before C. This method of processing is simple to understand, easy to create, and easy to troubleshoot. However, sometimes there are processes that make serial execution difficult or undesirable. In that situation, we can look at using jobs as a method to start a task, and then move it to the background so that we can begin the next task.

A common situation I ran into is needing to get information, or execute a command, on multiple computers. If it is only a handful of systems, standard scripting works fine. However, if there are dozens, or hundreds of systems, a single slow system can slow down the entire process.

Additionally, if one of the systems fails to respond, it has the possibility of breaking my entire script, causing me to scramble through the logs to see where it failed and where to pick it back up. Another benefit of using jobs is that each job has the ability to execute independent of the rest of the jobs. This way, a job can fail, without breaking the rest of the jobs.

How to do it...

In this recipe, we will create a long-running process and compare the timing for serial versus parallel processing. To do this, carry out the following steps:

1. Create a long-running process in serial:

    ```
    # Function that simulates a long-running process
    $foo = 1..5
    Function LongWrite
    {
        Param($a)
        Start-Sleep 10
        $a
    }
    $foo | ForEach{ LongWrite $_ }
    ```

2. Create a long-running process using jobs:

    ```
    # Long running process using jobs
    ForEach ($foo in 1..5)
    {
        Start-Job -ScriptBlock {
        Start-Sleep 10
        $foo } -ArgumentList $foo -Name $foo
    }
    Wait-Job *
    Receive-Job *
    Remove-Job *
    ```

How it works...

In the first step, we create an example long-running process that simply sleeps for 10 seconds and returns its job number. The first script uses a loop to execute our `LongWrite` function in a serial fashion five times. As expected, this script takes just over 50 seconds to complete.

The second step executes the same process five times, but this time using jobs. Instead of calling a function, this time we are using `Start-Job` that will simultaneously create a background job, start the job, and then return for more. Once all the jobs have been started, we use `Wait-Job *` to wait for all running jobs to complete. `Receive-Job` retrieves the output from the jobs, and `Remove-Job` removes the jobs from the scheduler.

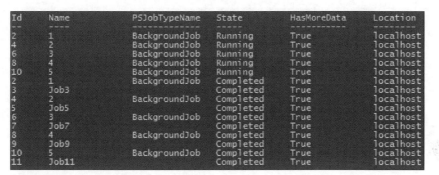

```
Id    Name    PSJobTypeName    State        HasMoreData    Location
--    ----    -------------    -----        -----------    --------
2     1       BackgroundJob    Running      True           localhost
4     2       BackgroundJob    Running      True           localhost
6     3       BackgroundJob    Running      True           localhost
8     4       BackgroundJob    Running      True           localhost
10    5       BackgroundJob    Running      True           localhost
2     1       BackgroundJob    Completed    True           localhost
3     Job3                     Completed    True           localhost
4     2       BackgroundJob    Completed    True           localhost
5     Job5                     Completed    True           localhost
6     3       BackgroundJob    Completed    True           localhost
7     Job7                     Completed    True           localhost
8     4       BackgroundJob    Completed    True           localhost
9     Job9                     Completed    True           localhost
10    5       BackgroundJob    Completed    True           localhost
11    Job11                    Completed    True           localhost
```

Because of the setup and teardown process required for creating and managing jobs, the process runs for more than the expected 10 seconds. In a test run, it took approximately 18 seconds total to create the jobs, run the jobs, wait for the jobs to complete, retrieve the output from the jobs, and remove the jobs from the scheduler.

There's more...

▶ Scaling up: While moving from 50 seconds to 18 seconds is impressive in itself (decreasing it to 36 percent of the original run-time), larger jobs can give even better results. By extending the command to run 50 times (instead of the original 5), run-times can decrease to 18 percent of the serial method.

▶ Working with remote resources: Jobs can be used both locally and remotely. A common need for a server admin is to perform a task across multiple servers. Sometimes, the servers respond quickly, sometimes they are slow to respond, and sometimes they do not respond and the task times out. These slow or unresponsive systems greatly increase the amount of time needed to complete your tasks. Parallel processing allows these slow systems to respond when they are available without impacting the overall performance.

By using jobs, the task can be launched among multiple servers simultaneously. This way, the slower systems won't prompt other systems from processing. And, as shown in the example, a success or failure report can be returned to the administrator.

See also

More information on using jobs in PowerShell can be found at:

▶ http://blogs.technet.com/b/heyscriptingguy/archive/2010/03/16/
hey-scripting-guy-march-16-2010.aspx

▶ http://blogs.technet.com/b/heyscriptingguy/archive/2012/12/31/
using-windows-powershell-jobs.aspx

▶ http://blogs.technet.com/b/heyscriptingguy/archive/2012/02/02/
speed-up-excel-automation-with-powershell-jobs.aspx

Dealing with errors in PowerShell

When creating a script in any language, error handling is needed to ensure proper operations. Error handling is useful when debugging scripts and ensuring scripts work properly, but they can also present alternative methods of accomplishing tasks.

How to do it...

Carry out the following steps:

1. Create a simple function that uses no error handling

   ```
   Function Multiply-Numbers
   {
       Param($FirstNum, $SecNum)

       Write-Host ($FirstNum * $SecNum)
   }
   ```

2. Test the function using various arguments:

3. Update the function using a `Try/Catch` block:

```
Function Multiply-Numbers
{
    Param($FirstNum, $SecNum)
    Try
    {
        Write-Host ($FirstNum * $SecNum)
    }
    Catch
    {
        Write-Host "Error in function, present two numbers to
multiply"
    }
}
```

4. Test the `Multiply-Numbers` function using various arguments:

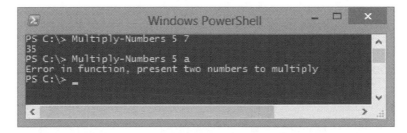

5. In the PowerShell console, execute a command to generate an error such as `Get-Item foo`.

6. View the `$Error` variable to return the error code history.

```
PS C:\> Get-Item foo
Get-Item : Cannot find path 'C:\foo' because it does not exist.
At line:1 char:1
+ Get-Item foo
+ ~~~~~~~~~~~~
    + CategoryInfo          : ObjectNotFound: (C:\foo:String) [Get-Item], Item
NotFoundException
    + FullyQualifiedErrorId : PathNotFound,Microsoft.PowerShell.Commands.GetIt
emCommand


PS C:\> $Error
Get-Item : Cannot find path 'C:\foo' because it does not exist.
At line:1 char:1
+ Get-Item foo
+ ~~~~~~~~~~~~
    + CategoryInfo          : ObjectNotFound: (C:\foo:String) [Get-Item], Item
NotFoundException
    + FullyQualifiedErrorId : PathNotFound,Microsoft.PowerShell.Commands.GetIt
emCommand
```

How it works...

In the first step, we create a function that takes two numbers, multiplies them, and returns the result. As we see in the second step, the function operates normally as long as two numbers are presented, but if something other than a number is presented, then an unfriendly error is returned.

In the third step, our updated script uses a Try/Catch block to find errors and return a more friendly error. The `Try` block attempts to perform the multiplication, and if an error is returned then processing exits. When the `Try` block fails for any reason, it then executes the `Catch` block instead. In this case, we are returning a command specific error message, in other scenarios we could initiate an alternative task or command that was based on the error.

The fifth and sixth steps generate an error in the PowerShell console, and then show the `$Error` variable. The `$Error` variable is an in-built array that automatically captures and stores errors as they happen. You can view the variable to report all errors listed, or you can use indexing such as `$Error[1]` to return specific errors.

There's more...

> ▸ Clearing error codes: By default, the `$Error` array will retain a number of error codes. These errors are only removed from the array when it reaches its maximum size, or when the user session is ended. It is possible to clear out the array before doing a task, so that you can then review the `$Error` array after and know that all the alerts are relevant.
>
> ```
> $Error.Count
> $Error.Clear()
> $Error.Count
> ```
>
> This example starts by returning the number of items in the array. Then `$Error.Clear()` is called to empty the array. Lastly, the number of array items is returned to confirm that it has been cleared.
>
> ▸ `$ErrorActionPreference`: In many programming/scripting languages, there are methods to change the default action when an error occurs. In VBScript, we had the option "On Error Resume Next", which told the script to continue on as though no error had occurred. In PowerShell, we have the `$ErrorActionPreferece` variable. There are four settings for this variable:
>> ❑ **Stop**: Whenever an error occurs, the script or process is stopped. This is the default action.

    ❑   **Continue**: When an error occurs, the error will be reported and the process will continue.

    ❑   **SilentlyContinue**: When an error occurs, PowerShell will attempt to suppress the error and the process will continue. Not all errors will be suppressed.

    ❑   **Inquire**: When an error occurs, PowerShell will prompt the operator to take the correct action.

To set your preference, simply set the variable to the desired string value as shown in the following code:

```
$ErrorActionPreference = "Stop"
```

Tuning PowerShell scripts for performance

In PowerShell, as with most things with computers, there is often more than one way to accomplish a task. Therefore the question is not always *how* to accomplish a task, it is *how best* to accomplish the task. Often times the answer comes down to how fast a certain method performs.

In this recipe, we will look at different methods to retrieve the local groups on a member server. The different methods will be benchmarked to determine the optimal method.

Getting ready

In this example, we will be listing the NT groups on the local computer. To do this we will be querying the **Win32_Group** WMI class. This class however, returns all local computer groups, as well all domain groups. If you have a domain environment with a large number of groups, this process can be extensive.

How to do it...

Carry out the following steps:

1.   Start by identifying different methods to list local groups on a computer:

```
Get-WmiObject -Class Win32_Group | Where-Object Domain -eq
$env:COMPUTERNAME
Get-WmiObject -Query "select * from Win32_Group where
Domain='$env:ComputerName'"
```

2. Benchmark the first task using `Measure-Command`:

```
Administrator: Windows PowerShell                       _  □  x

PS C:\> Measure-Command { Get-WmiObject -Class Win32_Group | where Domain -eq $e
nv:COMPUTERNAME }


Days              : 0
Hours             : 0
Minutes           : 6
Seconds           : 28
Milliseconds      : 814
Ticks             : 3888143148
TotalDays         : 0.00450016568055556
TotalHours        : 0.108003976333333
TotalMinutes      : 6.48023858
TotalSeconds      : 388.8143148
TotalMilliseconds : 388814.3148


PS C:\>
```

3. Benchmark the second task using `Measure-Command`:

```
Administrator: Windows PowerShell                       _  □  x

PS C:\> Measure-Command { Get-WmiObject -Query "select * from Win32_Group where
Domain='$env:ComputerName'" }


Days              : 0
Hours             : 0
Minutes           : 0
Seconds           : 0
Milliseconds      : 79
Ticks             : 796743
TotalDays         : 9.2215625E-07
TotalHours        : 2.213175E-05
TotalMinutes      : 0.001327905
TotalSeconds      : 0.0796743
TotalMilliseconds : 79.6743


PS C:\>
```

How it works...

Both of these commands perform the same task, querying WMI for local groups on our server.

- The first command retrieves all groups from WMI (local and domain), then filters based on the domain name attribute

- The second command uses a query against WMI with a filter applied based on the domain name, WMI then returns the group objects to PowerShell

In this situation, the first command took several minutes to complete, while the second command took only 79 milliseconds. Both commands result in returning the same data, so this suggests the second method is more ideal for my current situation.

There's more...

Neither of these tasks is right nor wrong, they simply differ where the filtering process took place. However, the first method may be preferred based on what else is being done. For instance, if I was doing a large amount of work with groups and group membership, both in the domain and local system, the first method may be preferred.

If the results of the first WMI command were saved to a variable prior to filtering, then different filtering could be applied after. This one object could be filtered multiple times to provide different information, instead of requiring multiple queries against WMI.

Creating and using Cmdlets

In the past, each system or application would have its own set of tools used to manage it. Each tool had its own nomenclature, input, and output methods, and differing levels of manageability. In PowerShell, this all changes with Cmdlets.

PowerShell creates a consistent run-time for toolsets to be created that function and operate in a consistent manner. Input parsing, error presentation, and output formatting are all managed via PowerShell. This means that the developer does not need to spend a large amount of time filtering input and guessing at the output the administrator needs.

Cmdlets allow you to use the full power of custom C# code, without having to worry about input or output functions. Cmdlets also utilize native .NET framework classes that allow for managed code and working with objects.

This section shows how to use Visual Studio to create a custom Cmdlet and then utilize the functions exposed in that Cmdlet. Specifically, we will be creating a Cmdlet that queries the performance counters on a system and returns how long the system has been online.

Getting ready

Unlike functions and modules, to create a Cmdlet we require specialized tools. The first item we need is Visual Studio. If you don't have Visual Studio currently, there are "express" versions available that provide a free, but limited feature set. Alternatively, you can use the command line if you are familiar with compiling .NET classes from command line.

Additionally, you will need to download and install the Windows SDK. The SDK provides several system and .NET components necessary to create our Cmdlet.

How to do it...

Carry out the following steps:

1. Open Visual Studio and select to create a new **Class Library** project.

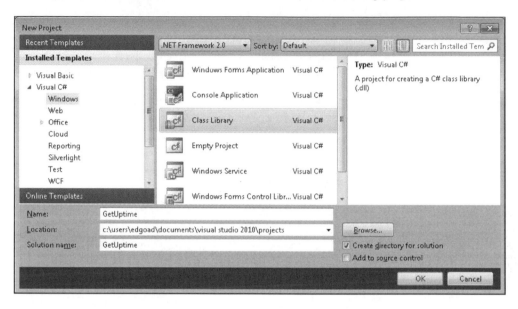

2. Import the references.

    ❑   In **Solution Explorer**, right-click on **References** and then we select **Add Reference**. On the **Browse** tab, browse to `C:\Program Files (x86)\Reference Assemblies\Microsoft\WindowsPowerShell\v3.0\` and select `System.Management.Automation.dll`.

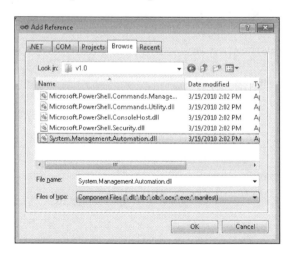

❑ In **Solution Explorer**, we right-click on **References** and then we select **Add Reference**. On the **.NET** tab, select **System.Configuration.Install**.

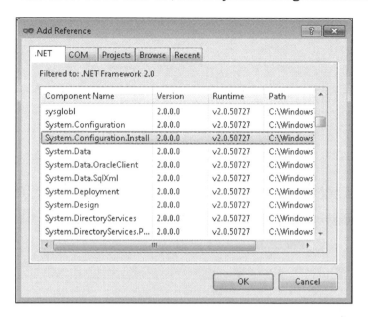

❑ **Solution Explorer** should now look similar to the following screenshot:

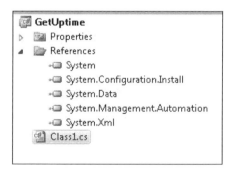

3. Add Cmdlet code:

```
[Cmdlet(VerbsCommon.Get, "Uptime")]
public class GetUptimeCommand : Cmdlet
{
    protected override void ProcessRecord()
    {
        using (var uptime = new PerformanceCounter("System",
"System Up Time"))
        {
```

```
                    uptime.NextValue();
                    WriteObject(TimeSpan.FromSeconds(uptime.
NextValue()));
                }
            }
        }
```

4. Add specific items for creating a Cmdlet:

```
        [RunInstaller(true)]
        public class GetUptimePSSnapIn : PSSnapIn
        {
            public GetUptimePSSnapIn()
                : base()
            {
            }
            public override string Name
            {
                get { return "GetUptimePSSnapIn"; }
            }
            public override string Vendor
            {
                get { return "Ed"; }
            }
            public override string Description
            {
                get { return "Returns the uptime of the system"; }
            }
            public override string VendorResource
            {
                get
                {
                    return "GetUptimePSSnapIn,Ed";
                }
            }
        }
```

5. Compile the project.

    ❑   On the **Menu** bar, select **Build | Build GetUptime**

6. If the folder for the module doesn't exist yet, create the folder.

```
$modulePath = "$env:USERPROFILE\Documents\WindowsPowerShell\
Modules\GetUptime"
if(!(Test-Path $modulePath))
{
    New-Item -Path $modulePath -ItemType Directory
}
```

7. Copy `GetUptime.dll` from the output of Visual Studio to the new module folder.

```
$modulePath = "$env:USERPROFILE\Documents\WindowsPowerShell\
Modules\GetUptime"
Copy-Item -Path GetUptime.dll -Destination $modulePath
```

8. In a PowerShell console, execute `Get-Module –ListAvailable` to list all the available modules:

```
PS C:\> Get-Module -ListAvailable


    Directory: C:\Users\Ed\Documents\WindowsPowerShell\Modules


ModuleType Name                                ExportedCommands
---------- ----                                ----------------
Binary     GetUptime                           Get-Uptime
Manifest   Hello                               {Get-Hello, Get-Hello2}
```

9. Use the Cmdlet by calling the included commands:

```
PS C:\> Get-Uptime

Days              : 3
Hours             : 22
Minutes           : 48
Seconds           : 42
Milliseconds      : 750
Ticks             : 3413227500000
TotalDays         : 3.95049479166667
TotalHours        : 94.811875
TotalMinutes      : 5688.7125
TotalSeconds      : 341322.75
TotalMilliseconds : 341322750


PS C:\>
```

How it works...

In the first step, we are creating a Visual Studio project for a class library. In this instance, I used Visual C# due to both to personal preference and the fact that there is more information available for creating Cmdlets with C#. Visual Basic could have been used as well.

> I configured the Visual Studio session as a .NET framework 2.0 project. This could have been 3.0, 3.5, or 4.0 instead.

In the second step, we add the necessary references to create and install our Cmdlet. The first reference—System.Managment.Automation.dll—loads the necessary components to tag this project as a Cmdlet. The second reference—System.Configuration.Install—loads the components necessary to install the Cmdlet on a system.

In the third step, we add the code for our Cmdlet. The code section can be broken into four sections: class attribute, class, ProcessRecord, and C# code.

- The Cmdlet code begins with the line [Cmdlet(VerbsCommon.Get, "Uptime")], which is an attribute that describes the class and what it does. In this case, it defines the class as a PowerShell Cmdlet with a verb-noun pair of Get-Uptime.

- The GetUptimeCommand class is a standard C# class and inherits from the Cmdlet class.

- The ProcessRecord is the section that is executed when the Cmdlet is called. There is also an optional BeginProcessing and EndProcessing section that can be added to provide a build-up and tear-down process. The build-up and tear-down can be used to load information before processing and clear out variables and other objects when done processing

- The C# code is the basic code and can be almost anything that would normally be included in a class project.

In the fourth step, we create the Cmdlet installer named GetUptimePSSnapin. The installer is a fairly simple class, similar to the Cmdlet class, which inherits the PSSnapin class and contains overrides that return information about the Cmdlet. In many scenarios, this section can be copy/paste into new projects and simply updated to reflect the new Cmdlet name.

In the fifth step, we compile the project. It is important to review the output from Visual Studio at this point to ensure no errors are reported. Any errors shown here may stop the project from compiling correctly and stop it from functioning.

Next, we create a folder to hold the compiled Cmdlet. This process is the same as we performed in the *Creating and using modules* recipe.

Lastly, we execute our commands to confirm the module loaded properly.

There's more

Cmdlet naming convention: Cmdlets are traditionally named in a verb/noun pair. The verb describes the action, such as get, set, or measure. The noun describes that object the action is being performed on or against. It is best practice to build functions and Cmdlets using this same naming convention for easy use.

For more information about which verbs are available and when they should be used, run `Get-Verb` from within PowerShell.

See also

▶ For more information on creating Cmdlets, see `http://msdn.microsoft.com/en-gb/library/windows/desktop/dd878294(v=vs.85).aspx`

2
Managing Windows Network Services with PowerShell

In this chapter we will cover the following recipes:

- ▸ Configuring static networking
- ▸ Installing domain controllers
- ▸ Configuring zones in DNS
- ▸ Configuring DHCP scopes
- ▸ Configuring DHCP server failover
- ▸ Converting DHCP addresses to static
- ▸ Building out a PKI environment
- ▸ Creating AD users
- ▸ Searching for and reporting on AD users
- ▸ Finding expired computers in AD
- ▸ Creating and e-mailing a superuser report

Introduction

Setting up a new Active Directory environment can be either exciting or boring. If you have rarely built out new domain and networking environments, the process is probably new and very exciting. However, if you are constantly building out new environments for test labs or other business needs, the process can be fairly long and drawn out. Instead, you are mostly interested in automating the process to require minimal user input and maintain consistency between builds.

This chapter covers the installation and configuration of Active Directory, DNS, DHCP, and Certificate Services. This chapter should cover everything necessary to prepare an environment as a fully functioning Active Directory domain for use in labs or new domain environments.

Configuring static networking

TCP/IP is the primary technology used for communicating between computers today. When first building out an environment, one of the first items to accomplish is to define and apply an IP addressing scheme. Once the addressing scheme is defined, we can create static addresses for our first servers. Later, we will configure DHCP in case static addressing is not desired for all of the systems in your environment.

Getting ready

From the following diagram we can see that we have already defined our addressing scheme using both IPv4 and IPv6. At the start of our network, we have a router acting as a default gateway, and we will configure two servers in preparation for becoming domain controllers. The default gateway router is already statically assigned with IPv4 and IPv6 addresses:

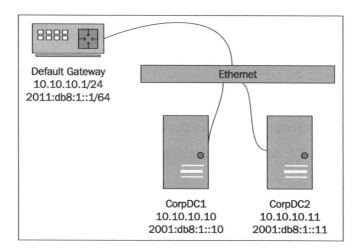

All three of these components are connected to a common Ethernet segment to communicate with each other.

 Before defining any networking configuration, we should confirm that our addresses do not conflict with other networks in our environment. Even when building out isolated environments, it is best to use different network addresses in case of accidental conflict with production environments.

How to do it...

Carry out the following steps to configure static networking:

1. Find the interface to set by executing Get-NetIPInterface:

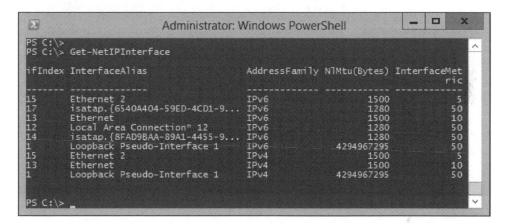

2. Set the IP information using `New-NetIPAddress`:

```
New-NetIPAddress -AddressFamily IPv4 -IPAddress 10.10.10.10
-PrefixLength 24 -InterfaceAlias Ethernet
```

```
Administrator: Windows PowerShell                                _  □  X

PS C:\> New-NetIPAddress -AddressFamily IPv4 -IPAddress 10.10.10.10 -PrefixLengt
h 24 -InterfaceAlias Ethernet

IPAddress           : 10.10.10.10
InterfaceIndex      : 13
InterfaceAlias      : Ethernet
AddressFamily       : IPv4
Type                : Unicast
PrefixLength        : 24
PrefixOrigin        : Manual
SuffixOrigin        : Manual
AddressState        : Tentative
ValidLifetime       : Infinite ([TimeSpan]::MaxValue)
PreferredLifetime   : Infinite ([TimeSpan]::MaxValue)
SkipAsSource        : False
PolicyStore         : ActiveStore

IPAddress           : 10.10.10.10
InterfaceIndex      : 13
InterfaceAlias      : Ethernet
AddressFamily       : IPv4
Type                : Unicast
PrefixLength        : 24
PrefixOrigin        : Manual
SuffixOrigin        : Manual
AddressState        : Invalid
ValidLifetime       : Infinite ([TimeSpan]::MaxValue)
PreferredLifetime   : Infinite ([TimeSpan]::MaxValue)
SkipAsSource        : False
PolicyStore         : PersistentStore

PS C:\>
```

3. Set DNS Servers using `Set-DnsClientServerAddress`:

```
Set-DnsClientServerAddress -InterfaceAlias Ethernet
-ServerAddresses "10.10.10.10","10.10.10.11"
```

```
Administrator: Windows PowerShell                                _  □  X

PS C:\> Set-DnsClientServerAddress -InterfaceAlias Ethernet -ServerAddresses "10
.10.10.10","10.10.10.11"
PS C:\>
```

4. Set the default route using `New-NetRoute`:

```
New-NetRoute -DestinationPrefix "0.0.0.0/0" -NextHop "10.10.10.1"
-InterfaceAlias Ethernet
```

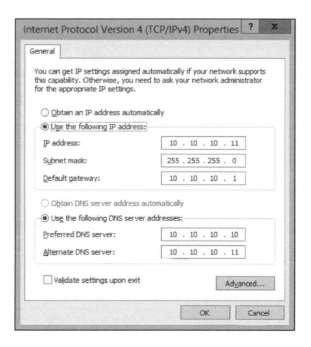

Administrator: Windows PowerShell

```
PS C:\> New-NetRoute -DestinationPrefix "0.0.0.0/0" -NextHop "10.10.10.1" -Inter
faceAlias Ethernet

ifIndex DestinationPrefix                            NextHop
------- -----------------                            -------
13      0.0.0.0/0                                    10.10.10.1
13      0.0.0.0/0                                    10.10.10.1

PS C:\>
```

How it works...

In the first step we list out the network adapters available on the server. Windows Servers often include several network adapters of different types, and depending on the features installed, there can be several more. By executing `Get-NetworkIPInterface`, we list the interface names and indexes that we will use to identify the specific interface we desire to configure.

The second and third steps use `New-NetIPAddress` and `Set-DnsClientServerAddress` to configure the identified interface with IPv4 address and DNS targets for the specified interface.

The last step uses `New-NetRoute` to define a network route. The `-DestinationPrefix 0.0.0.0/0` parameter identifies this route as the default route, or default gateway. The `-NextHop 10.10.10.1` parameter is the router address to forward traffic into if another route does not take precedence.

The following screenshot shows the IPv4 address properties after finalizing configuration via PowerShell:

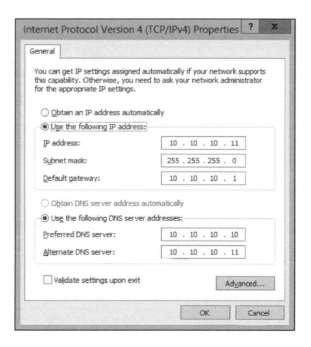

There's more...

There are a few more features provided by PowerShell. They are as follows:

▶ **IPv6 addressing**: In addition to configuring IPv4, PowerShell can also configure IPv6 addresses. The process for configuring static IPv6 addressing is exactly the same as IPv4, the only change is the addresses themselves.

Following are examples of configuring IPv6 on the same host. Note that both IPv4 and IPv6 addressing can coexist on the same server without issue:

```
New-NetIPAddress -AddressFamily IPv6 -IPAddress 2001:db8:1::10 `
-PrefixLength 64 -InterfaceAlias Ethernet
New-NetRoute -DestinationPrefix ::/0 -NextHop 2001:db8:1::1 `
-InterfaceAlias Ethernet
Set-DnsClientServerAddress -InterfaceAlias Ethernet `
-ServerAddresses "2001:db8:1::10","2001:db8:1::11"
```

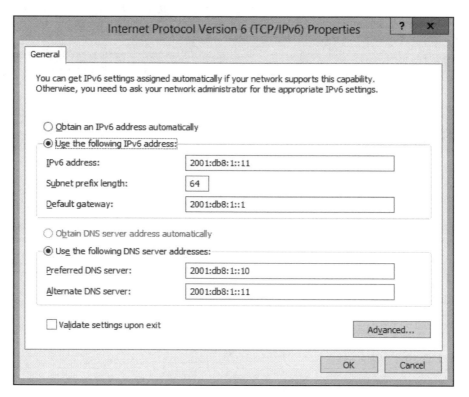

► **Additional IP addresses**: By using the `New-NetIPAddress` function, an interface can be configured with multiple IP addresses simultaneously. This configuration is often used for clustering or load balancing within Windows. Following is an example of configuring an additional address:

```
New-NetIPAddress -AddressFamily IPv4 -IPAddress 10.10.10.250
-PrefixLength 24 -InterfaceAlias Ethernet
```

▶ **Additional routes**: Windows has the ability to route network packets to more locations than the default gateway. Say for instance, there are two routers on your network: the default gateway and a second gateway. The second gateway is used to access the `10.10.20.0/24` network, and the Windows server needs to be configured to route to it:

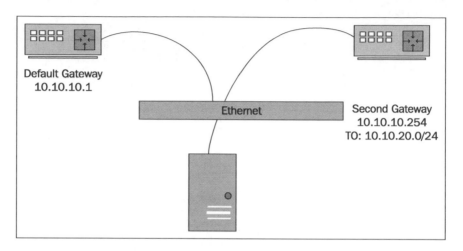

By executing the `New-NetRoute` command again, with the `-DestinationPrefix` and `-NextHop` addresses changed appropriately, we add a specific route to the server:

```
New-NetRoute -DestinationPrefix "10.10.20.0/24" -NextHop
"10.10.10.254" -InterfaceAlias Ethernet
```

 In some cases, such as a dedicated management network, the secondary network may be connected to a different network interface. If that is the situation, change the `-InterfaceAlias` parameter to target the second interface.

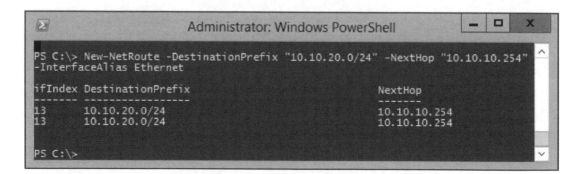

The full list of routes can be viewed by running `Get-NetRoute`. This will return all IPv4, IPv6, default, and static routes that are defined on the system:

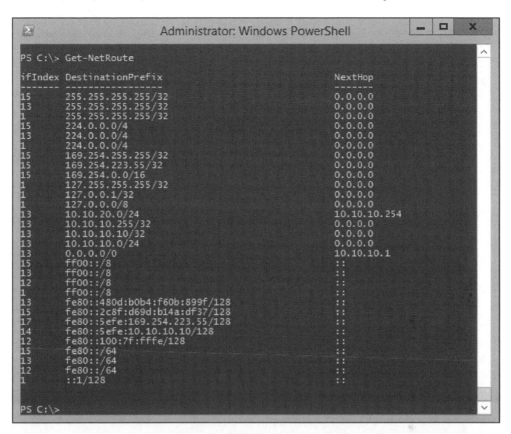

Installing domain controllers

Once the TCP/IP networking is set up and working, the next step to tackle is installing the domain controllers. In a Windows Active Directory domain, the domain controllers can be viewed as the core of the network. Domain controllers provide user authentication, group policy information, time synchronization, and access to Active Directory objects. Additionally, domain controllers often provide several network services such as DNS, DHCP, certificate services, and more.

This recipe will set up and install the first domain controller, creating a new domain in a new forest. Once completed, the second domain controller will be remotely installed and promoted. Additionally, we will install DNS on both domain controllers to provide name resolution services.

Getting ready

This recipe assumes a server and networking configuration setup similar to the prior recipe. We will be working with newly installed servers without any additional roles or software installed. To complete these tasks, you will need to log on to the server as the local administrator.

How to do it...

Carry out the following steps to install the domain controller:

1. As an administrator, open a PowerShell.

2. Identify the Windows Features to install:

   ```
   Get-WindowsFeature | Where-Object Name -like *domain*
   Get-WindowsFeature | Where-Object Name -like *dns*
   ```

3. Install the necessary features:

   ```
   Install-WindowsFeature AD-Domain-Services, DNS -
   IncludeManagementTools
   ```

4. Configure the domain:

   ```
   $SMPass = ConvertTo-SecureString 'P@$$w0rd11' -AsPlainText -Force
   Install-ADDSForest -DomainName corp.contoso.com -
   SafeModeAdministratorPassword $SMPass -Confirm:$false
   ```

How it works...

The first step executes the `Get-WindowsFeature` Cmdlet to list the features necessary to install domain services and DNS. If you are unsure of the exact names of the features to install, this is a great method to search for the feature names using wildcards. The second step uses `Install-WindowsFeature` to install the identified features, any dependencies, and any applicable management tools.

The third step calls `Install-ADDSForest` to create a new domain/forest named `corp.contoso.com`. Before promoting the server to a domain controller, we create a variable named `$SMPass`, which will hold a secure string that can be used as a password when promoting the server. This secure string is then passed as `-SafeModeAdministratorPassword` to the server, allowing access to the server if the domain services fail to start in the future:

You're about to be signed off

The computer is being restarted because Active Directory Domain Services was installed or removed.

Close

You will see a notice similar to the preceding screenshot when installation is finished. The system will automatically restart and the domain controller install will be complete.

There's more...

The following lists what more can be done with the domain controller:

- **Joining a computer to domain**: Once the domain has been created, computers can be joined to the domain manually or via automation. The following example shows how to use PowerShell to join the `CorpDC2` computer to the `corp.contoso.com` domain.

  ```
  $secString = ConvertTo-SecureString 'P@$$w0rd11' -AsPlainText
  -Force
  $myCred = New-Object -TypeName PSCredential -ArgumentList "corp\
  administrator", $secString
  Add-Computer -DomainName "corp.contoso.com" -Credential $myCred -
  NewName "CORPDC2" -Restart
  ```

  Similar to creating the domain, first a `$secString` variable is created to hold a secure copy of the password that will be used to join the computer to the domain. Then a `$myCred` variable is created to convert the username/password combination into a `PSCredentntial` object that will be used to join the computer to the domain. Lastly, the `Add-Computer` Cmdlet is called to join the computer to the domain and simultaneously, rename the system. When the system reboots, it will be connected to the domain.

- **Push install of domain controller**: It is normally considered best practice to have at least two **domain controllers (DCs)** for each domain. By having two DCs, one can be taken offline for maintenance, patching, or as the result of an unplanned outage, without impacting the overall domain services.

Once a computer has been joined to the domain, promoting the system to a DC can be performed remotely using PowerShell:

```
Install-WindowsFeature -Name AD-Domain-Services, DNS
-IncludeManagementTools -ComputerName CORPDC2
Invoke-Command -ComputerName CORPDC2 -ScriptBlock {
$secPass = ConvertTo-SecureString 'P@$$w0rd11' -AsPlainText -Force
$myCred = New-Object -TypeName PSCredential -ArgumentList "corp\
administrator", $secPass
$SMPass = ConvertTo-SecureString 'P@$$w0rd11' -AsPlainText -Force
Install-ADDSDomainController -DomainName corp.contoso.com -
SafeModeAdministratorPassword $SMPass -Credential $myCred -
Confirm:$false
}
```

First, the Domain and DNS services and appropriate management tools are installed on the remote computer. Then, using the `Invoke-Command` Cmdlet, the commands are executed remotely to promote the server to a domain controller and reboot.

 To create a new domain/forest, we used the `Install-ADDSForest` command. To promote a computer into an existing domain/forest, we use the `Install-ADDSDomainController` command.

Configuring zones in DNS

Windows domains rely heavily on DNS for name resolution and for finding appropriate resources. DNS is composed primarily of zones, each of which contains records. These zones and records provide name to address and address to name resolution for clients.

Here we will install and configure the DNS service and configure zones for servicing clients.

Getting ready

This recipe assumes a server and networking configuration similar to what is created in the first recipe. For DNS services to operate, the server does not need to be a member of an Active Directory domain, and in some scenarios, such as internet facing systems, Active Directory membership is discouraged.

We will be configuring our DNS servers with the following zones:

Zone	Type
corp.contoso.com	AD integrated
10.10.10.in-addr.arpa	AD integrated reverse lookup
20.168.192.in-add.arpa	AD integrated reverse lookup
contoso.com	Standard primary
fabrkam.com	Conditional forwarder to 192.168.99.1
corp.adatum.com	Secondary zone referencing 192.168.1.1

How to do it...

Carry out the following steps to configure zones in DNS:

1. Identify features to install:

   ```
   Get-WindowsFeature | Where-Object Name -like *dns*
   ```

2. Install DNS feature and tools (if not already installed):

   ```
   Install-WindowsFeature DNS -IncludeManagementTools -
   IncludeAllSubFeature
   ```

3. Create a reverse lookup zone:

   ```
   Add-DnsServerPrimaryZone -Name 10.10.10.in-addr.arpa -
   ReplicationScope Forest
   Add-DnsServerPrimaryZone -Name 20.168.192.in-addr.arpa -
   ReplicationScope Forest
   ```

4. Create a primary zone and add static records:

   ```
   Add-DnsServerPrimaryZone -Name contoso.com -ZoneFile contoso.com.
   dns
   Add-DnsServerResourceRecordA -ZoneName contoso.com -Name www -
   IPv4Address 192.168.20.54 -CreatePtr
   ```

5. Create a conditional forwarder:

   ```
   Add-DnsServerConditionalForwarderZone -Name fabrikam.com
   -MasterServers 192.168.99.1
   ```

6. Create a secondary zone:

   ```
   Add-DnsServerSecondaryZone -Name corp.adatum.com -ZoneFile corp.
   adatum.com.dns -MasterServers 192.168.1.1
   ```

How it works...

The first two steps may have already been completed if your DNS server coexists on the domain controller. When viewing the output of `Get-WindowsFeature` in the first step, if `Install State` for the DNS features equals `Installed`, the roles are already installed. If the roles are already installed, you can still attempt to reinstall them without causing issues.

The third step creates two AD-integrated reverse lookup zones named `10.10.10.in-addr.arpa` and `20.168.192.in-addr.arpa`. These zones are used for IP-to-Name resolution for servers in the `10.10.10.0/24` (internal) and `192.168.20.0/24` (DMZ or untrusted) subnets. These reverse lookup zones are not automatically created when installing DNS or Active Directory and it is the administrator's responsibility to create it.

> It is considered a best practice to have a reverse lookup zone for all networks in your organization. This eases many operational tasks and some network tools fail to work properly if the reverse lookup zones don't exist.

The fourth step creates a standard primary zone named `contoso.com`. This zone is different from the `corp.contoso.com` zone that was automatically created during creation of the domain. This new zone will be used to host records used in an untrusted or DMZ environment. In this example we created a static record `www.contoso.com`, configured it with a target IP address, and configured the reverse lookup record as well.

> The steps shown here are an example of creating a primary zone. Additional steps may be needed to fully secure a DNS server that is accessible by the outside world.
>
> Additionally, standard primary zones cannot be AD-integrated and do not automatically replicate to other DNS servers. To replicate a standard primary zone, a secondary zone must be created on the target DNS server and authorized to replicate.

The fifth step creates a conditional forwarder named `fabrikam.com`. A conditional forwarder simply identifies the domain request and forwards it to the appropriate master servers.

The sixth step creates a secondary zone named `corp.adatum.com`. Unlike primary zones, secondary zones are read-only, and they only hold a copy of the zone data as pulled from the master server. To add or update records in this zone, the changes must be made at the master server, and then replicated to the secondary.

 Unlike primary zones and conditional forwarders, secondary zones cannot be AD-integrated and do not automatically replicate to other DNS servers in the domain. This means that the secondary zones must be configured on each DNS server that will host the zone.

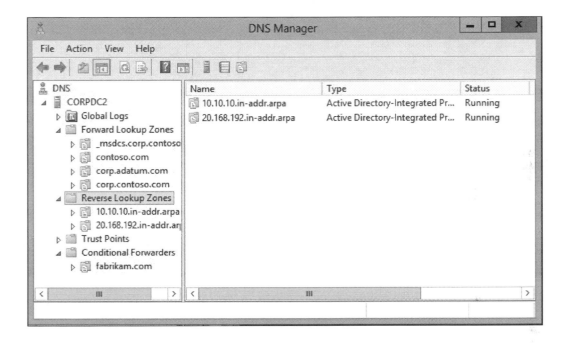

There's more...

The following lists the additional features of zones in DNS:

▸ **Listing all zones**: A full list of DNS zones on a server can be returned by executing the Get-DnsServerZone function:

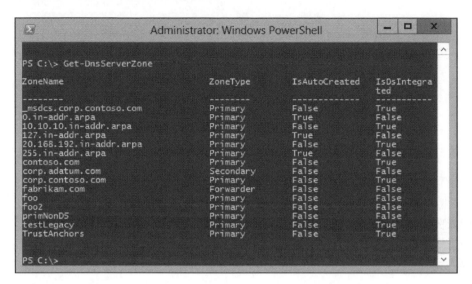

▸ **Updating DNS records**: When updating static records there are two options: delete and recreate, and update. The following is a simple function that gets a current resource record from DNS, updates it, and commits it back to DNS:

```
Function Update-DNSServerResourceRecord{
    param(
    [string]$zoneName = $(throw "DNS zone name required")
    ,[string]$recordName = $(throw "DNS record name required")
    ,[string]$newIPv4Address = $(throw "New IPv4Address required")
    )
    # Get the current record from DNS
    $oldRecord = Get-DnsServerResourceRecord -ZoneName $zoneName
-Name $recordName
    Write-Host "Original Value: " $oldRecord.RecordData.
IPv4Address

    # Clone the record and update the new IP address
    $newRecord=$oldRecord.Clone()
    $newRecord.RecordData.IPv4Address = [ipaddress]$newIPv4Address
```

```
# Commit the changed record
Set-DnsServerResourceRecord -ZoneName $zoneName
-OldInputObject $oldRecord -NewInputObject $newRecord
    Write-Host "New Value: " (Get-DnsServerResourceRecord
-ZoneName $zoneName -Name $recordName).RecordData.IPv4Address
}
```

Configuring DHCP scopes

As an alternative to statically assigned TCP/IP addresses, Windows supports the **Dynamic Host Configuration Protocol** (**DHCP**). This service allows for provisioning of IP addresses, default gateways, DNS information, and even more advanced information such as boot servers.

This recipe will set up the basic DHCP features on a domain controller and configure an initial DHCP scope.

Getting ready

This recipe assumes a server, networking, and domain configuration similar to what is created in the *Installing domain controllers* recipe.

How to do it...

Carry out the following steps to configure DHCP scopes:

1. Install DHCP and management tools:

   ```
   Get-WindowsFeature | Where-Object Name -like *dhcp*
   Install-WindowsFeature DHCP -IncludeManagementTools
   ```

2. Create a DHCP scope

   ```
   Add-DhcpServerv4Scope -Name "Corpnet" -StartRange 10.10.10.100
   -EndRange 10.10.10.200 -SubnetMask 255.255.255.0
   ```

3. Set DHCP options

   ```
   Set-DhcpServerv4OptionValue -DnsDomain corp.contoso.com -DnsServer
   10.10.10.10 -Router 10.10.10.1
   ```

4. Activate DHCP

   ```
   Add-DhcpServerInDC -DnsName corpdc1.corp.contoso.com
   ```

How it works...

The first step uses `Install-WindowsFeature` to install the DHCP feature and management tools on the currently logged on system. Once installed, the second step calls `Add-DHCPServerv4Scope` to create a DHCP scope named `Corpnet`, providing dynamic IPs on the `10.10.10.0/24` subnet.

The third step uses `Set-DhcpServerv4OptionValue` to set up common DHCP options, such as the DNS servers and default gateway address. This command can include other common options such as the DNS domain name, WinsServer, and Wpad location. Additionally, any extended DHCP option ID can be configured using the `Set-DhcpServerv4OptionValue` command.

The last step calls `Add-DHCPServerInDC` to activate the DHCP service on the computer in Active Directory. This authorizes the DHCP service to provide addresses to clients in the domain.

There's more...

The following lists the additional features of DHCP:

- **Adding DHCP reservations**: In addition to creating and activating DHCP scopes, we can also create reservations in DHCP. A reservation matches a network adapter's MAC address to a specific IP address. It is similar to using a static address, except the static mapping is maintained on the DHCP server:

  ```
  Add-dhcpserverv4reservation -scopeid 10.10.10.0 -ipaddress
  10.10.10.102 -name test2 -description "Test server" -clientid 12-
  34-56-78-90-12
  Get-dhcpserverv4reservation -scopeid 10.10.10.0
  ```

- **Adding DHCP exclusions**: Additionally, we can create DHCP exclusions using PowerShell. An exclusion is an address, or range of addresses that the DHCP server won't provide to clients. Exclusions are often used when individual IP addresses within the scope have been statically assigned:

  ```
  Add-DhcpServerv4ExclusionRange -ScopeId 10.10.10.0 -StartRange
  10.10.10.110 -EndRange 10.10.10.111
  Get-DhcpServerv4ExclusionRange
  ```

Configuring DHCP server failover

Prior to Server 2012, there were limited methods of ensuring DHCP was redundant and always available to service requests. One of the most common methods was to split DHCP scopes between multiple servers, with each server providing a subset of the scope. If one system was unavailable, the other system was still able to provide a subset of addresses. However, this caused problems because if a DHCP server was unavailable, there may not be enough addresses available to service all of your clients. Other redundancy options involved clustering or other expensive technologies that were difficult to manage.

In Server 2012 DHCP server failover is a built-in feature. This feature allows servers to share a common DHCP database to provide leases and provide redundancy. To use DHCP failover, the DHCP feature just needs to be installed and configured across servers. This recipe will walk through the configuration of DHCP failover.

Getting ready

This recipe assumes a server, networking, and domain configuration similar to what is created in the *Installing domain controllers* recipe. A minimum of two servers will be needed to configure as DHCP servers. Additionally, it assumes one of the domain controllers already has DHCP installed and configured.

How to do it...

Carry out the following steps to configure DHCP server failover:

1. Install DHCP on the second server either locally or remotely:

    ```
    Install-WindowsFeature dhcp -IncludeAllSubFeature -ComputerName
    corpdc2
    ```

2. Authorize DHCP on the second server:

    ```
    Add-DhcpServerInDC -DnsName corpdc2.corp.contoso.com
    ```

3. Configure DHCP failover:

    ```
    Add-DhcpServerv4Failover -ComputerName corpdc1 -PartnerServer
    corpdc2 -Name Corpnet-Failover -ScopeId 10.10.10.0 -SharedSecret
    'Pa$$w0rd!!'
    ```

How it works...

The first and second steps are responsible for installing and authorizing DHCP on CorpDC2. This is the same process used in the previous recipe to install DHCP on the first domain controller. Once installed, we use Add-DhcpServerInDC to authorize the server to act as a DHCP server.

The third step calls Add-DHCPServerv4Failover to configure DHCP failover across CorpDC1 and CorpDC2. This command identifies the scope 10.10.10.0 for failover and configures a shared key for authenticating communication between the servers.

At this point the failover configuration is complete and both DHCP servers will begin providing addresses. If you open the DHCP administration console, you will see that both domain controllers have DHCP installed and servicing clients. Additionally, you will see that both servers have the same client lease information, making the solution truly redundant:

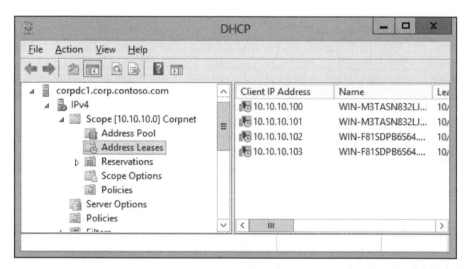

Converting DHCP addresses to static

While DHCP is an easy way to manage network addresses, especially, in dynamic environments, it does have its drawbacks. If something happens on your physical network or to your DHCP server, clients may not be able to receive or renew their addresses. And due to the dynamic nature of DHCP, addresses may change, causing issues with firewalls and DNS records.

This is normally fine for desktop environments, but in server environments, we want to minimize any possibility for an outage. As such, at some point you may want to convert your dynamically addressed hosts to use static addresses.

Getting ready

This recipe assumes a basic server configuration with a single interface using a single IP address via DHCP. The script works best when run locally on the target server.

How to do it...

Log on to the target server interactively and execute the following script:

```
# Identify all adapters that recieved an address via DHCP
$adapters = Get-WmiObject -Class Win32_NetworkAdapterConfiguration |
Where-Object {($_.IPAddress) -and $_.DHCPEnabled -eq 'True' }

# Iterate through each adapter
foreach($adapter in $adapters)
{
    # Get current adapter and IP information
    $adapIndex = $adapter.InterfaceIndex
    $ipAddress = $adapter.IPAddress[0]
    $subnetMask = $adapter.IPSubnet[0]
    $defaultGateway = $adapter.DefaultIPGateway[0]
    $prefix = (Get-NetIPAddress -InterfaceIndex $adapIndex -
AddressFamily IPv4).PrefixLength
    $dnsServers = $adapter.DNSServerSearchOrder
    [ipaddress]$netAddr = ([ipaddress]$ipAddress).Address -band
([ipaddress]$subnetMask).Address

    # Identify the DHCP server
    $dhcpServer = $adapter.DHCPServer
    $dhcpName = ([System.Net.DNS]::GetHostEntry($dhcpServer)).HostName

    # Add an exclusion to DHCP for the current IP address
    Invoke-Command -ComputerName $dhcpName -ScriptBlock{
        Add-DhcpServerv4ExclusionRange -ScopeId $args[0] -StartRange
$args[1] -EndRange $args[1]
    } -ArgumentList $netAddr.IPAddressToString, $ipAddress

    # Release the DHCP address lease
    Remove-NetIPAddress -InterfaceIndex $adapIndex -Confirm:$false

    # Statically assign the IP and DNS information
    New-NetIPAddress -InterfaceIndex $adapIndex -AddressFamily
IPv4 -IPAddress $ipAddress -PrefixLength $prefix -DefaultGateway
$defaultGateway
    Set-DnsClientServerAddress -InterfaceIndex $adapIndex
-ServerAddresses $dnsServers
}
```

How it works...

The first part of the script queries WMI for all network adapters that both have an active IP address, and are using DHCP. The results from the WMI query are placed into a variable named $adapters and are iterated in a for each loop, where the adapter and IP information is collected.

 A network adapter can hold multiple IP addresses, but this script is only capable of handling the first IPv4 address of each adapter.

Once all of the network information is collected, Invoke-Command is used to connect to the DHCP server that issued the address and creates an exclusion. The exclusion record's start and end address is the IP address assigned to the client. This prevents the IP address from being reused by another host at a later time.

Lastly, the adapter is changed to a static address. Remove-NetIPAddress is used to release the DHCP address from the interface. Once cleared, New-NetIPAddress is used to statically configure the interface with the same IPv4 address, subnet, and gateway that was previously held. Finally, Set-DnsClientServerAddress assigns the DNS server addresses.

There's more...

This script can be run against a system remotely using a PSSession, with the exception of creating the DHCP exclusion. When using a PSSession to a remote computer, you cannot create another session to a third computer. As such, the script will run and successfully set the local interfaces to static, but it won't exclude DHCP from providing those addresses to another client.

Building out a PKI environment

Windows Active Directory domains are a great way to authenticate users and computers. Using a central store of accounts and passwords, requests can be easily authenticated, and accounts can be quickly added, updated, or removed as needed. While this is a great method for authentication within the domain, it does not work as well outside of the domain. Situations, where the domain controller may not be accessible, where the authority of the domain controller is in question, or when accessing resources outside of a domain, call for alternative authentication methods.

Certificates allow for creation of an authentication infrastructure by using a series of trusts. Instead of joining a domain, and thereby trusting the domain controllers, you trust a **Certificate Authority (CA)**. The CA is responsible for handing out certificates that authenticate the user or computer. By trusting the CA, you implicitly trust the certificates it produces.

Windows server has the ability to operate both as an Active Directory domain and a Certificate Authority. This provides the basis for several technologies in a domain such as secure web servers, IPSec, and DirectAccess. The following will cover the necessary steps to install and configure a **Private Key Infrastructure** (**PKI**) environment.

Getting ready

This particular recipe installs and configures an enterprise root CA, which requires a domain environment to operate. If you do not have a domain environment, this can still be used, but the CAType needs to be changed to support a standalone system.

How to do it...

Carry out the following steps to build a PKI environment:

1. Install certificate server:

   ```
   Get-WindowsFeature | Where-Object Name -Like *cert*
   Install-WindowsFeature AD-Certificate -IncludeManagementTools
   -IncludeAllSubFeature
   ```

2. Configure the server as an enterprise CA:

   ```
   Install-AdcsCertificationAuthority -CACommonName corp.contoso.com
   -CAType EnterpriseRootCA -Confirm:$false
   ```

3. Install root certificate to trusted root certification authorities store:

   ```
   Certutil -pulse
   ```

4. Request machine certificate from CA:

   ```
   Set-CertificateAutoEnrollmentPolicy -PolicyState Enabled -Context
   Machine -EnableTemplateCheck
   ```

How it works...

The first two steps install and configure the certificate services on the target server. The certificate server is configured as an enterprise root CA named corp.contoso.com, with the default configuration settings.

The third step uses the Certutil.exe utility to download and install the root CA to the trusted root certification authorities store. Lastly, a machine certificate is requested using the default autoenrollment policy.

There are four types of Certificate Authorities supported by Windows server:

- ► Enterprise root CA
- ► Enterprise subordinate CA
- ► Standalone root CA
- ► Standalone subordinate CA

The two enterprise CA types are designed to integrate with Active Directory domains and provide more flexibility in AD environments. Standalone CA types operate similar to third party CAs and don't integrate with AD. Additionally, the subordinate CA types are child authorities that have been delegated permission from the root authorities to create certificates.

There's more...

Once the PKI environment is implemented, the next step is to create a group policy to have clients autoenroll. Unfortunately, there is not a built-in function to edit the group policy objects we need, so we have to perform the task manually. Following are the steps necessary to set up the autoenroll GPO:

1. Open **Server Manager** and select **Tools | Group Policy Management**:

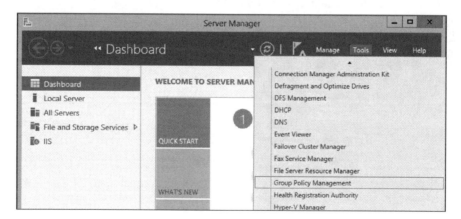

2. Browse to **Group Policy Management | Forest <forestname> | Domains | <domainname>**.

3. Right-click on **Default Domain Policy** and select **Edit**:

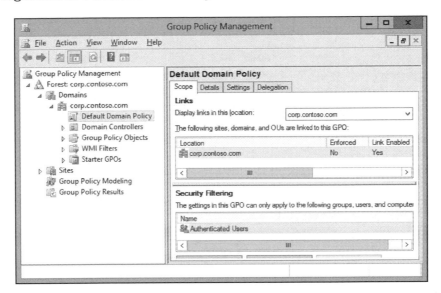

4. In the **Group Policy Management Editor**, browse to **Default Domain Policy | Computer Configuration | Policies | Windows Settings | Security Settings | Public Key Policies**:

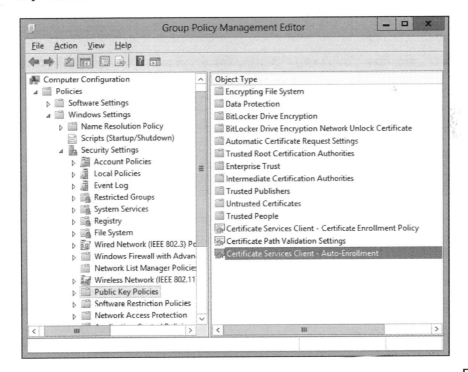

5. Right-click on **Certificate Services Client – Auto-Enrollment** and select **Properties**.

6. In the **Enrollment Policy Configuration** window, set the following fields:

   ❑ **Configuration Model: Enabled**

   ❑ Check the **Renew expired certificates, update pending certificates, and remove revoked certificates** checkbox

   ❑ Check the **Update certificates that use certificate templates** checkbox

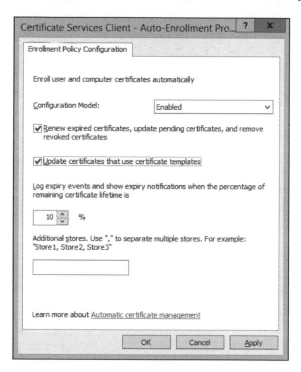

7. Click on **OK** and close the **Group Policy Management Editor**.

Creating AD users

When working in a test or lab environment, it is useful to have a number of test accounts to use. These accounts can have different access permissions and simulate different types of users doing specific tasks. These AD users are normally made up of simple accounts with a common password.

Additionally, when setting up a new production environment, it may be necessary to populate users into AD. These usernames and e-mail addresses are predefined and the passwords must be unique.

In this recipe we will use a PowerShell script to create both types of users.

Getting ready

To use this recipe properly, you need an AD environment with credentials capable of creating user accounts. Additionally, if you want to create specific users, you will need a CSV file with headers of **LastName,FirstName** as shown in the following screenshot that contains the users to create:

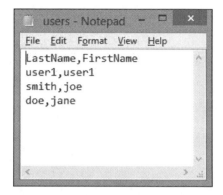

How to do it...

Carry out the following steps to create AD users:

1. To create a single Active Directory user account, use the following command:

    ```
    New-ADUser -Name JSmith
    ```

2. To create multiple Active Directory user accounts, we use the following functions:

    ```
    Function Create-Users{
        param($fileName, $emailDomain, $userPass, $numAccounts=10)
        if($fileName -eq $null ){
            [array]$users  = $null
            for($i=0; $i -lt $numAccounts; $i++){
                $users += [PSCustomObject]@{
                FirstName = 'Random'
                LastName = 'User' + $i
                }
            }
        } else {
            $users = Import-Csv -Path $fileName
        }
    ```

```powershell
    ForEach($user in $users)
    {
        $password = ''
        if($userPass)
        {
            $password = $userPass
        } else {
            $password = Get-RandomPass
        }
        Create-User -firstName $user.FirstName `
        -lastName $user.LastName -emailDomain $emailDomain `
        -password $password
    }
}


Function Create-User
{
    param($firstName, $lastName, $emailDomain, $password)
    $accountName = '{0}.{1}' -f $firstName, $lastName
    $emailAddr = '{0}@{1}' -f $accountName, $emailDomain
    $securePass = ConvertTo-SecureString $password -AsPlainText
-Force

    New-ADUser -Name $accountName -AccountPassword $securePass `
    -ChangePasswordAtLogon $true -EmailAddress $emailAddr `
    -Displayname "$FirstName $Lastname"  -GivenName $Firstname `
    -Surname $LastName -Enabled $true

    Write-Host "$LastName,$FirstName,$AccountName,$emailAddr,$pass
word"
}

function Get-RandomPass{
    $newPass = ''
    1..10 | ForEach-Object {
        $newPass += [char](Get-Random -Minimum 48 -Maximum 122)
    }
    return $newPass
}
```

How it works...

This script is composed of three functions: `Create-Users`, `Create-User`, and `Get-RandomPass`. The first function starts by checking if a value was passed for the `$fileName` parameter. If no value was included, it creates an array named `$Users` and populates it with the number of test accounts defined by `$numAccounts`. If `$fileName` exists, it imports the target file as a CSV and populates the `$Users` array.

 The loading of the CSV file has no error checking included, so it is important to review the contents of the file before starting. Specifically, confirm that the first line has the column headers as expected.

Once the user list has been determined, each user account is cycled through. Additional account properties, such as the e-mail address and username, are populated based on user information, and if a password was not predefined, a random password is generated. Once the password is defined, then `Create-User` is called.

The `Create-User` function defines the `$accountName` and `$emailAddr` of the user account by combining various attributes. It then converts the password into a secure string that can be used when creating the user account. Lastly, `New-ADUser` is called to create the user account in Active Directory with the defined user properties, and the user information is echoed to the console.

The third function named `Get-RandomPass` uses a loop to create a 10 random characters, which are combined and returned as a random password. The function begins by creating a `$newPass` variable as an empty string. The numbers 1 through 10 are passed into a `ForEach-Object` loop that chooses a random character and appends it to the `$newPass` variable. Once 10 characters have been added to the variable, the results are returned to whatever called the function.

 This password generator is very basic and may not meet your organization's complexity requirements. If this occurs, the account will still be created but will be disabled. A new password can be applied at a later time that meets the necessary complexity requirements.

Example output of creating multiple accounts is shown in the following screenshot:

```
PS C:\> Create-Users -emailDomain corp.contoso.com -numAccounts 10
User0,Random,Random.User0,Random.User0@corp.contoso.com,u2GPGiSWDu
User1,Random,Random.User1,Random.User1@corp.contoso.com,q:@ReIT9O8
User2,Random,Random.User2,Random.User2@corp.contoso.com,bx;Yo4k_WR
User3,Random,Random.User3,Random.User3@corp.contoso.com,cBoVkO@AWk
User4,Random,Random.User4,Random.User4@corp.contoso.com,OoR7[GhI7^
User5,Random,Random.User5,Random.User5@corp.contoso.com,?C^:1wqgZC
User6,Random,Random.User6,Random.User6@corp.contoso.com,xmykB_EcaF
User7,Random,Random.User7,Random.User7@corp.contoso.com,9B\]clV4xX
User8,Random,Random.User8,Random.User8@corp.contoso.com,EQWsCP]eUm
User9,Random,Random.User9,Random.User9@corp.contoso.com,XRaCl\p'ou
PS C:\>
```

There's more...

The following lists the additional features of AD users:

- **Additional AD properties**: The script as presented here sets only a minimum number of properties necessary for functional users. Several additional properties are as follows:
  - ❑ Personal information, such as home address and phone numbers
  - ❑ Organizational information, such as manager and office location
  - ❑ Remote access settings
  - ❑ AD information, such as home directory and logon script
  - ❑ Workstations the user is allowed to log on to

- **Template user**: Instead of creating a new account for each user, it is possible to create a template account that is used for all new accounts. Template accounts are useful for maintaining common settings, such as logon script or home directory location, and then not keep the setting for all future accounts. To use a template account, simply load the account using Get-ADUser and reference the account using the -Instance parameter. Refer the following example:

```
$templateUser=Get-ADUser -Identity Administrator
New-ADUser -Name Admin2 -Instance $templateUser -AccountPassword
$securePass
```

See also

For a full list of available user properties that can be configured, see http://technet.microsoft.com/en-us/library/hh852238.

Searching for and reporting on AD users

Once your AD environment has existed for some time, finding and changing settings in your environment can become difficult. For example, let's say when the domain was first created, all the users had the same logon script named `logon.bat`. Over time, specific needs arose that caused the creation of `logon2.bat`, and `new_logon.bat`, and `testlogon.bat`, with different users assigned to each script.

As an administrator, you want to consolidate all these logon scripts into one, but you need to know what this will impact. You need to know which logon scripts are being used, who is using which ones, and why the different scripts exist. Thanks to the capabilities of AD and PowerShell queries, these items can easily be found.

In this recipe we will perform multiple queries against Active Directory. We will be returning different information.

How to do it...

Carry out the following steps to search for and report on AD users:

1. To report on all users and their logon scripts execute the following code:

```
Get-ADUser -Filter * -Properties SamAccountName, DisplayName, `
ProfilePath, ScriptPath | `
Select-Object SamAccountName, DisplayName, ProfilePath, ScriptPath
```

2. To find all disabled user accounts execute the following code:

```
Get-ADUser –Filter 'Enabled -eq $false'
```

3. To find users who haven't logged in for 30 days execute the following code:

```
$logonDate = (Get-Date).AddDays(-30)
Get-ADUser -Filter 'LastLogonDate -lt $logonDate' | Select-Object
DistinguishedName
```

4. To find accounts with multiple logon failures execute the following code:

```
$primaryDC = Get-ADDomainController -Discover -Service PrimaryDC
Get-ADUser -Filter 'badpwdcount -ge 5' -Server $primaryDC.Name `
-Properties BadPwdCount | Select-Object DistinguishedName,
BadPwdCount
```

How it works...

The first example uses `Get-ADUser` and queries Active Directory for all `User` objects, and returns them to PowerShell. The accounts are then piped through `Select-Object` to return the username, profile location, and logon script to the screen.

The second example creates a simple filter for AD to show accounts that are not enabled. `Get-ADUser` is called with this filter and it returns the appropriate accounts.

The third example creates a slightly more robust AD filter that identifies users, who have not logged in for more than 30 days. We start by creating the `$logonDate` variable and assigning it with the date 30 days ago. We then call `Get-ADUser` with a filter based on the `LastLogonDate` attribute, and lastly return `Distinguished Name` of the users that match the filter. These may be users who have been on vacation, extended work trips and have not been able to log on to the domain, or user accounts that no longer are needed.

The fourth example provides a simple filter based on the number of bad password attempts for an account. We start by identifying the **primary domain controller** (**PDC**) in the environment. When a bad password attempt occurs, it is tracked on the domain controller initially queried, as well as the PDC emulator. This allows us to query a single server instead of all the DCs. If a particular account has a high number of password failures, it can be a sign of possible hacking attempt. As such, it is always helpful to have a script similar to this available so that the entire domain can be reviewed at a glance to determine if one user is having a problem, or if it is wide spread issue.

Finding expired computers in AD

As domains grow and change, one of the largest polluters of AD is expired machine accounts. Whenever a computer is joined to the domain, a machine account is created. However, when a machine is retired, the machine account is often left. There are no built-in tools to remove these machine accounts from the domain, and unlike user accounts, they are rarely audited. This becomes a problem as the environment grows, and auditing of the computer accounts becomes difficult.

This recipe will show how to search AD for expired, or nearly expired, machine accounts.

How to do it...

Carry out the following steps to find expired computers in AD:

1. To find recently aged accounts execute the following code:

```
$30Days = (Get-Date).AddDays(-30)
Get-ADComputer -Properties lastLogonDate -Filter 'lastLogonDate
-lt $30Days' | Format-Table Name, LastLogonDate
```

2. To find older accounts execute the following code:

```
$60Days = (Get-Date).AddDays(-60)
Get-ADComputer -Properties lastLogonDate -Filter 'lastLogonDate
-lt $60Days' | Format-Table Name, LastLogonDate
```

How it works...

By default, machine accounts are reset every 30 days, regardless of the user password expiration policy. With this in mind, we can search for accounts that haven't updated in 30 days in order to find recently aged accounts. In the first step we create a variable named $30Days. We call Get-Date to return the current date and time, and then use AddDays to add a negative 30 days. This date is then stored in our variable.

We then call Get-ADComputer to search AD for our computer accounts. We apply a filter on the lastLogonDate attribute and search for accounts that haven't logged in for more than 30 days. We then output the computer name and when it last logged on to the domain. Once the aging accounts are identified, we can proactively find and troubleshoot the machines to ensure there is no loss of services.

In the second step we perform the same function, but this time allowing for 60 days. In this scenario, since the machines haven't logged into the domain in twice the maximum normal, we can likely assume these systems are no longer in our environment. At this point we can additionally pipe the output of this command into Disable-ADAccount or Remove-ADComputer to disable or delete the account in AD.

See also

More information about machine account passwords and reset policies can be found at http://blogs.technet.com/b/askds/archive/2009/02/15/test2.aspx.

Creating and e-mailing a superuser report

One of the questions I receive every time there is a security audit or review is *How many super users are there?* To find this out, I have to manually open up Active Directory and look at the membership of Domain Admins and Enterprise Admins groups. Once I have identified the users, the security team then wants a documented list of who has superuser rights, when they got them, and why.

If your environment is anything like mine, looking at the Domain Admin group membership will be very surprising. Even though we work hard to limit who has access, more and more users creep into these groups throughout the year. By the time they are identified, finding out when, why, and how they were added can be exceedingly difficult. What is needed is a method of keeping up on the changes as they happen.

In this recipe we will create a superuser report that reports on membership of these critical groups. This report will show which accounts are in each group, and even highlight any changes that occurred since the last run. Additionally, the report will be e-mailed for easy access and retention.

Getting ready

To perform this recipe you will need to be in an Active Directory domain, with a service account that has access to query AD groups. The script runs on a system as a scheduled job and saves files to a local directory.

How to do it...

To create the superuser report, we create the following PowerShell script:

```
[Object[]]$oSuperUsers = New-Object PSObject

# Query the super-user groups for members
$oSuperUsers += Get-ADGroupMember -Identity 'Domain Admins' `
-Recursive | Select-Object @{Name='Group';expression={'Domain
Admins'}}, `
Name, objectClass
$oSuperUsers += Get-ADGroupMember -Identity 'Enterprise Admins' `
-Recursive | Select-Object @{Name='Group';expression={'Enterprise
Admins'}}, `
Name, objectClass
```

```
# Report on current membership
$strMessage = $oSuperUsers | Format-Table Name, objectClass `
-GroupBy Group | Out-String

$exportFile = "c:\temp\superusers.clixml"
if(Test-Path $exportFile)
{
    # Import the results from the last time the script was executed
    $oldUsers = Import-Clixml $exportFile

    # Identify and report on the changes
    $strMessage += "Changes`n"
    $strMessage += Compare-Object -ReferenceObject $oldUsers `
    -DifferenceObject $oSuperUsers | Select-Object @{Name="Group"; `
    expression={$_.InputObject.Group}}, @{Name="Name";expression=`
    {$_.InputObject.Name}}, @{Name="Side";expression={$_.
SideIndicator}}`
    | Out-String
}

# Export results from this execution
Export-Clixml -InputObject $oSuperUsers -Path $exportFile

# Email report to the administrator
Send-MailMessage -From reports@corp.contoso.com -Subject `
"Weekly SuperUser Report" -To admin@contoso.com -Body $strMessage `
-SmtpServer mail.contoso.com
```

How it works...

The first thing the script does is create a custom PowerShell object named $oSuperUsers to hold the group, name, and class information. A custom object is used here to make the results easier to manage and flexible further down the script. Get-ADGroupMember is then called against the Domain Admins and Enterprise Admins groups and populate the custom object. The membership of these two groups are organized by the group name and stored in the $strMessage variable.

An external file, c:\temp\superusers.clixml, is checked to see if this script has been executed before. If the file exists, it is loaded into the $oldUsers variable using Import-Clixml. This file holds an exported version of the $oSuperUsers object from the last run of the script. The two objects are compared using the Compare-Object command to highlight any differences and appended to $strMessage. Lastly, the current $oSuperUsers object is exported and overwrites the external file.

Finally, Send-MailMessage combines the group membership and changes into a simple text e-mail message. The message is sent via SMTP to a mail server and it will appear in the administrator's mailbox.

There's more...

To make full use of this script, it would be best to schedule it to run every week. To schedule the task, we save the command as a `.PS1` file and use the following script to add the script into Windows Task Scheduler:

```
# Define the action to be executed
$taskAction = New-ScheduledTaskAction -Execute `
"%SystemRoot%\system32\WindowsPowerShell\v1.0\powershell.exe" `
-Argument "C:\scripts\superUser.ps1"

# Define the execution schedule
$taskTrigger = New-ScheduledTaskTrigger -Weekly -WeeksInterval 1 -At 5am `
-DaysOfWeek Sunday

# Define the user account to execute the script
$taskUser = "Corp\ScriptAdmin"
$taskPassword = 'P@$$w0rd'

# Name the task and register
$taskName = "Super User Report"
Register-ScheduledTask -TaskName $taskName -Action $taskAction `
-Trigger $taskTrigger -User $taskUser -Password $taskPassword
```

The script starts by creating `New-ScheduledTaskAction`. This command identifies the command to execute, in this case `PowerShell.exe`, and any additional arguments, such as our `superUser.ps1` file. The `-Argument` option can be updated based on the location of your scripts.

Next, we define the schedule for the task. We do this by creating `New-ScheduledTaskTrigger` and define a start time and recurrence cycle. In this case we are executing our script at 5 a.m. every Sunday.

Next, we define our username and password to execute the script. In this situation we are using a predefined service account and storing the password in plain text.

Lastly, we use `Register-ScheduledTask` to save the task. Once completed, the task will appear in Windows Task Scheduler as shown in the following screenshot:

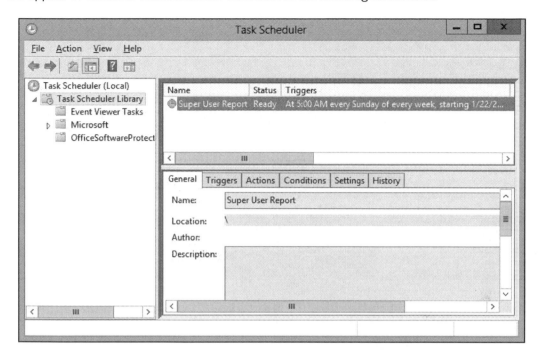

3
Managing IIS with PowerShell

In this chapter we will cover the following recipes:

- ▶ Installing and configuring IIS
- ▶ Configuring IIS for SSL
- ▶ Configuring a Central Certificate Store
- ▶ Configuring IIS bindings
- ▶ Configuring IIS logging
- ▶ Managing log files
- ▶ Configuring NLB across multiple servers
- ▶ Monitoring load balancing on NLB nodes
- ▶ Placing NLB nodes into maintenance
- ▶ Configuring a development/staging/production site scheme
- ▶ Promoting content in websites
- ▶ Reporting on website access and errors

Introduction

Internet Information Services (IIS) has become a key component in Windows Server. With IIS you can host publicly facing websites and internal intranets, as well as integrate with enterprise applications, such as SharePoint, Exchange, and System Center. IIS provides a central component of Windows Server that allows systems and applications to be expanded into more complex configurations.

This chapter covers how to install, configure, manage, and maintain IIS websites on Windows Server 8. In addition to basic management of IIS, this will also cover monitoring and reporting on IIS, using NLB for load balancing, and utilizing a development/staging/production configuration/promotion scheme.

Installing and configuring IIS

Websites are useful for multiple every day needs, from hosting static content, such as pictures, to dynamic content, such as calendars, and even web services. IIS in Windows Server 8 is extended greatly with additional PowerShell commands and functions.

This recipe will cover how to set up a basic IIS website and configure binding information.

Getting ready

For installing IIS, we will be using a basic Windows Server without any features installed.

How to do it...

Carry out the following steps to install and configure IIS:

1. Open a PowerShell console and install IIS:

   ```
   Get-WindowsFeature | Where-Object Name -likeweb*
   Install-WindowsFeature Web-WebServer -IncludeManagementTools
   ```

2. Use `Import-Module` to load the `WebAdministration` PowerShell module.

3. Use `Get-ChildItem` to view the IIS sites:

   ```
   Get-ChildItem IIS:\Sites
   ```

   When completed, you should see the configured sites similar to the following screenshot:

   ```
   PS C:\> Import-Module WebAdministration
   PS C:\> Get-ChildItem IIS:\Sites

   Name             ID   State     Physical Path                  Bindings
   ----             --   -----     -------------                  --------
   Default Web Site 1   Started   %SystemDrive%\inetpub\wwwroot  http *:80:
   ```

How it works...

In the first step we show all of the IIS-related features (over 50 of them) and their current install state. At this point we are looking to install only the basic IIS features. This includes the ability to present web static pages via HTTP, define a default document, perform logging, present error messages, compress static content to make it easier to send over the internet, and the management console.

When installing the `Web-Webserver` feature, it automatically includes the following features:

- `Web-Default-Doc`
- `Web-Dir-Browsing`
- `Web-Http-Errors`
- `Web-Static-Content`
- `Web-Http-Logging`
- `Web-Stat-Compression`
- `Web-Filtering`
- `Web-Mgmt-Console`

In the second step we load the `WebAdministrator` module. In PowerShell 3.0 modules are autoloading, and normally it isn't necessary to use `Import-Module`. PowerShell automatically loads modules when commands within the modules are executed, however, not when accessing the PSDrives presented by the module.

Lastly, we use `Get-ChildItem` to view the existing IIS websites. The sites are stored in the `IIS: PSDrive` under the `\Sites` directory. The command returns all websites on the system and information regarding their configuration.

There's more...

A **PSDrive**, or PowerShell Drive, is a logical drive that has been presented to PowerShell. This includes local drives on the computer, such as `C:\`, as well as mapped network drives. PSDrives also include drives presented by PowerShell providers, such as the Registry, Active Directory, and IIS.

A full list of PSDrives can be viewed by executing `Get-PSDrive`:

```
PS C:\> Get-PSDrive

Name          Used (GB)     Free (GB)  Provider       Root
----          ---------     ---------  --------       ----
A                                      FileSystem     A:\
AD                                     ActiveDire...  //RootDSE/
Alias                                  Alias
C                 20.42         39.23  FileSystem     C:\
Cert                                   Certificate    \
D                                      FileSystem     D:\
E                 35.77         24.23  FileSystem     E:\
Env                                    Environment
Function                               Function
HKCU                                   Registry       HKEY_CURRENT_USER
HKLM                                   Registry       HKEY_LOCAL_MACHINE
IIS                                    WebAdminis...  \\CORPDC1
Variable                               Variable
WSMan                                  WSMan

PS C:\>
```

Configuring IIS for SSL

The most common way of securing web traffic is to use SSL encryption. SSL signs and encrypts traffic between a web server and client in a way that is difficult for an outsider to view, change, or impersonate. If you have ever purchased something online, the web page that accepted your credit card details was likely encrypted using SSL.

In this recipe we will cover how to configure an IIS site to use SSL encryption.

Getting ready

Two things are required to use SSL encryption: a certificate capable of encrypting SSL traffic and a website configured to support SSL. If the website will be publicly facing, it is suggested you use an SSL certificate from a public Certificate Authority that is by default trusted by most web browsers.

How to do it...

Carry out the following steps to configure IIS for SSL:

1. Request an SSL certificate from your Certificate Authority.

2. Install the certificate in the `Certificates (Local Computer)\Personal\` `Certificates` store. Assuming you are using an internal CA and permissions, the following command can request and install the certificate:

```
Get-Certificate -Template WebServer -DnsName NLB_IIS.corp.contoso.
com - CertStoreLocation Cert:\LocalMachine\My
```

The certificate should now appear in the store as shown in the following screenshot:

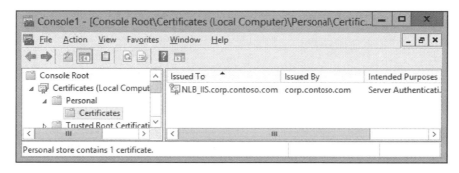

3. Create a new HTTPS binding on our website:

```
New-WebBinding -Name 'Default Web Site' -Protocol https -Port 443
```

4. Assign the certificate to the new binding:

```
$myCert = Get-Item Cert:\LocalMachine\My\* | `
Where-Object Subject -eq 'CN=NLB_IIS.corp.contoso.com'
$myCert | New-Item IIS:\SslBindings\0.0.0.0!443
```

After completing the preceding commands, you should see the following:

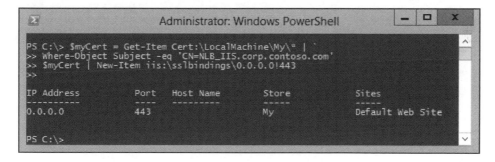

How it works...

We start by requesting and installing an SSL certificate on our web server. If the Certificate Authority is outside of your company, you will have to follow the instructions provided by the CA to request the certificate. Then we install the certificate to the local computer's personal store.

Next, we use `New-WebBinding` to create a new binding for the default website using HTTPS on port 443. Once the binding is created, we get the SSL certificate by ID and assign it to the binding.

To access the website, we now browse to `https://<servername>`. Note the `https` construct identifying the connection to use SSL.

There's more...

We can create a self-signed certificate for use with SSL. There are often times, where you need a certificate for SSL traffic but do not require a fully trusted environment. Working in a test/dev environment, where functionality is more important than security, you can use a self-signed certificate.

To create the certificate, on the web server run the following code:

```
New-SelfSignedCertificate -DnsName "test1.corp.contoso.com" -
CertStoreLocationCert:\LocalMachine\My
```

After completing the preceding commands, you should see the following:

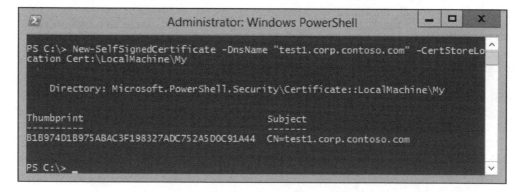

This process creates a new certificate for the DNS named `test1.corp.contoso.com`. This will allow the web server to sign all of its traffic, while allowing the clients to authenticate the server. In order for this certificate to work properly, it must be exported and installed in the Trusted Root Certificate Authorities certificate store on client machines.

To export the self-signed certificate from the web server to a file, execute the following:

```
$myCert = Get-ChildItem -Path Cert:\LocalMachine\My | `
Where-Object Subject -EQ 'CN=test1.corp.contoso.com'
Export-Certificate -Cert $myCert -FilePath C:\temp\test1.crt
```

To import the certificate to a client's Trusted Root Certificate Authorities store, copy the certificate to the client and execute the following:

```
Import-Certificate -FilePathC:\temp\test1.crt `
-CertStoreLocation Cert:\LocalMachine\Root
```

 A self-signed certificate should never be used in a production environment. Maintaining trusts and authentication with a self-signed certificate is difficult and insecure.

Configuring a Central Certificate Store

When working with IIS websites that use SSL, certificate management can often become difficult. The initial setup for one server or site may be simple, but every time you add or replace an IIS host, you need to confirm the SSL certificates are copied over and imported on the server. Additionally, when the certificate expires, the new certificate must be copied to all hosts that need it, and reregistered.

New in IIS8 is the ability to create a centralized certificate store that hosts certificates for all the websites in one place. Instead of manually copying and installing the certificates to each server, the web servers then simply access the centralized store and download the files as needed.

Getting ready

In this recipe we are going to publish the default website on a server with a precreated certificate for test1.corp.contoso.com. To begin, we create our certificate with both private and public keys and export it into a *.PFX file. This file is then copied to a network share, in our case a share on CorpDC1.

Additionally, a service account is created named SSLCerts that has access to this share only. We use a dedicated service account because we may want to save the setup commands, which contain the username/password, in our server build process. This way, the user account has limited access and the security threat is minimized.

How to do it...

Carry out the following steps to configure a Central Certificate Store:

1. Configure the certificate store:

    ```
    Install-WindowsFeature Web-CertProvider
    Enable-WebCentralCertProvider -CertStoreLocation \\corpdc1\certs
    -UserName'Corp\SSLCerts' -Password 'Pa$$w0rd!' -PrivateKeyPassword
    123456
    ```

2. Configure the site to use SSL:

    ```
    New-WebBinding -Name 'Default Web Site' -HostHeader Test1.corp.
    contoso.com -Protocol https -SslFlags 2
    ```

How it works...

Traditionally, installing certificates for SSL required copying the certificate to each server, and then importing it into the local computer certificate store. With the Central Certificate Store, we simply copy the certificates to a common file share, and configure a website to use the certificate.

In the first step, we install the Centralized SSL Certificate Support feature and enable the provider on our server. The provider is configured with the location, username, and password to access the network share, as well as the password used to encrypt the private key.

Certificates used for web servers contain two keys: a private key and a public key. The **private key** is used to sign and encrypt traffic, while the **public key** is used to authenticate the server and decrypt the traffic. The private key is encrypted within the certificate as an additional layer of security, and a password is required to access it.

When using a Central Certificate Store, it is important that all certificates in the store use the same private key password so that they can be decrypted by the store and provided to the web servers.

In the second step, we configure the default website to use the certificate test1.corp. contoso.com. In this situation we use the –HostHeader switch of Test1.corp. contoso.com to reference the certificate we are attempting to use. We also specify the – SslFlags switch with a value of 2, which instructs the web server to use a certificate from the Central Certificate Store. There are four options available for the –SslFlags switch:

Value	Description
0	Regular certificate in the Windows Certificate Store
1	SNI certificate in the Windows Certificate Store
2	Regular certificate in the Central Certificate Store
3	SNI certificate in the Central Certificate Store

There's more...

To access the website, register the address in DNS and access the site the same as any other HTTPS website. Of all the certificates in the store, IIS will determine which to use based on the name in the web request.

We can confirm the Central Certificate Store is functioning properly by accessing out the website via HTTPS. In Internet Explorer clicking on the lock icon displays information about the certificate used to sign the connection. As you can see from the following screenshot, we can confirm the certificate name matches the URL requested, and that the client trusts the CA that issued the certificate.

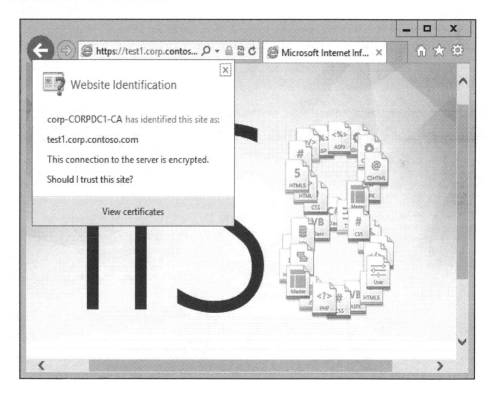

See also

More information regarding using SNI based certificates is included in the recipe, *Configuring IIS bindings*, in this chapter.

Configuring IIS bindings

By default, web servers operate on port 80 and only service a single website. However, often times there is a need to host multiple websites on the same server and use different IP addresses, IP ports, or even names to differentiate between the sites.

This recipe will show how to set up multiple websites on the same server using different forms of web bindings.

How to do it...

Carry out the following steps to configure IIS bindings:

1. Create a new website using a unique IP address

   ```
   New-Website -PhysicalPath C:\inetpub\IPBinding -Name IPBinding
   -IPAddress 10.10.10.250
   ```

   When finished, PowerShell will return information about the site and binding.

   ```
   PS C:\> New-Website -PhysicalPath C:\inetpub\IPBinding -Name IPBinding -IPAddres
   s 10.10.10.250

   Name              ID    State    Physical Path                Bindings
   ----              --    -----    -------------                --------
   IPBinding         4     Started  C:\inetpub\IPBinding         http 10.10.10.2
                                                                 50:80:
   ```

2. Create a new website using a unique TCP port:

   ```
   New-Website -PhysicalPath C:\inetpub\PortBinding -Name PortBinding
   -Port 88 -IPAddress *
   ```

   When finished, PowerShell will return information about the site and binding:

   ```
   PS C:\> New-Website -PhysicalPath C:\inetpub\PortBinding -Name PortBinding -Port
   88 -IPAddress *

   Name              ID    State    Physical Path                Bindings
   ----              --    -----    -------------                --------
   PortBinding       3     Started  C:\inetpub\PortBinding       http *:88:
   ```

3. Create a new website using host headers:

```
New-Website -PhysicalPath C:\inetpub\HostHeader -Name HostHeader
-HostHeader HostHeader
```

When finished, PowerShell will return information about the site and binding:

```
PS C:\> New-Website -Name HostHeader -PhysicalPath C:\inetpub\HostHeader -HostHe
ader HostHeader

Name            ID   State    Physical Path              Bindings
----            --   -----    -------------              --------
HostHeader      2    Started  C:\inetpub\HostHeader      http
                                                         *:80:HostHeader
```

4. Change the binding of a website:

```
Set-WebBinding -Name PortBinding -BindingInformation "*:88:"
-PropertyName Port -Value 89
```

How it works...

In the first step we create a new website and bind it to a dedicated IP address. Our web server has an additional IP address of 10.10.10.250 assigned specifically for use by our new site. We create the new site named IPBinding with the address assigned. Because no port was defined, IIS defaults to assigning port 80.

In the second step we create a new website and bind it to a specific port. In this instance we are telling IIS that any traffic received on port 88 should be directed to the website named PortBinding. To access the site, users will need to type http://server:88 to instruct the web client to use an alternate port.

 This website is configured to listen on all IP addresses (demonstrated by the * in the binding command). If the server has multiple addresses assigned, this may not be the desired configuration.

In the third step we create a website and bind it using host headers. Host headers are alternative names that a server can be accessed by and often need to be registered in DNS for clients to find and connect. To access this site, users will need to type http://HostHeader for the web server to identify the request and return the appropriate result.

As we can see in the following screenshot, we can easily support multiple sites on a single IIS server using different binding types:

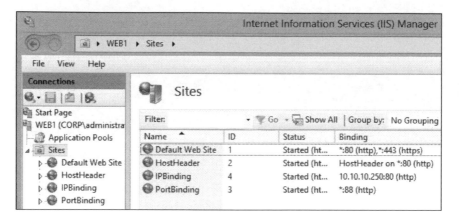

Lastly, we call `Set-WebBinding` to change the binding of an existing site. To make the change we identify the site and existing binding information, and then specify the property we are changing and the new value. In this case we are changing the port used for the `PortBinding` site, however this command can be used for host headers and IP addresses as well.

`Set-WebBinding` doesn't return any output to the screen. To view the new binding information for a site, use `Get-WebBinding`.

```
Get-WebBinding -Name PortBinding
```

There's more...

The following is more information about binding:

> ▶ **Port binding limitations**: Port binding can result in problems in some environments because it passes web traffic on non-standard ports. Some environments are configured to transfer only HTTP (80) or HTTPS (443) traffic between networks. Often times this is due to security requirements, other times it is due to restrictions of firewalls and proxies.

> ▶ **Host header limitations**: Host headers are often the easiest method to set up multiple websites on a single server; however, they also has the most restrictions. Because host headers rely on the name of the site being accessed to distinguish which data to return, if the site name is not given, the wrong data may be returned.

> Say for instance, you think your client may be having issues with DNS. In order to test this you type in the IP address of the website instead of the name. In this case, the web server does not know which site you requested and possibly will return the wrong site.

▶ **Host headers with SSL**: New in IIS 8 is the ability to support **Server Name Indicators** (**SNI**), which allows the server to support multiple SSL sites using the same address and port. Both the web client and web server must support the use of SNI. Most modern browsers already support this feature.

See also

More information on using Server Name Indicators can be found at:

▶ `http://en.wikipedia.org/wiki/Server_Name_Indication`

▶ `http://blogs.msdn.com/b/kaushal/archive/2012/09/04/server-name-indication-sni-in-iis-8-windows-server-2012.aspx`

Configuring IIS logging

By default, IIS logs nearly every transaction clients perform against the server. This is a great repository of information when debugging issues or when trying to profile your users and identify which resources are popular, which are not popular, and which are generating errors.

This recipe will cover how to configure IIS logging.

How to do it...

Carry out the following steps to configure IIS logging:

1. Change the IIS logging directory:

   ```
   Set-ItemProperty 'IIS:\Sites\Default Web Site' -Name logFile.
   directory -Value 'C:\Logs\IIS'
   ```

2. Change the logging type:

   ```
   Set-ItemProperty 'IIS:\Sites\Default Web Site' -Name logFile.
   logFormat 'W3C'
   ```

3. Change logging frequency:

   ```
   Set-ItemProperty 'IIS:\Sites\Default Web Site' -Name logFile.
   period -Value Weekly
   ```

4. Change logging to use a maximum size:

   ```
   Set-ItemProperty 'IIS:\Sites\Default Web Site' -Name logFile.
   period -Value MaxSize
   Set-ItemProperty 'IIS:\Sites\Default Web Site' -Name logFile.
   truncateSize 9000000
   ```

5. Disable logging:

```
Set-ItemProperty 'IIS:\Sites\Default Web Site' -Name logFile.
enabled -Value False
```

How it works...

The first step changes the location for log files for the default website instance. In this situation we are updating the `logFile.directory` property and changing the log directory to `C:\Logs\IIS`. To view the location of the log files, instead of executing `Set-ItemProperty`, we use `Get-ItemProperty`, as follows:

```
Get-ItemProperty 'IIS:\Sites\Default Web Site' -Name logFile.
directory.value
```

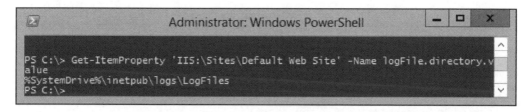

The second step changes the logging type for the default website instance. In this case we are updating the `logFile.logFormat` property and changing the logging format to W3C; acceptable values are:

- IIS
- NCSA
- W3C
- Custom

The third step updates the `logFile.period` property and changes the logging frequency for the default website instance. This is the frequency at which IIS will create new log files for the website. Acceptable values are:

- Hourly
- Daily
- Weekly
- Monthly
- Maximum size

In the fourth step we are updating the `logFile.period` and `logFile.truncateSize` parameters in order to configure logging to create a new log file once it reaches a certain size. Instead of creating a new file every hour, day, or week, they will continue to grow until they reach their maximum size and then create a new log.

The last step updates the `logfile.enabled` parameter in order to disable logging for the website. While this is not a best practice in most environments, there are situations where logging is unnecessary and can overwhelm the system. For example, if you have a web service which is accessed automatically by a large number of systems, this can cause issues by filling up the drives and generating excessive disk traffic. If the site is known to be stable, and there is no need to review the log files, you can simply disable logging.

Managing log files

By default, IIS is configured to create a separate log file for each day. Unlike many other applications such as Exchange, IIS does not contain a native method of maintaining the number or size of the log files.

As IIS saves log files, the log files' sizes and number can quickly grow out of control. For instance, a web server that has been in production for a year can have 365 log files (one for each day) or more. A busy website or web service can potentially fill the OS drive of a server within a few weeks or months.

While this is a great repository of information, we don't want our logging to negatively impact the server. Chances are that if we need to review the files, we will only need the last few days or few weeks of files, and can remove anything older.

This recipe shows how to filter through the log files and remove those older than a certain date.

Getting ready

In this recipe we will be searching for any log files older than seven days and deleting them. When first running this script, it should be against a test server to ensure the outcome is as desired.

 This example will delete log files from all websites on the target computer. Care should always be taken to ensure it is safe to remove the content prior to executing the script.

How to do it...

Open a PowerShell console and execute the following code:

```
$logDirs = Get-ChildItem -Path IIS:\Sites | Get-ItemProperty `
-name logFile.directory.value | Select -Unique
$numDays = -7
foreach ($myDir in $logDirs){
    $myDir = [Environment]::ExpandEnvironmentVariables($myDir)
    Get-ChildItem -Path $myDir -Recurse | Where-Object LastWriteTime
-lt `
    (Get-Date).AddDays($numDays) | Remove-Item
}
```

How it works...

The script begins by calling Get-ChildItem to list all of the websites in IIS. The websites are queried for logFile.directory.value for each site in order to determine the location of the log files. The output is then placed into the $logDirs variable.

Each logging directory is then cycled through in order. The first command, $myDir = [Env ironment]::ExpandEnvironmentVariables($myDir), is used to convert any system variables (such as %SystemDrive%) into its fully qualified path to be used by PowerShell.

Once the full path of the log file directory is defined, the script then recursively gets all items in the folder and subfolders. This list is filtered based on LastWriteTime to exclude files newer than seven days. Those files are then piped to Remove-Item in order to be deleted.

There's more...

You may want to keep your log files for more than seven days, but you don't want them to remain on the web server. This will allow you to retain a central repository for a longer time, but not overwhelm your web servers with log files. In that case the script can be modified to call Move-Item to move the log files to a remote location instead of deleting them.

Configuring NLB across multiple servers

One of the easiest methods of making a website highly available is to use a **Network Load Balancer** (**NLB**). The NLB role resides on the web servers themselves and provides a virtual IP address that balances traffic between the individual nodes. Clients make requests to the virtual address, and the web servers communicate with each other to determine which will service the request.

This results in a website that is highly available and can sustain individual server failures, but also provides a scale-out capability to grow websites quickly and easily.

This recipe will cover setting up and configuring an NLB cluster in order to provide a redundant website infrastructure.

Getting ready

To configure NLB, we will need a minimum of two servers with three static IP addresses, all connected via a common Ethernet segment. As you can see in the following diagram, I have predetermined my IP addresses of `10.10.10.241` for `Web1`, `10.10.10.242` for `Web2`, and `10.10.10.240` for the virtual address which we will name `NLB_IIS`.

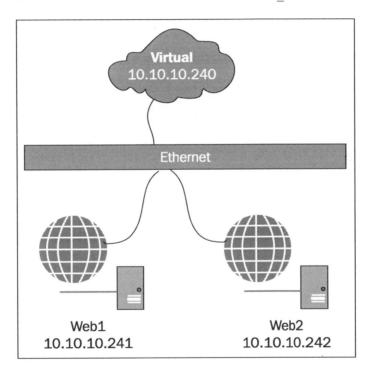

 If you are managing NLB clusters remotely, you will need to install the `RSAT-NLB` feature to install the NLB tools. This can be performed by executing `Install-WindowsFeature RSAT-NLB` on your management station.

How to do it...

Carry out the following steps for configuring NLB across multiple servers:

1. Install the NLB feature on the web servers:

```
Invoke-Command -ComputerName web1, web2 `
-ScriptBlock { Install-WindowsFeature NLB -IncludeManagementTools
}
```

2. Set up the NLB cluster on first host:

```
New-NlbCluster -HostName web1 -InterfaceName Ethernet `
-ClusterName NLB_IIS -ClusterPrimaryIP 10.10.10.240 `
-SubnetMask 255.255.255.0 -OperationMode Multicast
```

When completed, you will see confirmation of the new cluster and virtual IP address similar to the following screenshot:

```
PS C:\> New-NlbCluster -HostName web1 -InterfaceName Ethernet -ClusterName NLB_I
IS -ClusterPrimaryIP 10.10.10.240 -SubnetMask 255.255.255.0 -OperationMode Multi
cast

Name                IPAddress           SubnetMask          Mode
----                ---------           ----------          ----
NLB_IIS             10.10.10.240        255.255.255.0       MULTICAST
```

3. Add the second host to cluster:

```
Get-NlbCluster -HostName web1|Add-NlbClusterNode -NewNodeName web2
-NewNodeInterface Ethernet
```

When completed, you will see confirmation of the new node in the cluster with **HostID** of **2**.

```
PS C:\> Get-NlbCluster -HostName web1 | Add-NlbClusterNode -NewNodeName web2 -Ne
wNodeInterface Ethernet

Name        State           Interface       HostID
----        -----           ---------       ------
web2        Converged       Ethernet        2
```

4. Specify the ports for the cluster to balance:

```
Set-NlbClusterPortRule -HostName web1 -NewStartPort 80 -NewEndPort
80
```

When completed, the port configuration of the cluster will be displayed as shown in the following screenshot:

```
PS C:\> Set-NlbClusterPortRule -HostName web1 -NewStartPort 80 -NewEndPort 80

IPAddress State      Start      End       Protocol  Mode      Affinity  Timeout
--------- -----      -----      ---       --------  ----      --------  -------
All       Enabled    80         80        Both      Multiple  Single    0
```

How it works...

In the first step we use `Invoke-Command` to install the NLB feature on both web servers `Web1` and `Web2`.

In the second step we use `New-NlbCluster` to configure NLB on `Web1` and create the Cluster IP address of `10.10.10.240`. We also define the NLB cluster to operate in **multicast mode**, a special configuration that allows the NLB nodes to operate with only a single interface on the server.

Next, we configure call `Add-NlbClusterNode` to `Web2` as an additional member of the NLB cluster. Note that we do not have to identify the cluster address or operation mode like was done for the first server; instead, those attributes are inherited from the cluster itself.

Finally, we call `Set-NlbClusterPortRule` to configure NLB to listen only on port 80 for HTTP traffic. By default, NLB attempts to load balance all traffic on all ports; however, for our purposes we only need port 80. If we installed websites on multiple ports, or used HTTPS, we could then execute `Add-NlbClusterPortRule` to add additional ports to the NLB cluster.

There's more...

The following is more information about NLB configuration for websites:

- **Accessing the website**: Once the NLB cluster is set up and running, the only remaining task to access the website is to register the virtual IP address in DNS. In this scenario if we register the DNS record `NLB_IIS.corp.contoso.com` to `10.10.10.240` then open a web browser to `http://nlb_iis.corp.contoso.com`; the load balanced site is returned.

- **NLB modes**: There are three modes that an NLB cluster can operate in: multicast, unicast, and IGMP multicast. **Multicast**, as mentioned earlier, is the easiest to set up because it works well with a single network adapter. **IGMP multicast** is similar to multicast, but relies on IGMP communications between the servers to balance traffic. **Unicast** is preferred for large production environments as it separates the NLB communication and web traffic into separate interfaces.

Monitoring load balancing across NLB nodes

Once an NLB cluster is configured and running, one of the questions that is asked is why one host is working harder than another, or why one node has all the connections and the other has none. Normally, these questions are resolved by modifying the **Affinity** settings.

At its base, NLB balances traffic between different nodes in a cluster based on the total number of connections to each node. This information is then combined with the cluster's **Affinity** settings to group source hosts and networks onto the same node.

This recipe will cover the basic performance counters needed to identify if NLB is working and balancing load correctly.

Getting ready

In this recipe we will be working with the NLB configuration created in the prior recipe. In this case the cluster consists of only two nodes, but in production environments this can grow much larger.

How to do it...

Carry out the following steps to monitor load balancing across NLB nodes:

1. View the status of the hosts in the cluster:

   ```
   Get-NlbClusterNode -HostName web1
   ```

   When completed, the output will show the state of each node in the cluster:

   ```
   PS C:\> Get-NlbClusterNode -HostName web1

   Name                 State               Interface        HostID
   ----                 -----               ---------        ------
   Web1                 Converged(default)  Ethernet         1
   Web2                 Converged           Ethernet         2
   ```

2. View the cluster's **Affinity** settings:

   ```
   Get-NlbClusterPortRule -HostName web1
   ```

   When completed, the output will show the **Affinity** settings:

```
PS C:\> Get-NlbClusterPortRule -HostName web1

IPAddress State     Start    End     Protocol Mode     Affinity Timeout
--------- -----     -----    ---     -------- ----     -------- -------
All       Enabled   80       80      Both     Multiple Single   0
```

3. View the host connection count for each node:

```
$myNodes = Get-NlbClusterNode -HostName web1
$myCounter = $myNodes.Name | ForEach-Object {
    "\\$_\Web Service(_Total)\Current Connections"
}
Get-Counter -Counter $myCounter
```

When completed, the output will show the current number of connections to each node in the cluster:

```
PS C:\> Get-Counter -Counter $myCounter

Timestamp               CounterSamples
---------               --------------
9/25/2012 4:13:51 PM    \\web1\web service(_total)\current connections :
                        4

                        \\web2\web service(_total)\current connections :
                        5
```

How it works...

In the first step we view the status of the nodes in the cluster. This command will list all the nodes in the cluster, which interface they are attached to, and most importantly, the state of the node in the NLB cluster. In this case the state is **Converged**, which means the nodes are functioning properly. Additional values include **Shutting down**, **Stopped**, and **Suspended**.

Next, we use `Get-NlbClusterPortRule` to view the cluster's **Affinity** setting. By default the affinity is set to **Single**, meaning all traffic from a specific host is directed to the same cluster node, regardless of load. The default **Affinity** settings work well in many environments, however some firewalls and proxy servers pass traffic to the NLB nodes as though the firewall originated the request instead of the client. This then causes the NLB cluster to see all the traffic as originating from a single address and therefore passes the traffic to the same node. In this case, setting the affinity to **None** is preferable.

Lastly, we use PowerShell's `Get-Counter` command to retrieve performance counters on both NLB nodes. In this case we are looking at the `\Web Service(_Total)\Current Connections` counter to return the number of connections to the web server. If you are using NLB to balance something other than web services, you will need to find an appropriate connections counter.

There's more...

If you do not have a lot of traffic currently on your NLB site, and you want to generate a test load, the following script is a quick way to start. The script creates 10 background jobs, each downloading web pages from the target web server. Each job will download the default web page, sleep 2 seconds, and then repeat for 100 times before finally exiting. This should be long enough to confirm the balancing of your NLB cluster.

```
1..10 | ForEach-Object{
    Start-Job -ScriptBlock {
        $client = New-Object System.Net.WebClient
1..100 | ForEach-Object{
            $client.DownloadData("http://10.10.10.240")
            Start-Sleep 2
        }
    }
}
Wait-Job *
Remove-Job *
```

> All of the traffic in this test will be generated from the same host, and depending on the affinity rules, the NLB cluster may direct all of the traffic to the same node. If that occurs, you can run the test simultaneously from two hosts, or change affinity to **None**.

Placing NLB nodes into maintenance

One of the great benefits of NLB is the ability to remove one or more hosts from the cluster without affecting the overall service. This is often done when installing patches or upgrading code on a single server at a time. Removing hosts may result in degraded performance, and therefore, should only be done during a maintenance window, where performance is not an issue, but the overall service will remain online.

Getting ready

This recipe assumes you have a two-node cluster (Web1 and Web2) and Web2 is being taken offline to perform maintenance. The maintenance may require multiple reboots, so we will need to ensure the node remains offline until all work is finished.

How to do it...

Carry out the following steps to place NLB nodes into maintenance:

1. Safely shutdown and suspend the NLB node on Web2:

   ```
   $myCluster = Get-NlbCluster web1
   $myNode = $myCluster | Get-NlbClusterNode -NodeName web2
   $myNode | Stop-NlbClusterNode -Drain
   $myNode | Suspend-NlbClusterNode
   $myNode | Set-NlbClusterNode -RetainSuspended $true
   ```

2. Perform maintenance on the server.

3. Once the maintenance is complete, restart the node and add it into production:

   ```
   $myCluster = Get-NlbCluster web1
   $myNode = $myCluster | Get-NlbClusterNode -NodeName web2
   $myNode|Resume-NlbClusterNode
   $myNode | Start-NlbClusterNode
   ```

How it works...

The first step starts by connecting to the NLB cluster, and then to the specific node that places the node object into the $myNode variable. The node is then stopped with the –drain switch, which tells the node to stop accepting new connections, but continue servicing existing connections. This is used to ensure that active sessions are not dropped and active users aren't affected, however this can result in the stop process to take several minutes, hours, or in extreme cases, days.

Once the node is safely stopped, it is then suspended and configured to remain suspended. This allows us to reboot the host if needed, and keeps the NLB service from unexpectedly starting and servicing clients. At this point we can safely perform maintenance on the server.

The third step is essentially the opposite of the first. The script starts by connecting to the cluster and node and placing the node object into the $myNode variable. The node is then resumed, or unsuspended. Lastly, the node is started to begin servicing requests.

There's more...

If you execute Get-NlbClusterNode during the shutdown process, you will see that the NLB node proceeds through multiple states before finally suspending. Each of these states may remain for quite some time depending on the number of connections and lifetime of those connections.

Configuring a development/staging/production site scheme

Many websites use a multi-tiered infrastructure to promote content between development and production environments. One of the simplest is a three-tier development, staging, and production configuration. In this scenario the website and code is developed on a development instance. Once the code is ready, it is promoted to staging, where it is tested and confirmed to be working properly. Finally, it is promoted to production for general use.

In this recipe we will set up a basic three-tier website scheme on a single website in an NLB configuration. The same process can be performed for a non-NLB website by only providing one computer name to the scripts.

Getting ready

This recipe assumes an NLB web server configuration as shown in the *Configuring NLB across multiple servers* recipe in this chapter.

How to do it...

Carry out the following steps to configure this three-tier site scheme:

1. Create the folders on the web servers:

```
Invoke-Command -ComputerName web1, web2 -ScriptBlock {
    New-Item "C:\InetPub\wwwDev" -ItemType Directory
    New-Item "C:\InetPub\wwwStage" -ItemType Directory
    New-SmbShare -NamewwwDev -Path C:\InetPub\wwwDev `
    -FullAccess corp\administrator
}
```

2. Create the sites and configure them to use host headers:

```
Invoke-Command -ComputerName web1, web2 -ScriptBlock {
    New-Website -Name "Development.corp.contoso.com" `
    -HostHeader "development" -PhysicalPath "C:\InetPub\wwwDev\"
    New-Website -Name "Staging.corp.contoso.com" `
    -HostHeader "staging" -PhysicalPath "C:\InetPub\wwwStage\"
}
```

3. Register DNS for host headers:

```
Add-DnsServerResourceRecord -CName -HostNameAlias www.corp.
contoso.com `
-Name development -ZoneName corp.contoso.com `
-ComputerName corpdc1.corp.contoso.com
```

```
Add-DnsServerResourceRecord -CName -HostNameAlias www.corp.
contoso.com `
-Name staging -ZoneName corp.contoso.com `
-ComputerName corpdc1.corp.contoso.com
```

How it works...

In the first step we are creating directories on our web servers to hold our development and staging environments. We create two directories, C:\InetPub\wwwDev and C:\InetPub\wwwStage, to hold the development and staging environments. The production environment will remain at C:\InetPub\wwwRoot.

In addition to creating the necessary folders, the script also calls New-SmbShare to create a Windows share for the C:\InetPub\wwwDev directory on both servers. This directory is shared so that code can be synchronized between the servers.

The second step calls New-Website to configure two new websites for the development and staging folders. These websites are configured to use the host headers of development and staging, leaving the default website to service production requests.

Lastly, Add-DnsServerResourceRecord is used to register the CName records. The CName records are used to register additional names to the same Alias record. These records point to www.corp.contoso.com, which returns the IP address of the production website.

Promoting content in websites

Once our three-tier website scheme is set up, the next step is to configure the content promotion method. This recipe shows how to promote content between the various environments.

Getting ready

This recipe assumes the development/staging/production website configuration created in the prior recipe.

How to do it...

Carry out the following steps to promote content in websites:

1. Copy the content between the web servers:

   ```
   Copy-Item -Path \\web1\wwwDev -Destination \\web2\wwwDev -Verbose
   -Recurse -Force
   ```

2. Copy the files from development to staging:

```
Invoke-Command -ComputerName web1, web2 -ScriptBlock {
    Copy-Item -Path C:\inetpub\wwwDev -Destination C:\inetpub\
wwwStage -Verbose -Force -Recurse
}
```

3. Copy files from staging to production:

```
Invoke-Command -ComputerName web1, web2 -ScriptBlock {
    Copy-Item -Path C:\inetpub\wwwStage -Destination C:\inetpub\
wwwRoot -Verbose -Force -Recurse
}
```

How it works...

The first step copies files between the web servers in order to synchronize the content. The assumption here is that development has occurred solely on Web1, so Web2 needs to be updated with the latest version of code. If necessary, this script can also be reversed to copy content from Web2 into Web1.

The second step promotes content from development into staging. Similar to the prior example, this script uses Copy-Item to copy content from one folder to the other, but in this case, the content does not traverse servers; instead, it is promoted within each server.

The last step promotes content from staging into production. This step is the same as the previous one, only changes are the source and destination folders.

There's more...

There are a couple of extensions that can be added to these scripts to improve their functionality. The first command would be to execute Remove-Item on the target location prior to the Copy-Item command. An example of what the code would look like is as follows:

```
Invoke-Command -ComputerName web1, web2 -ScriptBlock {
    Remove-Item -Path C:\inetpub\wwwStage -Force -Recurse
-Confirm:$false
    Copy-Item -Path C:\inetpub\wwwDev -Destination C:\inetpub\wwwStage
-Verbose -Force -Recurse
}
```

This will cause the folders and files in the target location to be removed entirely prior to being promoted. If your environment is highly dynamic and files are being removed or moved consistently, this may be needed to ensure the content is correct.

The second extension would be to copy the files to a temporary target, and then rename the folders when the copying is finished. For instance, instead of wwwStage, the Copy-Item command is changed to copy to a wwwStageTmp folder. Once the data is copied to the wwwStagetmp folder, Rename-Item is called to rename the original folder and the new folder.

```
Invoke-Command -ComputerName web1, web2 -ScriptBlock {
    Copy-Item -Path C:\inetpub\wwwDev -Destination C:\inetpub\
wwwStageTmp -Verbose -Force -Recurse
    Rename-Item -Path C:\inetpub\wwwStage -NewName wwwStageOld -Force
-Confirm:$false
    Rename-Item -Path C:\inetpub\wwwStageTmp -NewName wwwStage -Force
-Confirm:$false
}
```

This will result in the promotion of the code to not occur until the very end of the script, but will have the added benefit of limiting the amount of time that the content is in an unknown state. This script also has the benefit of ensuring no old content is retained once the promotion occurs.

This script could be separated into two components, allowing the copying of content to occur separately from the ultimate promotion. For instance, if the website is very large in size, and you have a minimal amount of time to promote the content, the data can be copied to the temporary location ahead of time. Then, during your change window, the folders are quickly renamed, resulting in minimal downtime of the site.

Lastly, this script also has the benefit of providing a rollback method. If a change is made to the site and it is promoted, but then an issue is found, the content can be rolled back by simply renaming the folders. In the example shown, we could delete the wwwStage folder (because it exists in wwwDev, there is no need to keep the contents) and rename wwwStageOld back to wwwStage and the site will be the same as before the promotion.

Reporting on website access and errors

After a website has been active for some time, you will likely want to review the logs to see which content is popular and which is not. Assuming you have kept the default logging method of W3C, and the default sections, the script explained in this recipe should give a high-level view of your website.

How to do it...

Here, we are using a PowerShell script to parse the IIS log files and generate a report:

```
Function Parse-IISLogs
{
    # Identify the IIS logging directory
```

```
Import-Module WebAdministration
$logFile = Get-ItemProperty 'IIS:\Sites\Default Web Site' `
-Name logFile.directory.value
$logFile = [Environment]::ExpandEnvironmentVariables($logFile)

# Export log files to a temporary CSV file
$logFile += "\*\*.log"
(Get-Content $logfile | Where-Object {$_ -notlike "#[S,V,D]*"}) `
-replace "#Fields: ","" | Out-File $env:temp\webLog.csv

# Import the CSV file to memory
$webLog = Import-Csv $env:temp\webLog.csv -Delimiter " "

# Parse the CSV file for the top files
Write-Host "Top 3 files`n"
$webLog | Group-Object -property 'cs-uri-stem' | Sort-Object `
-Property Count -Descending | Select-Object Count, Name `
-First 3 | Out-String

# Parse the CSV file for the top 3 referers
Write-Host "Top 3 referers`n"
$webLog | Group-Object -property 'cs(Referer)' | Sort-Object `
-Property Count -Descending | Select-Object Count, Name `
-First 3 | Out-String

# Parse the CSV file for the top 3 useragent
Write-Host "Top 3 agents`n"
$webLog | Group-Object -property 'cs(User-Agent)' | Sort-Object `
-Property Count -Descending | Select-Object Count, Name `
-First 3 | Out-String

# Parse the CSV file for the top 3 404 errors
Write-Host "Top 3 File Not Found (404)`n"
$webLog | Where-Object sc-status -eq 404 | Group-Object `
-Property 'cs-uri-stem' | Sort-Object -Property Count -Descending|
`
Select-Object Count, Name -First 3 | Out-String

# Clean up
Remove-Item $env:temp\webLog.csv
}
```

How it works...

This script begins by importing the `WebAdministration` module in order to make the `IIS:\` PSDrive available. The script then finds the location of the log files for the default website.

We want to open the log files themselves, so we append `\*\*.log` to the `$logFile` variable. This adds wildcards that will include all log files one directory below the folder initially listed. `Get-Content` is called to read the log files and the contents are then piped to `Where-Object` to filter out the first three lines of the log which contain information about the log itself.

The new first line of the log file should now contain the column names for the file. We remove the initial `#Fields` content and then export the information to a CSV file. Once exported, we import the CSV file in a format that can be easily searched and filtered.

Once the CSV file has been imported, finding the data is matter of selecting and filtering for the data we need. To find the most accessed files or pages, we use `Group-Object` on the `cs-uri-stem` column to find the number of times an object is referenced. The column is then sorted based on the number of times a file has been accessed, and then limited to the first three. This combination of grouping, sorting, and selecting the first three items allows us to identify the most popular content.

The next two blocks perform the same tasks: grouping, sorting, and filtering, each on different columns. First we group by the `cs(referer)` column to report on where traffic is coming from. Then we group by the `cs(user-agent)` column to report on the type of clients accessing our website.

Lastly, we filter on the `sc-status` column to return all web requests that resulted in a 404, or file not found error. We then group by the `cs-uri-stem` column to report the top files that resulted in the 404 error.

A sample report of the website report is shown in the following screenshot:

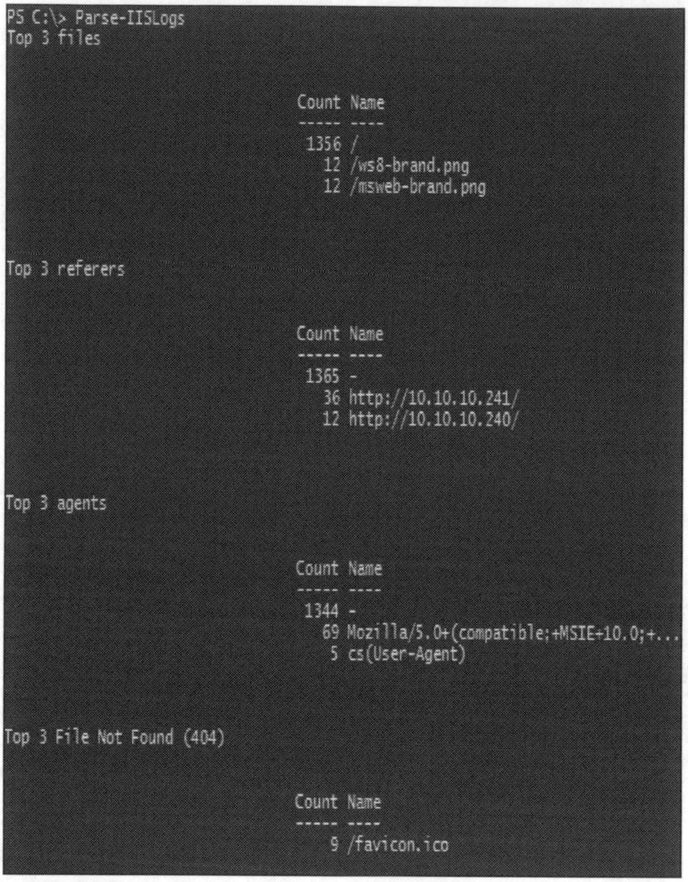

```
PS C:\> Parse-IISLogs
Top 3 files


                                 Count Name
                                 ----- ----
                                  1356 /
                                    12 /ws8-brand.png
                                    12 /msweb-brand.png




Top 3 referers


                                 Count Name
                                 ----- ----
                                  1365 -
                                    36 http://10.10.10.241/
                                    12 http://10.10.10.240/




Top 3 agents


                                 Count Name
                                 ----- ----
                                  1344 -
                                    69 Mozilla/5.0+(compatible;+MSIE+10.0;+...
                                     5 cs(User-Agent)




Top 3 File Not Found (404)


                                 Count Name
                                 ----- ----
                                     9 /favicon.ico
```

There's more...

This script is far from complete and can easily be extended to return information on different areas of network. For example, the report can be configured to report on which clients generate the most traffic, which IP blocks are requesting the most data, and even which content is taking the longest to return.

4
Managing Hyper-V with PowerShell

In this chapter we are going to cover the following recipes:

- ▶ Installing and configuring Hyper-V
- ▶ Configuring NUMA
- ▶ Securing Hyper-V
- ▶ Hyper-V networking
- ▶ Creating virtual machines
- ▶ Managing VM state
- ▶ Configuring VM networking
- ▶ Configuring VM hardware
- ▶ Quickly deploying VMs using a template
- ▶ Managing and reporting on VM snapshots
- ▶ Monitoring Hyper-V utilization and performance
- ▶ Synchronizing networks between Hyper-V hosts
- ▶ Hyper-V replication
- ▶ Migrating VMs between hosts
- ▶ Migrating VM storage between hosts
- ▶ Using failover clustering to make VMs highly available

Introduction

Microsoft Hyper-V is a hardware virtualization platform by Microsoft that allows a single physical machine to host multiple virtual operating systems. Hyper-V allows for more efficient utilization of physical resources by sharing disk, network, memory, and CPU among multiple virtual computers. Microsoft released Hyper-V 2012 in two versions: as a feature of the standard OS, and as a free standalone Hyper-V Server. The commands in this chapter can be performed in both environments.

In addition to basic management of Hyper-V, this chapter also covers how to automate the deployment and management of guest **virtual machines** (**VMs**), manage VM snapshots, migrate VMs between hosts and preparing a host for maintenance, and how to utilize clustering to make highly available VMs. This chapter should cover everything necessary to set up and manage an enterprise Hyper-V farm; including reporting, performing maintenance, and monitoring performance.

Installing and configuring Hyper-V

To begin virtualizing with Hyper-V Server, the first thing we need to do is install and configure the Hyper-V Server feature. In this recipe we will configure the physical drives used by Hyper-V. The steps in this recipe can be used to configure the Server 2012 Standard and Datacenter editions, as well as the free Hyper-V Server edition.

Getting ready

In this recipe we will set up and configure Hyper-V on our first server named HV01. The operating system should already be installed on the C:\ drive and configured with a network address. A separate disk, E:\, will be used to hold our VM and VHDx files.

To simplify management of the Hyper-V Server, the system is joined to a domain:

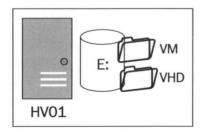

How to do it...

Carry out the following steps to install and configure Hyper-V:

1. Create the folders for the VM and VHDx files.

   ```
   New-Item E:\VM -ItemType Directory
   New-Item E:\VHD -ItemType Directory
   ```

2. If you are not using the free Hyper-V Server, install Hyper-V role. The server will reboot to enable the Hyper-V role:

   ```
   Install-WindowsFeature Hyper-V -IncludeManagementTools -Restart
   ```

 This step is only necessary if you are using a Windows Server 2012 Standard and Datacenter edition. If you are using the free Hyper-V Server 2012, the role is already installed.

3. If you are administering the server remotely, install the Hyper-V management tools on another system. This will install both the GUI and PowerShell administration tools:

   ```
   Install-WindowsFeature RSAT-Hyper-V-Tools
   ```

4. Configure Hyper-V to use the target folders:

   ```
   Set-VMHost -ComputerName HV01 -VirtualHardDiskPath E:\vhd `
   -VirtualMachinePath E:\vm
   ```

5. Confirm the settings by executing the following:

   ```
   Get-VMHost -ComputerName HV01| Format-List *
   ```

   When executed, you will see a screen similar to the following screenshot:

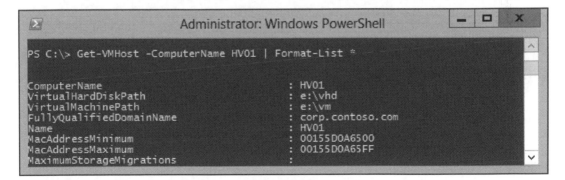

How it works...

In the first step we create the target folders that will host the VM and VHDx files. By default, Windows stores these files at `C:\ProgramData\Microsoft\Windows\Hyper-V` and `C:\Users\Public\Documents\Hyper-V\Virtual Hard Disks` respectively. For performance reasons, these files should be stored separately from the OS disk. Depending on the number of virtual machines being hosted, and the disk utilization of those VMs, a disk array or SAN should be used.

In the second step we use `Install-WindowsFeature` to install the `Hyper-V` role on the server and instruct it to reboot when finished. When finished, the server will automatically reboot to complete the installation. This step is not necessary for the free Hyper-V Server edition.

In the third step we are installing the Hyper-V management tools on a remote system. This will allow management of our Hyper-V Server without requiring us to log onto the server console. In a production environment this is often preferred as it minimizes the overhead needed to manage the system, and the server can be dedicated to running virtual machines.

In the fourth step we execute `Set-VMhost` to configure the target folders for Hyper-V. This command uses the `-ComputerName` switch to reference the system HV01. This allows the command to be executed on the Hyper-V Server remotely and non-interactively. To execute the command locally, simply remove the switch and the task will affect the local server.

Lastly, we call `Get-VMHost` to confirm the configuration of the Hyper-V Server. Here we see `VirtualHardDiskPath` and `VirtualMachinePath` are located in our new directories on the `E:\` drive.

There's more...

In this example we are using a different drive as the default location for our VMs. We are doing this for two primary reasons: ease of management, and performance. Management is improved by keeping all of the VM configurations and hard disks on a separate drive, and we do not have to worry as much about day-to-day server management. Tasks such as deleting old user profiles or old files on the OS drive, should not affect the virtual machines.

Additionally, moving the virtual disks to separate physical drives results in improved performance by increasing the total disk capability. Additional disk spindles means more IOPs, more throughput, and potentially faster response time. Once there are more than a few VMs operating on the server, you will begin to see the difference multiple disks provide.

When sizing the disks for a large VM, such as a busy SQL server, it is best practice to begin by identifying the requirements as if it was a physical server. Once the number, size, and performance needed for the physical environment are identified, the same numbers can often be applied to the virtual environment.

Configuring NUMA

In older multiprocessor systems, multiple processor clustering methods were used to provide access to the computer resources to all processors. Most resources were easily accessed by multiple processors, with the exception of memory.

In newer multiprocessor systems the use of **Non-Uniform Memory Architecture (NUMA)** has become standard. NUMA allows for the system memory to be split between the available processors, creating NUMA zones, with each zone *owning* its memory.

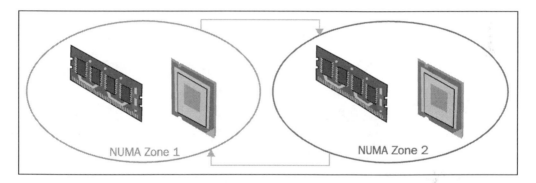

When a processor needs to access memory that is owned by another processor, the first processor asks the second processor to perform the request. When this memory request occurs, it takes slightly longer to be fulfilled because of the hand-off to the second processor. Because the timing to fulfill memory requests changed, it is referred to as being non-uniform.

By default, NUMA spanning is enabled on Hyper-V. There are multiple reasons for disabling NUMA and for leaving NUMA enabled. Enabling NUMA allows for operating large VMs that require more memory than a single NUMA zone contains. Additionally, it can allow for operating of more VMs on the system at a time.

Enabling NUMA however results in a performance impact for any VMs shared across zones. Because accessing memory owned by a different zone takes longer than accessing local memory, this can cause the VM performance to degrade.

Getting Ready

For this recipe we will be working with a server with the Hyper-V feature installed. This server needs to have at least two physical processors for NUMA spanning to operate.

How to do it...

Execute the following commands to change the NUMA configuration:

1. Disable NUMA spanning:

```
Invoke-Command -ComputerName HV01 -ScriptBlock {
    Set-VMHost -NumaSpanningEnabled $false
    Restart-Service vmms
}
```

2. View the NUMA status:

```
Get-VMHost -ComputerName HV01 | Format-List *
```

When executed, you will see a screen similar to the following screenshot:

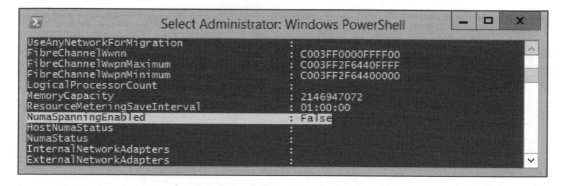

3. Re-enable NUMA spanning:

```
Invoke-Command -ComputerName HV01 -ScriptBlock {
    Set-VMHost -NumaSpanningEnabled $true
    Restart-Service vmms
}
```

How it works...

In the first step we disable NUMA spanning on our server. In this instance we are managing a remote Hyper-V Server, so we are using `Invoke-Command` to execute the steps on the server `HV01`. First, we use `Set-VMHost` with the `-NumaSpanningEnabled` switch set to `$false`. Next, we restart the **Virtual Machine Management Service (VMMS)** of Hyper-V for the change to take effect.

> Restarting the Virtual Machine Management Service of Hyper-V will cause all running VMs on the server to be stopped. Depending on your environment this may cause a service outage and should only be performed while the system is in maintenance.

In the second step we call `Get-VMHost` to view the server configuration. As we can see, the `NumaSpanningEnabled` switch is set to `False`, this confirms that our change has taken effect.

Lastly, we re-enable NUMA spanning on our server. This process is the same as the first step, however this time we set the `-NumaSpanningEnalbed` switch to `$true`.

See also

More information about the Non-Uniform Memory Access architecture can be found at `http://en.wikipedia.org/wiki/Non-Uniform_Memory_Access`.

Securing Hyper-V

Because a Hyper-V Server may host dozens of virtual machines, properly securing the Hyper-V Server itself is critical. In a Hyper-V Server there are two primary groups used for managing the system: the Administrators group and the Hyper-V Administrators group that is created when the Hyper-V feature is installed. These two groups provide full access to the Hyper-V Server, and potentially, access to all virtual machines operating on the server.

In addition to managing the Hyper-V Server itself, administrators can use the Virtual Machine Connection tool of Hyper-V to access the virtual machines. This tool provides the virtual equivalent of physically accessing the system. Administrators can access the keyboard, video, and mouse of the system, change the power state, modify the virtual hardware, and boot from CD/DVD.

In this recipe we will cover securing the administrative functions on the Hyper-V Server and individual virtual machines.

Getting ready

In this example we are securing a single Hyper-V Server in a domain environment. Following standard Windows security practices, we will be using security groups to grant access to the resources on the Hyper-V Server:

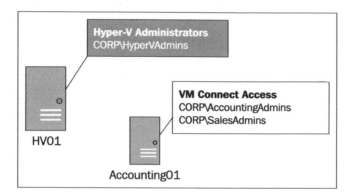

In this recipe we are securing our Hyper-V Server, HV01. We will add a domain group named CORP\HyperVAdmins to the local Hyper-V Administrators group. Additionally, we will grant VM Connect Access to the CORP\Accounting01 group.

 Because we are changing permissions on the Hyper-V Server, these steps must be executed using an account with administrative level rights.

How to do it...

Execute the following steps to secure hyper-V:

1. Add users to the Hyper-V Administrators group:

```
$userGroup = [ADSI]("WinNT://CORP/HyperVAdmins")
$hvComp = [ADSI]("WinNT://HV01,computer")
$hvGroup = $hvComp.PSBase.Children.Find("Hyper-V Administrators")
$hvGroup.PSBase.Invoke("Add",$userGroup.PSBase.Path)
```

2. View the current list of Hyper-V Administrators:

```
[ADSI]$userGroup = "WinNT://HV01/Hyper-V Administrators,group"
$groupMembers = $userGroup.PSBase.Invoke("Members")
$groupMembers | ForEach-Object {
    $_.GetType().InvokeMember("Name", 'GetProperty', $null, $_,
$null)
}
```

3. Grant remote connect access:

```
Grant-VMConnectAccess -ComputerName HV01 -VMName Accounting01 `
-UserName AccountingAdmins
```

4. Review who has remote connect access:

```
Get-VMConnectAccess -ComputerName HV01 -VMName Accounting01
```

After executing the command, you should see something similar to the following screenshot:

```
PS C:\> Get-VMConnectAccess -ComputerName HV01 -VMName Accounting01

UserName                 VMName        ComputerName
--------                 ------        ------------
CORP\SalesAdmins         Accounting01  HV01
CORP\AccountingAdmins    Accounting01  HV01
```

5. Revoke remote connect access:

```
Revoke-VMConnectAccess -ComputerName HV01 -VMName Accounting01 `
-UserName CORP\SalesAdmins
```

How it works...

In the first step we are using PowerShell to add a domain group to a local group on the Hyper-V Server. The script starts by searching Active Directory for a domain group named `Corp\HyperVAdmins`. This group was created to contain the administrators for all of the Hyper-V Servers in our environment. Next, the script searches Active Directory for the computer named `HV01`, and then searches within the server for a local group named Hyper-V Administrators. Lastly, the script adds the `Corp\HyperVAdmins` group into the `HV01\ Hyper-V Administrator` group.

The default permissions restrict this task from running remotely. To execute this function, the firewall needs to be reconfigured, or the commands must be executed locally by logging onto the server or by using a PSSession.

In the second step we review who has been added to the Hyper-V Administrator group on the local server. This will allow us to confirm that the correct users have been granted permission to our servers.

In the third step we use `Grant-VMConnectAccess` to grant access to the `Accounting01` virtual machine. In this situation we have a group of administrators named `AccountingAdmins`, who are responsible for managing this server, and we need to provide them access to the virtual machine.

In the fourth step we use `Get-VMConnectAccess` to query the Hyper-V Server to review who has access to the `Accounting01` virtual machine. In this situation we find that there are two groups with connect access: `SalesAdmins` and `AccountingAdmins`. Because this server is used by the Accounting department, we need to remove the Sales group from the server.

In the last step we use `Revoke-VMConnectAccess` to remove the `SalesAdmins` group from the `Accounting01` virtual machine.

There's more...

VMConnectAccess allows for a user to remotely connect to a virtual machine using the Hyper-V administration tools. This allows the user to use the VM as if they were at a physical computer. They can open the computer console, reboot the server, and load/unload ISO media. Administrators will initially use this feature when first setting up a virtual machine (installing the OS, configuring IP address, joining to domain, and so on) and it can be useful for several other tasks.

> Standard Windows security still applies, and the users must have accounts to access the server. However, the ability to restart the VM into safe mode or booting from ISOs may allow escalation of privileges.

Additionally, `VMConnectAccess` is not viewable or configurable via the Hyper-V administrative console. To grant, revoke, or view access, PowerShell must be used.

Hyper-V networking

In Hyper-V there are three types of network switches available: external, internal, and private. **External network** switches are tied to physical network adapters on the Hyper-V Server and they allow systems on the network to access remote systems and services. **Internal network** switches allow VMs on the Hyper-V Server to communicate with each other, and the Hyper-V Server itself. **Private network** switches allow VMs on the Hyper-V Server to communicate with each other, but not to the Hyper-V Server or outside of the Hyper-V server.

Getting ready

In this recipe we will be setting up the networks for an NLB cluster on our Hyper-V Server. To accomplish this, we will be creating three networks: production, management, and NLB Comm. The **production network** is an external network attached to a physical network adapter on the Hyper-V Server and it provides access to the Corp environment. The **NLB Comm network** is a private network used for intra-NLB communication. Lastly, the **management network** is an internal network that will be used for out-of-band management of the VMs on the server.

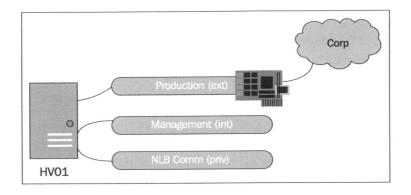

For this recipe we need a Hyper-V Server configured similar to the *Installing and configuring Hyper-V* recipe.

How to do it...

Carry out the following steps to set up the Hyper-V networks:

1. List the adapters on the Hyper-V Server and identify the name of the interface to connect the external network:

    ```
    $cim = New-CimSession -ComputerName HV01
    Get-NetAdapter -CimSession $cim
    ```

    When completed, the physical interfaces will be listed as shown in the following screenshot:

    ```
    PS C:\> $cim= New-CimSession -ComputerName HV01
    PS C:\> Get-NetAdapter -CimSession $cim

    Name                    InterfaceDescription                    ifIndex Statu
                                                                            s
    ----                    --------------------                    ------- -----
    Ethernet 3              Intel(R) 82574L Gigabit Network Co...#2       24 Up
    Ethernet                Intel(R) 82574L Gigabit Network Conn...       13 Up
    ```

2. Create the external network on the Hyper-V Server and attach it to the Ethernet interface:

    ```
    New-VMSwitch -ComputerName HV01 -Name "Production" `
    -NetAdapterName "Ethernet"
    ```

3. Create the internal network on the Hyper-V Server for management of the VMs:

    ```
    New-VMSwitch -ComputerName HV01 -SwitchType Internal -Name
    Management
    ```

4. Create the private network on the Hyper-V Server:

```
New-VMSwitch -ComputerName HV01 -SwitchType Private -Name "NLB
Comm"
```

5. View all of the networks on the Hyper-V Server:

```
Get-VMSwitch -ComputerName HV01
```

When executed, the virtual switches will be displayed as shown in the following screenshot:

```
PS C:\> Get-VMSwitch -ComputerName HV01

Name          SwitchType  NetAdapterInterfaceDescription
----          ----------  ------------------------------
Production    External    Intel(R) 82574L Gigabit Network Connection
Management    Internal
NLB Comm      Private
```

How it works...

The first step in creating our Hyper-V networks is to identify which network interfaces exist on the Hyper-V Server and their names. In this example, we use `New-CimSession` to connect remotely to our Hyper-V Server and then call `Get-NetAdapter` to list the network adapters. In this example, we have two interfaces available: Ethernet and Ethernet 3.

Once we have identified the physical network adapters, we use `New-VMSwitch` to create our first Hyper-V network. The first network we create is our production network, which is our external network. We use the `-NetAdapterName` switch with the name of our desired physical adapter to provide access to the external network.

In third and fourth step we create the internal and private networks by using the `-SwitchType` switch.

 The `-SwitchType` switch is only used when creating internal or private networks. If this switch is not included, the switch is assumed to be an external switch.

In the last step we use `Get-VMSwitch` to list out the switches that have been created on the Hyper-V Server.

There's more...

External and internal switches have an additional option to allow or disallow the Hyper-V Server from using a network. For instance, with this setting on an external switch, both the VMs and Hyper-V Server can use the same network interface. To enable or disable the setting, use the `Set-VMSwitch` command and specify the `-AllowManagementOS` switch:

```
Set-VMSwitch -ComputerName HV01 -name Production -AllowManagementOS
$false
```

 By default, `AllowManagementOS` is enabled for external switches and disabled for internal switches

Creating virtual machines

Once our Hyper-V Server environment is built and configured, we can begin hosting virtual machines on it. Creating VMs using the Hyper-V admin console is quick and easy if you only need to create two or three VMs. However, if you need to create more, or need to ensure the configurations remain the same, then PowerShell is the ideal tool.

In this recipe we will create and configure a new virtual machine on our Hyper-V Server.

Getting ready

For this recipe we need a functioning Hyper-V Server similar to the *Hyper-V networking* recipe in this chapter.

How to do it...

Carry out the following steps to create a new virtual machine:

1. Create the new virtual machine:

   ```
   New-VM -ComputerName HV01 -Name Accounting02 -MemoryStartupBytes
   512MB `
   -NewVHDPath "e:\VM\Virtual Hard Disks\Accounting02.vhdx" `
   -NewVHDSizeBytes 100GB -SwitchName Production
   ```

2. Configure the system for dynamic memory:

   ```
   Set-VMMemory -ComputerName HV01 -VMName Accounting02 `
   -DynamicMemoryEnabled $true -MaximumBytes 2GB
   ```

3. Review the virtual machine configuration:

   ```
   Get-VM -ComputerName HV01 -Name Accounting02 | Format-List *
   ```

When executed, the virtual machine configuration is displayed similar to the following screenshot:

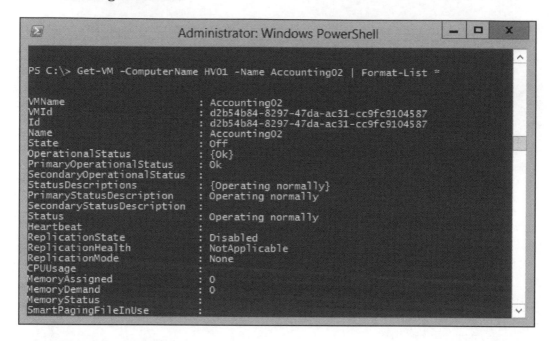

```
PS C:\> Get-VM -ComputerName HV01 -Name Accounting02 | Format-List *

VMName                      : Accounting02
VMId                        : d2b54b84-8297-47da-ac31-cc9fc9104587
Id                          : d2b54b84-8297-47da-ac31-cc9fc9104587
Name                        : Accounting02
State                       : Off
OperationalStatus           : {Ok}
PrimaryOperationalStatus    : Ok
SecondaryOperationalStatus  :
StatusDescriptions          : {Operating normally}
PrimaryStatusDescription    : Operating normally
SecondaryStatusDescription  :
Status                      : Operating normally
Heartbeat                   :
ReplicationState            : Disabled
ReplicationHealth           : NotApplicable
ReplicationMode             : None
CPUUsage                    :
MemoryAssigned              : 0
MemoryDemand                : 0
MemoryStatus                :
SmartPagingFileInUse        :
```

How it works...

The first step uses the `New-VM` command to create a virtual machine on the Hyper-V Server HV01. Here we create a new VM named `Accounting02`. Multiple switches are used to define the various aspects of the virtual machine:

- `MemoryStartupBytes` defines the guaranteed minimum memory resources when the system is switched on

- `NewVHDPath` defines the name and location Hyper-V should create in the VHDx file for the VM

- `NewVHDSizeBytes` defines the size of the hard disk for the VM

- `SwitchName` defines the networking switch for the VM

Some PowerShell switches, such as `MemoryStartupBytes`, accept values presented as `Bytes`. However, PowerShell is capable of automatically calculating the `Byte` equivalent when a value is passed as KB, MB, GB, or TB.

For instance, here we specify `MemoryStartupBytes` as 512 MB, which is shorthand for 536,870,912 bytes.

Once the virtual machine is created, we then use Set-VMMemory to configure the virtual machine to use dynamic memory. Dynamic memory allows Hyper-V to increase or decrease the memory used by a VM as needed. In this instance we enable dynamic memory and specify the maximum amount of memory to allocate is 2 GB.

Lastly, we execute Get-VM to list the VM properties. Here, we can view the memory configuration to confirm that DynamicMemoryEnabled is set to true, the MemoryMinimum is configured to guarantee a minimum of 512 MB of RAM, and that MemoryMaximum allows the VM to burst up to 2 GB of RAM if needed.

Managing VM state

Scripting the state of virtual machines allows us to quickly and easily manage all of the virtual machines in your environment. This will allow us to power systems on or off individually, as a group, or as a job that occurs automatically based on the time of day, or triggered by external processes.

Getting ready

In this recipe we will be working with the Accounting02 virtual machine created in the *Creating virtual machines* recipe.

How to do it...

Carry out the following steps to manage VM state:

1. View the current virtual machine state:

    ```
    Get-VM -ComputerName HV01 -Name Accounting02
    ```

    When executed, you should see a screen similar to the following screenshot:

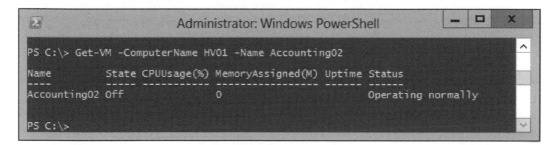

```
PS C:\> Get-VM -ComputerName HV01 -Name Accounting02

Name          State CPUUsage(%) MemoryAssigned(M) Uptime Status
----          ----- ----------- ----------------- ------ ------
Accounting02  Off               0                        Operating normally

PS C:\>
```

2. Power on the virtual machine:

```
Start-VM -ComputerName HV01 -Name Accounting02
```

When executed, you can call `Get-VM` again to confirm the change:

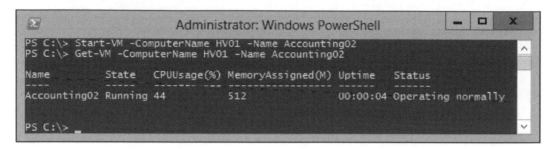

3. Suspend the virtual machine:

```
Save-VM -ComputerName HV01 -Name Accounting02
```

When executed, you can call `Get-VM` again to confirm the change:

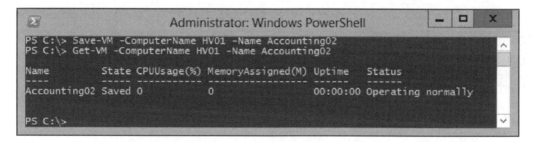

4. Resume the virtual machine:

```
Start-VM -ComputerName HV01 -Name Accounting02
```

5. Shut down the virtual machine:

```
Stop-VM -ComputerName HV01 -Name Accounting02
```

6. Power off the virtual machine:

```
Stop-VM -ComputerName HV01 -Name Accounting02 -TurnOff
```

How it works...

Managing the state of virtual machines in Hyper-V is relatively easy.

In the first step we are using `Get-VM` to view the state of the `Accounting02` virtual machine on the Hyper-V Server `HV01`. The results confirm that the VM is currently powered off and not consuming any resources.

In the second step we call `Start-VM` to power on the virtual machine. This is the virtual equivalent of powering on a physical server. When started, our VM will power on, progress through the BIOS, boot from the defined media, and load the operating system. We can then call `Get-VM` again to confirm the VM is powered on and consuming CPU and memory.

In the third step we are using `Save-VM` to suspend our virtual machine. Saving the VM is similar to suspending or hibernating a laptop computer. When this occurs, all activity on the computer is suspended, and the contents of memory are written to disk to be accessed later. When we call `Get-VM`, we see that the state of the VM is **Saved**, meaning we can resume it at a later time without losing information.

In the fourth step we are using `Start-VM` to resume our VM from its saved state. Because the system state and contents of memory are saved on disk, the VM is quickly resumed to an operational state, instead of performing the full boot and startup process.

Next, we use `Stop-VM` to shut down the virtual machine. This process will attempt to use the Hyper-V integration tools to perform a clean shutdown and switch off from within the guest OS. If the tools are not available for some reason, the command will prompt you to forcibly switch off the server.

Lastly, we use `Stop-VM` with the `-Turnoff` switch to switch off the virtual machine. This is the virtual equivalent of removing the power cord from the system and all processing will cease. This should only be performed as a last step as an unclean shutdown may cause loss of data or corruption of files.

There's more...

Using `Save-VM` and `Start-VM` is a great method to allow for maintenance tasks on Hyper-V Servers. For instance, let's assume we need to install a new network adapter in your Hyper-V Server and we need to accomplish this with minimal downtime to the guest VMs. Because we are changing the hardware of the Hyper-V Server, we will need to switch off the server, however with these tools, we don't have to shut down the VMs.

In this scenario we can use `Save-VM` to pause the running VMs and save their state to disk. Once all the VMs are saved, we can shutdown the host and perform the necessary work. When finished, call `Start-VM` to return the VMs to their prior state. No shutdown of the VM is needed and the running configuration should be the same as before.

 Some applications do not work well when they are paused in this manner. Additionally, some applications are picky about resource availability, and the save/start order is important for the process to work properly.

Configuring VM networking

One of the many features that virtualization provides is the ability to easily change the configuration of a virtual machine. Changes to physical servers often require purchases of additional hardware, downtime of the server to install and reconfigure the hardware, and possibly running of new cables to provide networking, fiber channel, or additional capabilities to the server.

The flexibility of Hyper-V networking minimizes the amount of effort needed to make many of these changes. With Hyper-V, virtual NICs can be added or removed, network destinations can be changed, and **Virtual LANs (VLANs)** can be configured. These abilities allow for a more agile environment that can change as business needs change, security requirements update, or troubleshooting requires.

Getting ready

In this recipe we will add a new virtual NIC to our `Accounting02` VM from the *Creating virtual machines* recipe and configure it to operate on an additional network. This new network uses a virtual switch named `Extranet` and will utilize a VLAN to separate the traffic for the systems of the accounting department.

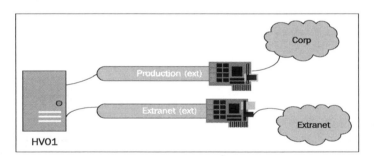

How to do it...

Carry out the following steps to configure VM networking:

1. Open PowerShell and add a new virtual NIC to the VM:

   ```
   Add-VMNetworkAdapter -ComputerName HV01 -VMName Accounting02 `
   -SwitchName Extranet
   ```

    The target virtual machine must be switched off to add a networker adapter.

2. Change the VLAN on the new virtual NIC:

```
Get-VMNetworkAdapter -ComputerName HV01 -VMName Accounting02 | `
Where-Object SwitchName -eq 'Extranet' | Set-VMNetworkAdapterVlan
`
-Access -VlanId 9
```

3. Review the virtual NIC configuration:

```
Get-VMNetworkAdapter -ComputerName HV01 -VMName Accounting02
Get-VMNetworkAdapter -ComputerName HV01 -VMName Accounting02 | `
Get-VMNetworkAdapterVlan
```

When executed, you should see something similar to the following screenshot:

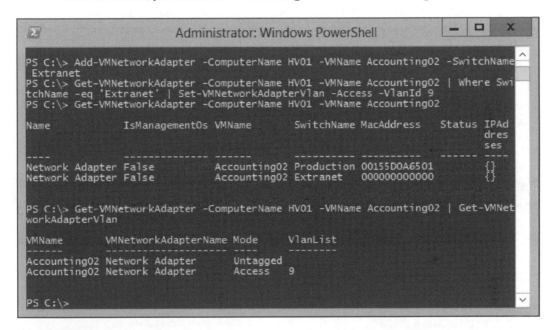

How it works...

In the first step we use `Add-VMNetworkAdapter` to create a new virtual adapter on our virtual machine. Here, we configure the adapter to be attached to the virtual switch named `Extranet`.

In the second step we query our virtual machine to list the current network adapters. We filter this list for an adapter attached to the `Extranet` switch to find the NIC we just created. Finally, we use `Set-VMNetworkAdapterVLAN` to configure the adapter to use VLAN number 9.

In the third step we call `Get-VMNetworkAdapter` to review our configuration. We call this command twice. First to view our adapters and confirm they are attached to the correct switches. We call `Get-VMNetworkAdapter` again to pipe the results into `Get-NetworkAdapterVlan` to confirm the VLAN configuration for the new NIC is correct.

There's more...

It is also possible to reassign the switch a network adapter is attached to. If instead of creating a second adapter, we simply wanted to reassign the adapter, the following commands would have worked:

```
Get-VMNetworkAdapter -ComputerName HV01 -VMName Accounting01 `
-Name "Network Adapter" | Connect-VMNetworkAdapter `
-SwitchName Extranet
Get-VMNetworkAdapter -ComputerName HV01 -VMName Accounting02 | `
Where-Object SwitchName -eq 'Extranet' | Set-VMNetworkAdapterVlan `
-Access -VlanId 9
```

In this example we begin by getting a reference to the adapter object on our virtual machine. Once we have the adapter, we call `Connect-VMNetworkAdapter` to reassign the adapter to the extranet switch. We then also call `Set-VMNetworkAdapterVLAN` to assign the correct VLAN to our adapter.

Configuring VM hardware

Occasionally, you will find that the initial configuration for a virtual machine needs to change to continue to support its role. Sometimes this is because the hardware is undersized and needs to be increased to meet the needs. Other times this is because the hardware is too big and needs to be decreased to free up resources for other VMs.

Getting ready

In this example we will be reconfiguring the hardware of our `Accounting02` virtual machine from the *Creating virtual machines* recipe. Specifically, we will be changing the memory configuration, adding additional hard drives, and changing the number of virtual CPUs on the VM.

 Most of these commands can only be performed while the VM is switched off.

How to do it...

Carry out the following steps to update the virtual hardware:

1. Change the memory configuration to increase the available RAM:

    ```
    Set-VMMemory -ComputerName HV01 -VMName Accounting02 -StartupBytes
    1GB
    ```

2. Enable dynamic memory on the VM:

    ```
    Set-VMMemory -ComputerName HV01 -VMName Accounting02 `
    -DynamicMemoryEnabled $true -MaximumBytes 2GB -MinimumBytes 128MB
    `
    -StartupBytes 1GB
    ```

3. Add an additional IDE hard disk:

    ```
    New-VHD -ComputerName HV01 `
    -Path "E:\vm\Virtual Hard Disks\Accounting02_1.vhdx" `
    -SizeBytes 50GB -Dynamic
    Add-VMHardDiskDrive -ComputerName HV01 -VMName Accounting02 `
    -Path "E:\vm\virtual hard disks\Accounting02_1.vhdx"
    ```

4. Change the number of virtual CPUs:

    ```
    Set-VMProcessor -ComputerName HV01 -VMName Accounting02 -Count 4
    ```

How it works...

In this recipe we begin by configuring the memory on our virtual machine. In the first step we are using `Set-VMMemory` to change the amount of RAM available to the VM and setting it to 1 GB.

In the second step we use `Set-VMMemory` again to change the memory configuration and enable dynamic memory. Dynamic memory allows Hyper-V to add and remove memory to a running VM based on the current need and available resources on the server. In this situation we also configure the `MinimumBytes` and `MaximumBytes` memory values for use with dynamic memory, as well as the guaranteed amount of memory available when the VM is switched on.

In the third step we are creating a new hard disk and attaching it to our virtual machine. We start by calling `New-VHD` to create a new VHDx file on the Hyper-V Server. Next, we use `Add-VMHardDiskDrive` to attach the disk as an IDE drive to the VM.

In addition to IDE drives, we can also attach the disk as a SCSI drive. To accomplish this, we use the `-ControllerType` and `-ControllerNumber` switches to define the disk as SCSI and which controller to use.

In the fourth step we are using `Set-VMProcessor` to change the number of virtual processors on the virtual machine.

Quickly deploying VMs using a template

Creating new virtual machines in Hyper-V is a relatively simple and automatable process, however the installation of an operating system on the VM can still take an extended period of time. Existing automated deployment tools help in the installation process, but most are slow and can be improved in a virtual environment.

Getting ready

In this recipe we will be using a VM with a basic installation of Server 2012 named `Server2012_template`:

1. Create a new VM using the steps in the *Creating virtual machines* recipe.

2. Install the Windows operating system on the new VM.

3. Execute `C:\Windows\System32\Sysprep\Sysprep.exe`.

4. Select **Enter System Out-of-Box Experience (OOBE)**, **Generalize**, and **Shutdown**:

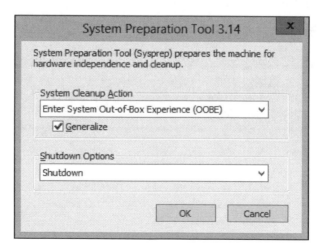

5. Click on **OK** to reconfigure and switch off the VM.

How to do it...

Complete the following steps to deploy a VM from the template:

1. Open PowerShell and create the new VHDx file:

   ```
   New-VHD -ComputerName HV01 `
   -ParentPath 'E:\vm\Virtual Hard Disks\Server8_template.vhdx' `
   -Path 'E:\vm\Virtual Hard Disks\Test01.vhdx'
   ```

2. Create the new VM and attach the VHDx file:

   ```
   New-VM -ComputerName HV01 -Name Test01 `
   -VHDPath 'E:\vm\Virtual Hard Disks\Test01.vhdx' -SwitchName
   Production
   ```

3. Configure the VM memory as dynamic:

   ```
   Set-VMMemory -ComputerName HV01 -VMName Test01 `
   -DynamicMemoryEnabled $true -MaximumBytes 2GB
   ```

4. Start the VM:

   ```
   Start-VM -ComputerName HV01 -Name Test01
   ```

How it works...

The recipe starts by using New-VHD to create a new virtual hard disk. Specifically, we are using the -ParentPath switch to create a differencing hard disk. This disk configuration is unique in the virtual machine. It will initially perform all reads from the parent disk and the child/destination disk will be empty. All writes or changes will be sent to the child disk, and then any reads for the new or changed blocks will come from the child disk.

In the second step we call New-VM to create a new VM named Test01. While creating the VM we use the -VHDPath switch to use the virtual hard disk we just created.

In the third step we use Set-VMMemory to configure the memory on our VM. In this instance we are configuring the VM for dynamic memory and a maximum value of 2 GB.

Lastly, we call Start-VM to start the virtual machine on the Hyper-V host. The VM will switch on, finalize the system preparation process, and prompt you for the administrator password, and then be available for logon.

There's more...

This type of VM deployment is ideal for a test lab or virtual desktop environment. This allows for quickly deploying multiple similar systems and having them operational with minimal user impact. Because the environment is quick and easy to deploy, you can also delete the systems when no longer using them, and redeploy them when needed. Assuming your environment uses network storage for user data, there should not be any possibility of losing information between rebuilds.

One thing to note in this configuration is that the template disk is used by all VMs that were deployed from the template. This single VHDx file can result in a performance bottleneck if the backend disks are not sized properly. If performance issues appear, you should look at the utilization of the template disk and potentially move it to a faster disk subsystem.

See also

More information about using SysPrep can be found at `http://technet.microsoft.com/en-us/video/creating-an-install-image-with-sysprep-in-windows-server-2012`.

More information about Hyper-V disk types can be found at `http://blogs.technet.com/b/yungchou/archive/2013/01/23/hyper-v-virtual-hard-disk-vhd-operations-explained.aspx`.

Managing and reporting on VM snapshots

One of the greatest features when using virtualization is the ability to use snapshots. Snapshots allow for a virtual machine state and configuration to be captured and then later, rolled back to undo any changes. This is a great method to test our changes on virtual machines, by snapshotting the VM prior to making the change, it can be rolled back if the result is undesired.

Getting ready

In this recipe we will be working with our `Accounting02` virtual machine created in the *Creating virtual machines* recipe.

In this fictional scenario we have an application team that is planning to make two different sets of changes to our VM. In order to facilitate troubleshooting and recovery, we will be creating several snapshots of the VM before and during the activity. If needed, we will rollback the snapshots to a working condition.

How to do it...

Complete the following steps to manage and report on VM snapshots:

1. Create a snapshot prior to any work occurring on the VM:

   ```
   Checkpoint-VM -ComputerName HV01 -VMName Accounting02 `
   -SnapshotName "First Snap"
   ```

2. Allow the application team to perform their first set of changes.

3. Once the application team is done with the first set of changes, create another snapshot:

   ```
   Checkpoint-VM -ComputerName HV01 -VMName Accounting02 `
   -SnapshotName "Second Snap"
   ```

4. When finished, review the snapshots for the VM:

   ```
   Get-VMSnapshot -ComputerName HV01 -VMName Accounting02
   ```

   When executed, we will see an output similar to the following screenshot:

```
PS C:\> Get-VMSnapshot -ComputerName HV01 -VMName Accounting02

VMName       Name        SnapshotType CreationTime            ParentSnapshotName
------       ----        ------------ ------------            ------------------
Accounting02 First Snap  Standard     10/7/2012 1:55:57 PM
Accounting02 Second Snap Standard     10/7/2012 1:56:00 PM    First Snap
```

5. Allow the application team to perform their second set of changes.

6. The application team requests to rollback the last change:

   ```
   Restore-VMSnapshot -ComputerName HV01 -VMName Accounting02 `
   -Name "Second Snap" -Confirm:$false
   ```

7. Remove all snapshots for the VM:

   ```
   Remove-VMSnapshot -ComputerName HV01 -VMName Accounting02 -Name *
   ```

How it works...

Prior to any work being performed on our virtual machine, we use `Checkpoint-VM` to create a snapshot of the virtual machine. This captures the state of the virtual machine as a snapshot named `First Snap` and will allow for a rollback to a known working state.

In the second step we alert the application team the snapshot is complete and they can proceed with their changes. Once the first set of changes is complete, we then create another snapshot named Second Snap. This provides for a second rollback point, allowing us to later choose between no changes and some changes.

In the fourth step we use Get-VMSnapshot to list the snapshots for the virtual machine. As we can see from the output we have our two snapshots. If you notice the column on the right, ParentSnapshotName, you will see that the snapshots use a parent-child relationship to minimize the resources each snapshot requires.

In the sixth step we use Restore-VMSnapshot to rollback the last set of changes performed. This rollback process not only rolls back any file changes to the system, but also any changes to memory contents and power state.

 When restoring a snapshot, the snapshots still remain, only the contents of the running VM are reset. Once finished working with the snapshots, we will still need to remove the snapshots.

In the last step we use Remove-VMSnapshot to delete all of the snapshots for this virtual machine. This process merges all of the changes that occurred between the snapshots and the current state into the source hard disk. If a large number of changes occurred, the merge process may take a while to complete.

There's more...

It is possible to export the contents of a VM snapshot from Hyper-V. This export can then be reimported later or imported onto another Hyper-V Server and then operate as a new system.

```
Export-VMSnapshot -ComputerName HV01 -VMName Accounting02 `
-Name "First Snap" "E:\vm\export\"
```

This command creates a temporary merged copy of the original VM and the snapshot is changed. The merged copy is then exported to the target folder. The export can then be imported into Hyper-V to replace the current VM or as a new VM.

Monitoring Hyper-V utilization and performance

Monitoring the performance and utilization of Hyper-V Server is a key component of ensuring your virtual environment is running properly. By monitoring you Hyper-V environment, you can identify VMs that are using more resources than expected, and when your environment needs additional resources.

Getting ready

This recipe will utilize the built-in Hyper-V performance counters to report on system utilization. This will report on the resources being used by each virtual machine and allow easy identification of problem systems. In this recipe we will be reporting on the CPU resources being used by the individual virtual machines.

For this example we will only be monitoring four performance counters related to the Hyper-V virtual CPUs shown as follows. Additional counters can be added to track memory, disk, and network utilization as well:

▶ `Hyper-V HyperVisor Virtual Processor\% Guest Run Time`

▶ `Hyper-V HyperVisor Virtual Processor\% Hypervisor Run Time`

▶ `Hyper-V HyperVisor Virtual Processor\% Remote Run Time`

▶ `Hyper-V HyperVisor Virtual Processor\% Total Run Time`

 In this example we are requesting the data from a remote system. Appropriate firewall rules must be applied to allow remote performance monitoring.

How to do it...

Carry out the following steps to manage the Hyper-V utilization and performance:

1. Open **Performance Monitor** by going to the **Start** menu and typing `Perfmon`.

2. On the **Performance Monitor** tab click on the green **+** button to select additional counters:

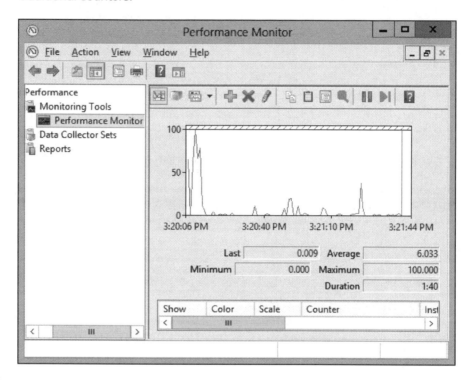

3. Under **Select counters from computer**, enter the name of your Hyper-V server and hit *Enter*.

4. On the **Add-Counters** page browse the Hyper-V counters and identify the counters to report on:

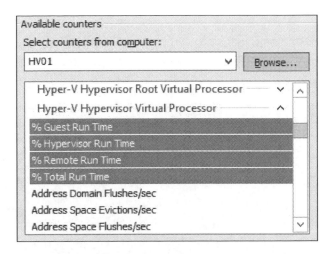

5. Create the counter array and query the Hyper-V Server:

```
$myNodes = "HV01","HV02"
$myCounter = $myNodes | ForEach-Object {
    "\\$_\Hyper-V Hypervisor Virtual Processor(*)\% Guest Run
Time"
    "\\$_\Hyper-V Hypervisor Virtual Processor(*)\% Hypervisor Run
Time"
    "\\$_\Hyper-V Hypervisor Virtual Processor(*)\% Remote Run
Time"
    "\\$_\Hyper-V Hypervisor Virtual Processor(*)\% Total Run
Time"
}
Get-Counter -Counter $myCounter
```

6. Select and format the data into a usable form:

```
$counterResults = Get-Counter -Counter $myCounter
$counterResults.CounterSamples | `
select @{
    Name="VM"; Expression={
        if($_.InstanceName.Contains(":")){
            $_.InstanceName.Substring(0,$_.InstanceName.
IndexOf(":"))
        } else {
            $_.InstanceName
        }
    }
```

```
}, InstanceName, @{ Name="Counter"; Expression={ $_.Path.
Substring( `
$_.Path.LastIndexOf("\")+1 ) } }, CookedValue | `
Sort-Object VM, Counter, InstanceName | `
Format-Table -Property VM, Counter, InstanceName, CookedValue
```

When executed, you should see a performance report similar to the
following screenshot:

VM	Counter	InstanceName	CookedValue
--	-------	------------	-----------
_total	% guest run time	_total	0.243339075574425
_total	% hypervisor run...	_total	0.911058810165034
_total	% remote run time	_total	0
_total	% total run time	_total	1.15439788573946
accounting01	% guest run time	accounting01:hv ...	0.658017736485815
accounting01	% hypervisor run...	accounting01:hv ...	2.29759251907583
accounting01	% remote run time	accounting01:hv ...	0
accounting01	% total run time	accounting01:hv ...	2.95561025556165
accounting02	% guest run time	accounting02:hv ...	0.558707156214382
accounting02	% guest run time	accounting02:hv ...	0
accounting02	% guest run time	accounting02:hv ...	0
accounting02	% guest run time	accounting02:hv ...	0
accounting02	% hypervisor run...	accounting02:hv ...	2.22662550323665
accounting02	% hypervisor run...	accounting02:hv ...	0.0112374568103762
accounting02	% hypervisor run...	accounting02:hv ...	0.00893884122390733
accounting02	% hypervisor run...	accounting02:hv ...	0.0109871185232676
accounting02	% remote run time	accounting02:hv ...	0
accounting02	% remote run time	accounting02:hv ...	0
accounting02	% remote run time	accounting02:hv ...	0
accounting02	% remote run time	accounting02:hv ...	0
accounting02	% total run time	accounting02:hv ...	2.78533265945104
accounting02	% total run time	accounting02:hv ...	0.0112374568103762
accounting02	% total run time	accounting02:hv ...	0.00893884122390733
accounting02	% total run time	accounting02:hv ...	0.0109871185232676

How it works...

In the first few steps we are using Windows Performance Monitor to review the available
performance counters on our Hyper-V Server. The Hyper-V role installs dozens of performance
counters providing information on the Hyper-V Server, the guest operating systems, CPU,
memory, networking, and even remote connections. In the fourth step we identify the Virtual
CPU counters we wish to monitor.

In the fifth step we start by creating an array of our Hyper-V Server named $myNodes. This
can be a single server, or an array of multiple servers. We pipe the server names into a
ForEach-Object loop to assign our server names to our identified counters. These counters
are then saved as an array named $myCounter. Lastly, we call Get-Counter to query our
Hyper-V Server.

Lastly, we sort the data to a format that is more easily viewed. We start by calling `Get-Counter` to query the performance counters and save the output into a variable `$counterResults`. We then pipe `$counterResults` into a `Select-Object` statement that returns the name of the VM, the counter and instance information, and the value. This information is then passed into `Sort-Object` and `Format-Table` to order the information and make it more usable.

As we can see from the results, the commands report on the CPU resources used by each virtual CPU on the system, as well as the total resources used for the entire system.

There's more...

In this example we have reported only on the CPU resources of a virtual machine, but this script can be expanded to monitor other components as well. Each virtual machine also has performance counters for memory utilization, disk access, and network utilization. Additionally, the Hyper-V Server itself can be monitored for total CPU, disk, network, and memory utilization to ensure the system is not running out of resources.

Synchronizing networks between Hyper-V hosts

When managing multiple Hyper-V Servers simultaneously, it is often best to keep the server configurations similar. This allows for easier management of the servers, as well as enabling portability of the virtual machines between the Hyper-V Servers. In this recipe we will synchronize the networking configuration between Hyper-V Servers.

Getting ready

To perform this recipe we will need two Hyper-V Servers with similar hardware configurations. We are assuming that the physical servers are configured similarly, specifically, with respect to the number, naming, and purpose of the network adapters.

How to do it...

Carry out the following steps to synchronize networks between Hyper-V hosts:

1. Open PowerShell and collect information on the `Private` and `Internal` switches:

   ```
   $HV01Switch = Get-VMSwitch -ComputerName HV01 -SwitchType Private,
   Internal
   $HV02Switch = Get-VMSwitch -ComputerName HV02 -SwitchType Private,
   Internal
   ```

2. Compare the switches and create new switches wherever necessary:

```
$HV01Switch | Where-Object {$HV02Switch.Name -NotContains $_.Name}
| `
ForEach-Object{ New-VMSwitch -ComputerName HV02 -Name $_.Name `
-SwitchType $_.SwitchType }
$HV02Switch | Where-Object {$HV01Switch.Name -NotContains $_.Name}
| `
ForEach-Object{ New-VMSwitch -ComputerName HV01 -Name $_.Name `
-SwitchType $_.SwitchType }
```

3. Compare and create `External` switches wherever necessary:

```
$HV01Switch = Get-VMSwitch -ComputerName HV01
$HV02Switch = Get-VMSwitch -ComputerName HV02
$HV01Switch | Where-Object {$HV02Switch.Name -NotContains $_.Name}
| `
ForEach-Object{
    IF($_.SwitchType -eq "External"){
        New-VMSwitch -ComputerName HV02 -Name $_.Name
-NetAdapterName `
        (Get-NetAdapter -CimSession (New-CimSession -ComputerName
HV01) | `
        Where-Object InterfaceDescription -eq `
        $_.NetAdapterInterfaceDescription).Name
    }
}
$HV02Switch | Where-Object {$HV01Switch.Name -NotContains $_.Name}
| `
ForEach-Object{
    IF($_.SwitchType -eq "External"){
        New-VMSwitch -ComputerName HV01 -Name $_.Name
-NetAdapterName `
        (Get-NetAdapter -CimSession (New-CimSession -ComputerName
HV02) | `
        Where-Object InterfaceDescription -eq `
        $_.NetAdapterInterfaceDescription).Name
    }
}
```

How it works...

In the first step we are using Get-VMSwitch to retrieve the switch configurations on the Hyper-V Servers. This is retrieving the Private and Internal switches on both Hyper-V hosts and placing them into arrays.

In the second step we are comparing the two arrays with each other. We start by comparing the virtual switches on HV01 against HV02. For each virtual switch that exists on the first server, but not the second, we call New-VMSwitch to create the switch on the host. We then reverse the process and create switches on HV01.

In the third step we requery the Hyper-V servers for all switches. We start by comparing the virtual switches on HV01 against HV02. If a switch exists on HV01 but not on HV02, it is created and attached the external interface based on the interface description. The process is then reversed to synchronize the virtual switches on the initial Hyper-V host.

Hyper-V replication

Hyper-V Server provides a built-in replication technology for dealing with planned and unplanned system failures. The replica technology allows for a virtual machine to be replicated from a source Hyper-V Server to a target Hyper-V Server and constantly kept up-to-date. In case of an outage the target VM can be switched on with minimal data loss. This replication works well within the same datacenter, as well as between different datacenters.

In this recipe we will set up a VM to be replicated between Hyper-V hosts and test failover.

Getting ready

To perform this recipe we will need a minimum of two Hyper-V Servers, each with their own storage. A virtual machine will operate on the first Hyper-V Server and it will be replicated to the second server as shown in the following diagram. We will perform failover tests to confirm the failover process operates as expected:

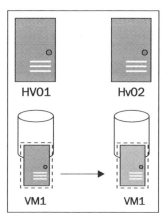

How to do it...

Carry out the following steps to configure replication:

1. Open **Active Directory Users and Computers** (dsa.msc) and open the computer properties of the Hyper-V Server HV01.

2. On the **Delegation** tab, select **Trust this computer for delegation to any service** and click on **OK**:

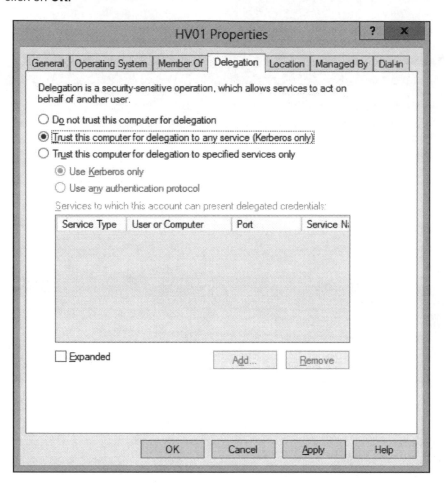

3. Reboot the server HV01 for the changes to take effect.

4. Configure the server HV02 as a Hyper-V replica server:

```
Invoke-Command -ComputerName HV02 -ScriptBlock{
    Enable-Netfirewallrule `
    -DisplayName "Hyper-V Replica HTTP Listener (TCP-In)"
    Set-VMReplicationServer -ReplicationEnabled $true `
    -AllowedAuthenticationType Kerberos `
    -KerberosAuthenticationPort 10000 `
    -DefaultStorageLocation "E:\vm" `
    -ReplicationAllowedFromAnyServer $true
}
```

5. Configure the virtual machine VM01 on HV01 as a replica source:

```
Invoke-Command -ComputerName HV01 -ScriptBlock{
    Enable-VMReplication -VMName "VM1" `
    -ReplicaServerName "HV02.corp.contoso.com" `
    -ReplicaServerPort 10000 -AuthenticationType Kerberos `
    -CompressionEnabled $true -RecoveryHistory 5
}
```

6. Begin replication:

```
Invoke-Command -ComputerName HV01 -ScriptBlock{
    $PrimaryVM1 = "VM1"
    Start-VMInitialReplication –VMName $PrimaryVM1
}
```

7. Monitor replication status:

```
Measure-VMReplication -ComputerName HV01
```

When executed, the results will be returned similar to the following screenshot:

```
PS C:\> Measure-VMReplication -ComputerName HV01

Name State                        Health LReplTime PReplSize(M) AvgLatency AvgR
                                                                           eplS
                                                                           ize(
                                                                           M)
---- -----                        ------ --------- ------------ ---------- ----
VM1  InitialReplicationInProgress Normal           2,716.00                0.00
```

8. Once the replication is finished, we can perform a failover test:

```
Invoke-Command -ComputerName HV02 -ScriptBlock{
    $TestReplicaVM1 = Start-VMFailover -AsTest -VMName "VM1" `
    –Confirm:$false
    Start-VM $TestReplicaVM1
}
```

9. Stop the failover test:

```
Invoke-Command -ComputerName HV02 -ScriptBlock{
    Stop-VMFailover –VMName "VM1"
}
```

10. Perform a planned failover:

```
Invoke-Command -ComputerName HV01 -ScriptBlock{
    Stop-VM "VM1"
    Start-VMFailover -VMName "VM1" -Prepare –Confirm:$false
}
Invoke-Command -ComputerName HV02 -ScriptBlock{
```

```
        Start-VMFailover -VMName "VM1"
        Set-VMReplication -Reverse -VMName "VM1"
        Start-VM "VM1"
    }
```

How it works...

In the first three steps we enable delegation on server HV01. When performing activities on a system, normally Kerberos authentication restricts how many systems, or hops, can be used. By enabling delegation, we are allowing the Hyper-V Server to use our credentials when accessing remote systems. This will allow the server to securely replicate with the target server.

In the fourth step we use `Invoke-Command` to connect to server HV02 in order to configure it as the replica target. We begin by calling `Enable-NetFirewallRule` to allow Hyper-V replication via HTTP. Then we use `Set-VMReplicationServer` to configure the server as the replication target. Authentication between the Hyper-V Servers is Kerberos operating over port 10000 (any port can be configured here). We configure the replica target location as `E:\VM` and allow replication from any source server.

In the fifth step we connect to the server HV01 to configure our VM as the replica source. We call `Enable-VMReplication` and identify VM1 as our source virtual machine and HV02 as the target Hyper-V Server. Authentication is configured and network compression is enabled. Lastly, replication is configured to keep the last five copies on the target server.

In the sixth and seventh steps we initiate and monitor the replication. The initial replication process is started by calling `Start-VMInitialReplication` and copies the entire source virtual machine to the target Hyper-V Server. Depending on the size of the virtual machine and the speed of the connection between the servers, this initial synchronization can take a while. We then use `Measure-VMReplication` to monitor the replication status.

In the eighth step we use `Start-VMFailover` with the `-AsTest` switch to perform a test of the failover process on the replica server. The failover test creates a copy of the VM on the replica server. This test VM is renamed and disconnected from the network. We then start the failover virtual machine and can access it via the Hyper-V console, or attach it to a network. When finished, we call `Stop-VMFailover` to stop the failover test and remove the copy of the VM.

Lastly, we perform a full failover of the VM to the target Hyper-V Server. This process starts by calling `Stop-VM` to stop the virtual machine on HV01 and then `Start-VMFailover` begins the failover process. By starting the failover process on the source server, we ensure that all changes are replicated to the target server before additional steps are performed. On the target server we call `Start-VMFailover` to finish the failover process and start the VM.

In addition to failing over the virtual machine, we also call `Set-VMReplication` in order to configure VM replication to occur in reverse, or from HV02 to HV01. This will then allow us to fail back to the initial server in the future.

To fail back, we will need to repeat the first and second steps on the alternate server.

See also

More information about Kerberos Delegation and Hyper-V can be found at `http://blogs.technet.com/b/matthts/archive/2012/06/10/configuring-kerberos-constrained-delegation-for-hyper-v-management.aspx`.

Migrating VMs between hosts

Hyper-V uses a process known as Live-Migration to migrate virtual machines between Hyper-V Servers without requiring downtime. The process utilizes shared storage (fiber channel, iSCSI, or CIFS) to host the virtual machines, and then copies the running VM process from one server to the other.

Getting ready

In this recipe we will be using a CIFS share to host our virtual machines. This allows us to keep a centralized store of virtual machines and easily share between the hosts. Additionally, this works using traditional Ethernet technology and doesn't require an expensive storage infrastructure:

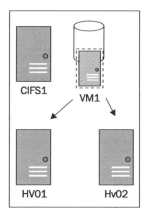

 Due to Kerberos Delegation restrictions, you must be actively logged on to the server initiating the VM migration tasks. Otherwise, an error will be returned regarding insufficient permissions on the CIFS share or Hyper-V Server.

How to do it...

Carry out the following steps to migrate VMs between hosts:

1. Create an SMB share on your file server. Ensure the Hyper-V Servers have full control access to the share and filesystem:

   `New-SmbShare -Name VMs -Path E:\Shares\VMs -FullAccess Everyone`

2. Open **Active Directory Users and Computers** (dsa.msc) and open the computer properties of the Hyper-V Server HV01.

3. On the **Delegation** tab, select **Trust this computer for delegation to any service** and click on **OK**:

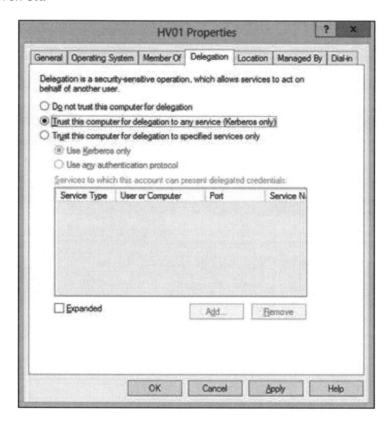

4. Reboot the server HV01 for the changes to take effect.

5. Repeat steps 2-4 for server HV02.

6. Log on to HV01 and create a virtual machine on the CIFS share:

```
New-VM -Name VM1 -MemoryStartupBytes 512MB -Path "\\CIFS1\VMs\VM1" `

-NewVHDPath "\\CIFS1\VMs\VM1.vhdx" -NewVHDSizeBytes 100GB `
-SwitchName Production
```

7. Switch on and configure the new virtual machine.

8. Enable the Hyper-V Servers for live migration:

```
Set-VMHost -ComputerName HV01,HV02 -UseAnyNetworkForMigration
$true `
-VirtualMachineMigrationAuthenticationType Kerberos
Enable-VMMigration -ComputerName HV01,HV02
```

9. Review the Hyper-V Server settings:

```
Get-VMHost -ComputerName HV01 | Format-List *
```

When executed, you will see output similar to the following screenshot:

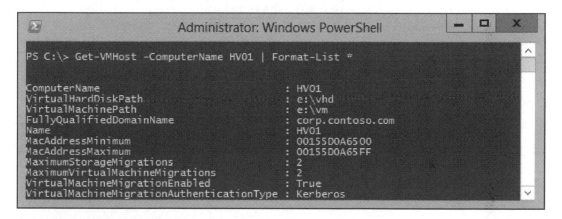

10. Migrate the VM to HV02:

```
Move-VM -Name VM1 -DestinationHost HV02
```

How it works...

We start the process by configuring the environment to support live migration. First, we use `New-SMBShare` to create a share on our file server and enable full control access to the `Everyone` group. This will provide sufficient permissions to our Hyper-V Servers.

Next, we enable delegation for both of our Hyper-V Servers. This delegation is needed to pass our credentials between the servers and enable the VMs to be shared between servers.

Next, we log onto the first Hyper-V Server `HV01` and use `New-VM` to create our virtual machine. We have to log on to the server directly so that the Kerberos Delegation will allow the Hyper-V server to place the `VHDx` file on the network share. We then create and install a virtual machine on the network share.

Next, we call `Set-VMHost` and `Enable-VMMigration` to enable live migration for both Hyper-V hosts. We configure the servers to use any available network for migration and to use Kerberos authentication for migration between servers.

We then call `Get-VMHost` to confirm our migration settings. As we can see from the output, `VirtualMachineMigrationEnabled` is set to `True`. Additionally, `VirtualMachineMigrationAuthenticationType` is set to `Kerberos`.

Lastly, we call `Move-VM` to migrate the VM between the Hyper-V Servers:

See also

More information about Kerberos Delegation and Hyper-V can be found at `http://blogs.technet.com/b/matthts/archive/2012/06/10/configuring-kerberos-constrained-delegation-for-hyper-v-management.aspx`.

Migrating VM storage between hosts

In environments without shared storage, Hyper-V operates using local storage on each server to hold the virtual machines. Hyper-V allows for migration of virtual machines and their virtual hard disks between Hyper-V Servers using local storage. This allows for VM portability between hosts without the additional cost of shared storage.

Getting ready

In this recipe we will be using two Hyper-V Servers, each with locally attached storage. The virtual machines reside on locally attached storage on the Hyper-V Servers and we will move the VM and its disk contents between the hosts. This process will occur without any downtime on the virtual machine:

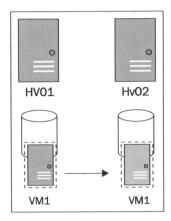

 Due to Kerberos restrictions, you must be logged on to the source server to properly authenticate to the target server.

How to do it...

Complete the following steps to migrate VM storage:

1. Log onto server HV01 and open a PowerShell console.

2. Execute the following to initiate the migration:

```
Move-VM -Name VM1 -DestinationHost HV02 `
-DestinationStoragePath E:\vm -IncludeStorage
```

How it works...

To move the virtual machines between hosts, we first log on to the server that currently hosts the virtual machine that is being migrated. Next, we use Move-VM to move the virtual machine and virtual hard disks to the target server.

 Depending on the size of the VM and the speed of the storage and networking, this process may take an extended period of time.

Using failover clustering to make VMs highly available

One of the more proven methods to make virtual machines highly available is to configure multiple Hyper-V Servers into a failover cluster. The virtual machines are then placed on the cluster nodes instead of the individual servers. The cluster is configured to migrate VMs from one host to another when instructed, when a host is placed into maintenance, or when a host unexpectedly fails.

Getting ready

For Hyper-V clustering to work properly, we will need two Hyper-V Servers with shared storage to host the virtual machines. In this example we are using a CIFS file share to host the virtual machines as shown in the recipe *Migrating VMs between hosts*.

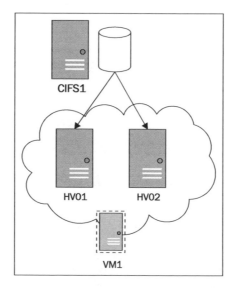

> This recipe will cover only one method of configuring a simple Hyper-V cluster. Additional options and configurations exist and may be more appropriate for your environment.

How to do it...

Carry out the following steps to set up failover clustering for Hyper-V:

1. Open **Active Directory Users and Computers** (dsa.msc) and open the computer properties of the Hyper-V Server HV01.

2. On the **Delegation** tab, select **Trust this computer for delegation to any service** and click on **OK**:

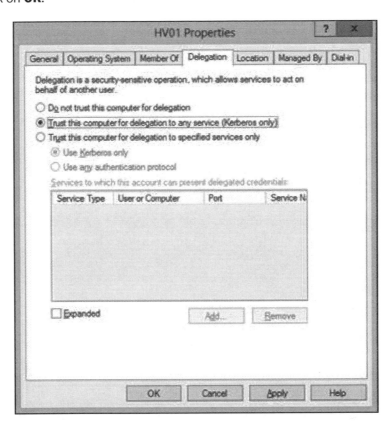

3. Reboot the server HV01 for the changes to take effect.

4. Repeat steps 1-3 for server HV02.

5. Install failover clustering on the Hyper-V Servers:

```
Invoke-Command -ComputerName HV01, HV02 -ScriptBlock {
    Install-WindowsFeature Failover-Clustering
-IncludeManagementTools
}
```

6. Configure the server as a cluster:

```
New-Cluster -Name HVCluster -Node "HV01","HV02"
```

7. Create the new virtual machine on the shared storage:

```
New-VM -Name VM1 -MemoryStartupBytes 512MB -Path "\\CIFS1\VMs\VM1" `

-NewVHDPath "\\CIFS1\VMs\VM1.vhdx" -NewVHDSizeBytes 100GB `
-SwitchName Production
```

8. Import the virtual machines to the cluster:

```
Add-VMToCluster -VMName VM1 -Cluster HVCluster
```

9. Move the virtual machine to a different node in the cluster:

```
Get-Cluster HVCluster | Move-ClusterVirtualMachineRole `
-MigrationType Live -Name VM1 -Node HV02
```

10. Place HV host into maintenance:

```
Suspend-ClusterNode -Cluster HVCluster -Name HV01 –Drain
```

11. Remove the HV cost from maintenance:

```
Resume-ClusterNode -Cluster HVCluster -Name HV01
```

How it works...

We start the process by configuring the Hyper-V Servers for delegation. Delegation is needed for the Hyper-V Servers to access the VMs on the network share. Once configured for delegation, we reboot the servers for the change to take effect.

Next, we use `Invoke-Command` to install the `Failover-Clustering` feature on our servers. Once installed, we use `New-Cluster` to create a new failover cluster named `HVCluster` with both nodes included.

Next, we create a new virtual machine on the shared storage. This step shows creating a new virtual machine with the `New-VM` command, but existing VMs can also be migrated onto the shared storage. To achieve this, the `Move-VMStorage` command is used and executed from the Hyper-V Server hosting the VM.

Once one VM is hosted on shared storage, we use `Add-VMToCluster` to import the VM as a cluster role. When called, this command automatically searches the nodes in the Hyper-V Server environment to find the VM by name. Once found, the VM is imported to the cluster and managed as a cluster resource.

Now that the cluster is configured and VMs are imported, we can migrate VMs between the hosts. In the ninth step, we use `Move-ClusterVirtualMachineRole` to perform a Live-Migration of `VM1` to the second Hyper-V Server. This occurs without requiring downtime of the virtual machine.

After we have proven that migration works between the nodes, we can then place one of the nodes into maintenance. By calling `Suspend-ClusterNode`, we are telling the failover cluster to stop processing on the node. We suspend the node with the `Drain` switch, which tells the cluster to migrate all running roles to other hosts in the cluster prior to suspending. When all roles have been migrated, the host is suspended to allow for maintenance tasks.

Finally, we call `Resume-ClusterNode` to resume our cluster node and enable it to host resources.

There's more...

When creating a VM cluster, there is often a question of how big to make the cluster. By having a minimum of resources, there is no waste of unused CPU or memory on the hosts. By having excess resources, it provides for flexibility in maintenance and expansion of the virtual environment.

I have found that sizing the environment into an N + 2 configuration optimal allows for a single host to be in maintenance mode, while still providing resources for an unplanned failover. Additionally, if the resource demands increase (such as adding additional VMs), the environment will only drop to an N + 1 configuration. At this point we can easily prove the need for additional compute resources without limiting our ability to perform failover or maintenance tasks.

See also

More information about Kerberos Delegation and Hyper-V can be found at `http://blogs.technet.com/b/matthts/archive/2012/06/10/configuring-kerberos-constrained-delegation-for-hyper-v-management.aspx`.

5
Managing Storage with PowerShell

This chapter covers the following topics:

- ▶ Managing NTFS file permissions
- ▶ Managing NTFS alternate streams
- ▶ Configuring NTFS deduplication
- ▶ Monitoring NTFS deduplication
- ▶ Configuring storage pools
- ▶ Reporting on storage pools
- ▶ Managing file quotas

Introduction

This chapter covers how to configure and manage storage using traditional disk, storage pools, and the new deduplication feature in Windows Server 2012.

Managing NTFS file permissions

NTFS file permissions are one of the cornerstones of Windows security. By managing the file permissions, we can decide who has access to which files or directories, and what kind of access they have: read, write, change permissions, and so on.

In this recipe we will cover basic management of file permissions using PowerShell.

Getting ready

All of the steps in this recipe are being performed on a single domain joined server acting as a file server. In this recipe we will be performing four tasks:

- Editing the permissions on an Excel spreadsheet
- Cloning permissions for a new folder
- Taking ownership and reassigning permissions
- Enabling inheritance

 These steps can be performed locally on the server, remotely using a PSSession, or remotely using file shares.

How to do it...

The tasks we are going to perform are as follows.

Editing the permissions on an Excel spreadsheet

The sales team has an Excel spreadsheet, M:\Sales\Goals.xls, on our file server that uses NTFS permissions to restrict access. The sales administrator has asked that the new employee, Joe Smith, be given full control access to the file. Perform the following steps:

1. Identify the file to update and open a PowerShell console.

2. Read the permissions file and save them into a variable called $acl:

   ```
   $acl = Get-Acl M:\Sales\goals.xls
   ```

3. Create new FileSystemAccessRule for the new user with the appropriate permissions:

   ```
   $ace = New-Object System.Security.AccessControl.
   FileSystemAccessRule "joe.smith","FullControl","Allow"
   ```

4. Append the permissions:

   ```
   $acl.SetAccessRule($ace)
   ```

5. Apply the permissions to the file:

   ```
   $acl | Set-Acl M:\Sales\goals.xls
   ```

Cloning permissions for a new folder

The marketing department has a folder on our file server named M:\Marketing and has requested a new folder named M:\Marketing2. Additionally, they want the new folder to have the same permissions as their current folder. Perform the following steps:

1. Open PowerShell and create the new folder

    ```
    New-Item M:\Marketing2 -ItemType Directory
    ```

2. Get the existing folder permissions

    ```
    $SrcAcl = Get-Acl M:\Marketing
    ```

3. Set the new permissions

    ```
    Set-Acl -Path M:\Marketing2 $SrcAcl
    ```

Taking ownership and reassigning permissions

The user, Ricardo Cuello, is on vacation and Joe Smith, their manager, needs access to files they were working on. All of the files are stored on our file server under M:\Groups\Projections, however, the user was the only person with access to the files. You have been asked to provide access for the manager. Perform the following steps:

1. Open PowerShell and take ownership of the folder:

    ```
    $folder = "M:\Groups\Projections"
    takeown /f $folder /a /r /d Y
    ```

2. Add permission for the manager:

    ```
    $acl = Get-Acl $folder
    $ace = New-Object System.Security.AccessControl.
    FileSystemAccessRule `
    "joe.smith","FullControl","Allow"
    $acl.SetAccessRule($ace)
    Set-Acl $folder $acl
    ```

3. Recursively overwrite permissions:

    ```
    Get-ChildItem $folder -Recurse -Force |`
    ForEach {
        Get-Acl $acl | Set-Acl -Path $_.FullName
    }
    ```

Enabling and disabling inheritance

A team has created a folder named Imaging under M:\Groups and asked that the default file permissions not be applied to their folder on the file server. Instead of inheriting permissions from the parent folder, they want to selectively choose who has access to the files. Perform the following steps:

1. Open PowerShell and gather the current permissions:

   ```
   $acl = Get-Acl M:\Groups\Imaging
   ```

2. Enable or disable inheritance:

   ```
   $acl.SetAccessRuleProtection($True, $False)
   #first option is to disable inheritance - true=disable
   #second option is to keep inherited permissions - false=discard
   ```

3. Commit the change:

   ```
   Set-Acl M:\Groups\Imaging $acl
   ```

How it works...

In the first step we are using Get-Acl and Set-Acl to add permissions to a file. We start by getting the current **Access Control List** (**ACL**) on the file and placing it into the variable $acl.

We then create new System.Security.AccessControlFileSystemAccessRule to create an **Access Control Entry** (**ACE**) named $ace. We then assign the FullControl permission to our user Joe Smith.

Lastly, we call $acl.SetAccesRule in order to add the new permissions. We then call Set-ACL to assign the updated permissions to our Excel document.

If we view the file properties, we can confirm that the new user has access to the file.

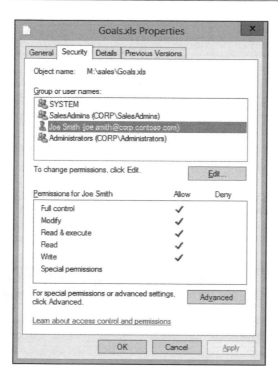

In the second step we start by calling `New-Item` to create the new directory for the Marketing department.

We then call `Get-Acl` against `M:\Marketing` to get the permissions on the existing folder. These permissions are saved in the variable `$srcAcl`.

Lastly, we use `Set-Acl` to apply the copied permissions to the new `M:\Marketing2` folder. This step overwrites any existing permissions on the new folder, leaving only the copied permissions.

In the third step we start by administratively seizing the ownership of the folder using the `takeown` command. `Takeown` is not a PowerShell command, but instead a tool included with Windows Server 2012 that allows an administrator to take ownership of a file or folder.

Once we have seized ownership of the folder, we create an access rule for the manager to access the folder. This process is the same as in the first step by reading the current file permissions, adding an ACE granting, and applying the permissions to the folder.

Lastly, we use `Get-ChildItem` to recursively move through the folders and files. For each file or folder, we use `Set-ACL` to set permissions.

> Seizing permissions requires the commands to be executed in an administrative session. Ensure PowerShell is running as an administrator when executing the commands.

In the last step we use the `SetAccessRuleProtection` command to configure permission inheritance. We begin by using `Get-ACL` to read the credentials of the current folder and storing the results in the variable `$acl`. We then use `$acl.SetAccessRuleProtection` to disable inheritance and discard any inherited permissions. Lastly, we use `Set-Acl` to apply the permissions to the folder.

The `SetAccessRuleProtection` command takes two inputs: the first to enable or disable inheritance, and the second to keep or discard inherited permissions. In this scenario we are disabling permission inheritance and discarding all inherited permissions. Only those permissions applied directly to the file will remain.

Managing NTFS alternate streams

In addition to NTFS permissions, Windows also tracks what is known as alternate streams regarding files. These **alternate streams** help identify where a file is originally from and what type of additional security to place on it.

In this recipe we will view the data streams on a file and unblock the file to allow full access.

Getting ready

One of the most common uses of alternate streams is when downloading files from the Internet. Windows will automatically tag these files and apply additional security when they are accessed. To access the files normally, you have to *unblock* the file.

For this recipe we will be downloading the `WMF 3.0 Release Notes.docx` file from `http://download.microsoft.com`. We will then use this file to review and change the data streams. Any other file downloaded from the Internet will work here as well.

How to do it...

Perform the following steps to manage NTFS alternate streams:

1. Open Internet Explorer and browse to `http://download.microsoft.com`.

2. Search for `Windows Management Framework 3.0`, and download the `WMF 3 Release Notes.docx` file:

By default, Windows will download the file to the `Downloads` folder in your user profile.

3. View the file and stream information on the downloaded files:

   ```
   Get-Item C:\Users\Ed\Downloads\*.* -Stream *
   ```

   When executed, we will see the list of streams similar to the following screenshot:

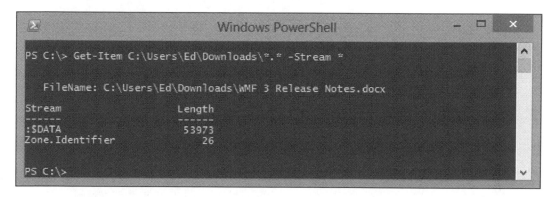

4. View the contents of the `Zone.Identifier` stream:

   ```
   Get-Content 'C:\Users\Ed\Downloads\WMF 3 Release Notes.docx:Zone.Identifier'
   ```

   When executed, we will see the contents of the stream:

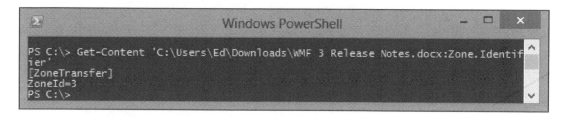

5. Unblock the file and confirm the `Zone.Information` stream is removed:

   ```
   Unblock-File 'C:\Users\Ed\Downloads\WMF 3 Release Notes.docx'
   Get-Item 'C:\Users\Ed\Downloads\*.*' -Stream *
   ```

When executed, we will see the original $DATA stream only:

```
Windows PowerShell                                    _  □  ×

PS C:\> Unblock-File 'C:\Users\Ed\Downloads\WMF 3 Release Notes.docx'
PS C:\> Get-Item C:\Users\Ed\Downloads\*.* -Stream *


    FileName: C:\Users\Ed\Downloads\WMF 3 Release Notes.docx

Stream                   Length
------                   ------
:$DATA                    53973

PS C:\> _
```

How it works...

We start by browsing to `http://download.microsoft.com` and searching for the WMF 3 Release Notes, which includes the release notes for PowerShell 3.0.

Next, we call `Get-Item` to view the files in our `Downloads` folder. Here, we use the `-Stream` switch to return both the files and all streams attached to the files. As we can see from the result, there are two streams for our file. The `:$DATA` stream is the content of the file itself. The `Zone.Identifier` stream identifies where the file originated.

We then use `Get-Content` to view the contents of the `Zone.Identifier` stream. To view the stream, we reference the filename, plus `:Zone.Identifier`. As we can see from the output, this stream contains a small amount of text that identifies the file as being from `ZoneId 3`, which means the file is from the Internet.

In the last step we use `Unblock-File` to remove the alternate stream. This is equivalent to pressing the `Unblock` button on the file properties as shown in the following screenshot. Once the file has been unblocked, we review the stream information and confirm that only the `:$DATA` stream remains. Because the additional stream has been removed, Windows now trusts the file.

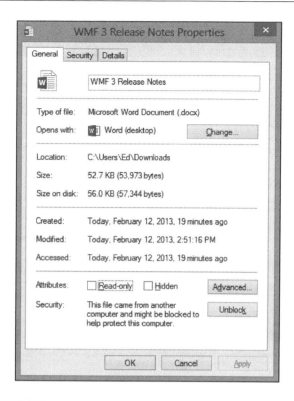

There's more...

NTFS alternate streams are actually hidden text files in the filesystem. They are seen by the operating system as additional file information and so aren't shown when listing the contents of a file.

We can also create our own alternate streams using a text editor. By following the same naming scheme shown previously, `filename.exe:Zone.Identifier`, we can add or edit the zone information for other files. There are six possible zones:

- NoZone = -1
- MyComputer = 0
- Intranet = 1
- Trusted = 2
- Internet = 3
- Untrusted = 4

Configuring NTFS deduplication

In previous versions of Windows Server, there was an option for Single Instance Storage. This allowed users to store the same file multiple times on a system, but the system only kept a single instance of the file. This was often used for **Remote Installation Services (RIS)**, which required multiple copies of the Windows installation disk, one for each installation source.

New in Server 2012 is the data deduplication feature. This feature allows for block-level deduplication of files, comparison and deduplication of smaller pieces or chunks of files. This allows for more storage savings between both similar and dissimilar files.

Getting ready

In this recipe we will be working with a new file server with minimal information on it. Specifically, we will be working with our M:\ drive. We know that usage of the server will increase, so we are configuring deduplication early.

How to do it...

Perform the following steps to enable deduplication:

1. Install the deduplication feature on the server:

   ```
   Add-WindowsFeature FS-Data-Deduplication
   ```

2. Use DDPEval to report on the estimated savings:

   ```
   ddpeval.exe M:\
   ```

   When completed, you will see the estimated results similar to the following screenshot:

```
PS C:\> ddpeval.exe M:\
Data Deduplication Savings Evaluation Tool
Copyright (c) 2012 Microsoft Corporation.  All Rights Reserved.

Evaluated folder: M:\
Evaluated folder size: 8.46 GB
Files in evaluated folder: 182

Processed files: 32
Processed files size: 8.45 GB
Optimized files size: 1.66 GB
Space savings: 6.80 GB
Space savings percent: 80

Optimized files size (no compression): 3.25 GB
Space savings (no compression): 5.20 GB
Space savings percent (no compression): 61

Files excluded by policy: 150
     Small files (<32KB): 150
Files excluded by error: 0
```

3. Configure the disk for deduplication:

    ```
    Enable-DedupVolume M:\
    ```

4. Set the deduplication age to 0 days to test deduplication process:

    ```
    Set-DedupVolume M: -MinimumFileAgeDays 0
    ```

5. Start the deduplication job:

    ```
    Start-DedupJob M: -type Optimization
    ```

How it works...

In the first step we are installing the FS-Data-Deduplication feature on the file server. Included with the deduplication feature is a tool named DDPEval that estimates the potential storage savings using deduplication. Once the feature is installed, we execute DDPEval to report on potential savings. In this scenario the tool reports that we can reclaim up to 80 percent of the currently used storage.

Next, we use Enable-DedupVolume to enable deduplication on the target drive. Enabling the volume includes it in the scheduled optimization jobs. Once the optimization job executes, duplicate data on the disk will be consolidated and free space will begin to be reclaimed.

In the fourth step we are calling Set-DedupVolume with the –MinimumFileAgeDays switch. This setting identifies how long a file should remain unchanged before deduplicating it. Because the deduplication/reduplication process slows access to the files on the server, it is normally best to deduplicate only on files that are infrequently accessed. In this case we are setting it to 0 days so we can test the deduplication process.

Lastly, we call Start-DedupJob to manually start the Optimization (deduplication) job on the target drive. Depending on the amount of data on the drive, the process can take an extensive amount of time.

There's more...

Historically, a common use for data deduplication is for storing backup information. When a system is backed up, the information is stored on a remote share and deduplicated against itself. When the next system is backed up, the information is deduplicated against itself, and also against the data from the other systems. This results in the backup system being able to perform full backups of multiple systems, and yet only store the unique data between the backups.

See also

For more information about data deduplication in Server 2012, refer the following websites:

▸ http://blogs.technet.com/b/filecab/archive/2012/05/21/introduction-to-data-deduplication-in-windows-server-2012.aspx

▸ http://technet.microsoft.com/en-us/library/hh831602.aspx

Monitoring NTFS deduplication

Once data deduplication is configured on a server, we can monitor the processing to ensure it is operating properly. Additionally, we will need to routinely review the amount of savings and schedules of the deduplication process.

Getting ready

In this recipe we are moving forward with the configuration of the prior recipe. Most deduplication settings are left to the defaults, except for the minimum file age which is set to 0.

How to do it...

Perform the following tasks to monitor deduplication:

1. Get the status of the deduplication process:

   ```
   Get-DedupJob
   ```

   When executed, we will see the status of any current deduplication processes:

   ```
   PS C:\> Get-DedupJob

   Type            ScheduleType        StartTime             Progress    State
   ----            ------------        ---------             --------    -----
   Optimization    Manual              4:43 PM               50 %        Running
   ```

2. Report on deduplication savings:

   ```
   Get-DedupStatus
   ```

When executed, we will see a brief report of deduplication status and current savings:

```
PS C:\> Get-DedupStatus

FreeSpace      SavedSpace    OptimizedFiles    InPolicyFiles    Volume
---------      ----------    --------------    -------------    ------
58.09 GB       6.8 GB        32                32               M:
```

3. View the deduplication jobs schedules:

   `Get-DedupSchedule`

   When executed, we will see the current deduplication job schedules:

```
PS C:\> Get-DedupSchedule

Enabled    Type                StartTime      Days        Name
-------    ----                ---------      ----        ----
True       Optimization                                  Back...
True       GarbageCollection   2:45 AM        Saturday    Week...
True       Scrubbing           3:45 AM        Saturday    Week...
```

How it works...

We start by viewing the status of any active deduplication jobs. We execute `Get-DedupJob` to report on all active deduplication jobs and their current status. One item to note here is `StartTime` of the job to confirm the job is still active.

Next, we use `Get-DedupStatus` to view the optimization statistics. This command returns information about how much data is being deduplicated and how much filesystem space is being saved because of deduplication.

Lastly, we call `Get-DedupSchedule` to view the schedule for the deduplication jobs. The optimization job runs hourly to continually deduplicate new data and update statistics. The other jobs run every week during expectedly slow times.

 Depending on your environment, the default schedules may not be optimal. They can be changed by using `Set-DedupSchedule`.

There's more...

There are three scheduled deduplication jobs: `Optimization`, `GarbageCollection`, and `Scrubbing`. The `Optimization` job is responsible for identifying duplicate data on the filesystem and freeing up the storage. Additionally, for data that cannot be deduplicated, the optimization job will compress. This job runs hourly, and once the initial job is complete, subsequent passes finish quickly as they only process new data.

The remaining jobs are responsible for reclaiming and maintaining the freed storage. The `GarbageCollection` job is responsible for removing deleted information from the deduplication store. The `Scrubbing` job performs maintenance on the deduplication store and repairs data if needed.

Configuring storage pools

New in Server 2012 is a feature to create and use storage pools. Storage pools work in a similar way to the **Redundant Array of Independent Disks** (**RAID**) configurations, but provide additional flexibility not available in traditional RAID. With storage pools, additional disks can be added and data will be automatically balanced between the disk, and we can also change the data protection type dynamically.

Getting ready

In this recipe we will be using three 100 GB drives in addition to our OS drive. Once joined into a storage pool, we will create a small virtual disk to hold test data.

How to do it...

Perform the following steps to set up storage pools:

1. List disks capable of pooling:

   ```
   Get-PhysicalDisk -CanPool $true
   ```

   After completing the command, we will see a list of disks available for pooling:

```
PS C:\> Get-PhysicalDisk -CanPool $true

FriendlyName  CanPool    OperationalS HealthStatus Usage              Size
                         tatus
------------  -------    ------------ ------------ -----              ----
PhysicalDisk1 True       OK           Healthy      Auto-Select      100 GB
PhysicalDisk2 True       OK           Healthy      Auto-Select      100 GB
PhysicalDisk3 True       OK           Healthy      Auto-Select      100 GB
```

2. Using the available disks, create a storage pool:

```
$poolDisks = Get-PhysicalDisk -CanPool $true
New-StoragePool -FriendlyName "MyPool" -PhysicalDisks $poolDisks `
-ProvisioningTypeDefault Thin `
-StorageSubSystemFriendlyName "Storage Spaces*"
```

3. Using the newly created storage pool, create a virtual disk:

```
Get-StoragePool -FriendlyName MyPool | `
New-VirtualDisk -FriendlyName "TestData" -Size 10GB `
-ProvisioningType Thin
```

After completing the command, we will receive confirmation that the virtual disk is created:

```
PS C:\> Get-StoragePool -FriendlyName MyPool | New-VirtualDisk -FriendlyName "Te
stData" -Size 10GB -ProvisioningType Thin

FriendlyName   ResiliencySet OperationalS HealthStatus IsManualAtta        Size
               tingName      tatus                     ch
------------   ------------- ------------ ------------ ------------        ----
TestData       Mirror        OK           Healthy      False              10 GB
```

4. Initialize, partition, and format the virtual disk:

```
Get-VirtualDisk -FriendlyName TestData | Initialize-Disk -PassThru
| `
New-Partition -AssignDriveLetter -UseMaximumSize | `
Format-Volume -Confirm:$false
```

How it works...

We start the process by calling Get-PhysicalDisk with the –CanPool switch to identify which disks are available and support pooling.

 Not all disks are supported in storage pools. For instance, to create a storage pool we need at least two physical disks 4 GB or larger in size.

Next, we create a new storage pool named MyPool. We add all of the available disks and set -ProvisioningType to Thin. The Thin provisioning allows us to present large disks to the operating system, but they only require enough storage to house the data on the drives. This is a common method to present large amounts of storage to users and applications, but only consumes what is needed.

Once the storage pool is created, we create a virtual disk on the storage pool. In this instance, we create a 10 GB disk and identify it to use thin provisioning. Once created, the virtual disk is presented to the operating system as a new drive. The disk is then initialized, partitioned, and formatted as any other drive.

There's more...

As we saw in the third step, Windows defaulted to creating new virtual disks with a `Mirror` configuration. We can confirm this by running `Get-StoragePool` and viewing the default resiliency setting:

```
PS C:\> Get-StoragePool | select FriendlyName, ResiliencySettingNameDefault

FriendlyName                              ResiliencySettingNameDefault
------------                              ----------------------------
MyPool                                    Mirror
Primordial                                Mirror
```

Because we are using more than two disks in our pool, we can change the default resiliency setting by using the `Set-StoragePool` command:

```
PS C:\> Get-StoragePool -FriendlyName MyPool | Set-StoragePool -ResiliencySettin
gNameDefault Parity
PS C:\> Get-StoragePool | select FriendlyName, ResiliencySettingNameDefault

FriendlyName                              ResiliencySettingNameDefault
------------                              ----------------------------
MyPool                                    Parity
Primordial                                Mirror
```

Reporting on storage pools

Once created, we need to routinely review the storage pools to ensure they are functioning properly. One item we need to pay attention to is the utilization of the thin pools and disks in our environment. If the underlying disks in a thin pool fill up, we can have unexpected results in the presented virtual disks.

Getting ready

In this recipe we will be working with the storage pool configuration created in the previous recipe. We will be reporting on the utilization of the storage pools and the virtual disks in the pools.

How to do it...

Perform the following steps to report on storage pools:

1. Report on storage pool usage:

```
Get-StoragePool | `
Format-Table FriendlyName, `
@{Name="AllocGB";Expression={$_.AllocatedSize/1GB}}, `
@{Name="SizeGB";Expression={$_.Size/1GB}}
```

When executed, we will see a status similar to the following screenshot:

```
PS C:\> Get-StoragePool | ft FriendlyName, @{Name="alocGB";Expression={$_.Alloca
tedSize/1GB}}, @{Name="SizeGB";Expression={$_.Size/1GB}}

FriendlyName                                    alocGB              SizeGB
------------                                    ------              ------
MyPool                                            3.25              297.75
Primordial                                299.619140625                360
```

2. Get virtual disk usage:

```
Get-VirtualDisk | `
Format-Table FriendlyName, `
@{Name="AllocGB";Expression={$_.AllocatedSize/1GB}}, `
@{Name="FootPrintGB";Expression={$_.FootprintOnPool/1GB}}, `
@{Name="SizeGB";Expression={$_.Size/1GB}}
```

When executed, we will see a status similar to the following screenshot:

```
PS C:\> Get-VirtualDisk | ft FriendlyName, @{Name="AlloocGB";expression={$_.Allo
catedSize/1GB}}, @{Name="FootPrintGB";Expression={$_.FootprintOnPool/1GB}}, @{na
me="SizeGB";expression={$_.Size/1GB}}

FriendlyName                 AlloocGB           FootPrintGB            SizeGB
------------                 --------           -----------            ------
TestData                            1                     2                10
```

How it works...

We start by using `Get-StoragePool` to view the pools on the server and their properties. Specifically, we are interested in the size of the pool (`SizeGB`) and the amount of space consumed (`AllocGB`). This quickly allows us to see how much storage has been consumed versus how much is available.

Next, we use `Get-VirtualDisk` to view the virtual disks and report on the utilization. In this instance we are reporting on how much data is in the virtual disk (`AllocGB`), how much raw disk space is consumed (`FootPrintGB`), and the maximum size of the virtual disk (`SizeGB`).

The FootPrintGB size shown is double the AllocGB size. This is because the virtual disk is provisioned as a mirror, meaning the data is stored twice in the storage pool.

There's more...

With server virtualization becoming a common technology, it is tempting to use storage pools inside of virtual machines. While this is possible, care needs to be taken on where the underlying disks are physically located.

Storage pools mirror and stripe the data among multiple disks to provide redundancy and improved performance. However, if a virtual machine's storage pool disks reside on the same physical disk, all of these benefits are lost. In reality, the striping and mirroring will decrease the performance of the storage pool.

Managing file quotas

Another great feature of Windows Server is the ability to place quotas on folders. Quotas allow an administrator to restrict the amount of data users can place on a server. A common use for quotas is with a user's home directory. By limiting the amount of data a user can place on the server, it prevents one user from unfairly using all of the available storage.

There are two types of quotas available for Server 2012: hard and soft. **Hard quotas** restrict how much data a user can store on the server and will block any usage above the defined quota limit. **Soft quotas** track how much data a user is consuming and alert when the limit is reached. Users will still be able to store additional information when soft quotas are exceeded.

Getting ready

In this recipe we will be working with our file server to create simple quotas for our users and groups. We will be using a soft quota and configuring the e-mail settings to enable alerts when quota thresholds are reached.

How to do it...

Perform the following steps to enable file quotas:

1. Install the File System Resource Manager:

```
Install-WindowsFeature FS-Resource-Manager -IncludeManagementTools
```

2. Get the current e-mail configuration, and configure e-mail alerting for the soft/hard quotas:

```
Get-FsrmSetting
Set-FsrmSetting -SmtpServer mail.corp.contoso.com `
-FromEmailAddress FSAdmin@corp.contoso.com
```

3. Create a template based on one of the built-in templates:

```
$myQuota = Get-FsrmQuotaTemplate -Name "Monitor 500 MB Share"
$myQuota | New-FsrmQuotaTemplate -Name HomeFolders
Set-FsrmQuotaTemplate -Name HomeFolders -Threshold $myQuota.
Threshold
```

4. Create auto-apply quota:

```
New-FsrmAutoQuota -Path E:\Users -Template HomeFolders
```

5. Create quota:

```
New-FsrmQuota -Path E:\Groups -Template HomeFolders
```

6. Generate a quota usage report:

```
New-FsrmStorageReport -Name "Quota Report" -Namespace "E:\" `
-ReportTypeQuotaUsage -Interactive -MailTo fsadmin@corp.contoso.
com
```

How it works...

In the first step we install the File Server Resource Manager feature on our server. This feature allows our file server to implement quotas on disks and folders as well as perform file classification.

In the second step we review the current configuration of the server, then update it to fit our environment. We use `Get-FsrmSetting` to return to the current settings. Note the `SMTPServer`, `FromEmailAddress`, and `AdminEmailAddress` settings. We configure the `SmtpServer` and `FromEmailAddress` settings to enable e-mailing in our environment.

In the third step, we are using the built-in Monitor 500 MB Share template to create a new template named `HomeFolders`. We start by calling `Get-FsrmQuotaTemplate` to save the existing template settings into the `$myQuota` variable. We then pipe the settings into `New-FsrmQuotaTemplate` to create the new template. Finally, we use `Set-FsrmQuotaTemplate` to assign the thresholds and actions. In this instance we are keeping the same settings; however, we could also update the hard/soft thresholds, and the actions that occur when the thresholds are met.

In the fourth and fifth steps we are applying quotas to our folders. First, we call `New-FsrmAutoQuota` in order to apply `Auto Quota` on the `E:\Users` folder. This setting automatically applies quota policies on all folders included in the quota. Next, we call `New-FsrmQuota` to apply a standard `Quota` on the `E:\Groups` folder. This quota includes subfolders, but additional quotas can be applied at subfolders.

In the last step we are calling `New-FsrmStorageReport` to use the built-in reporting features of the File Server Resource Manager. In this instance, we are generating a report immediately, instead of scheduling it, and e-mailing it to the file server administrator.

There's more...

Our template defaults to e-mailing the file server administrator when a user reaches 80 percent, 100 percent, and 120 percent of the quota limit. We can change these alerts to additionally e-mail the user when the thresholds are reached.

```
$myQuota = Get-FSRMQuotaTemplate HomeFolders
$myQuota.Threshold.Action | Where-Object  Type -eq Email | `
ForEach-Object {$_.MailTo = "[Admin Email];[Source Io Owner Email]"}
Set-FsrmQuotaTemplate -Name $myQuota.Name -Threshold $myQuota.
Threshold
```

The preceding code updates all of the e-mail alerts in our template. The script starts by using `Get-FsrmQuotaTemplate` to retrieve a reference to our quota template and placing it into the `$myQuota` variable. We filter `$myQuota` based on the action performed when a threshold is reached. For each of these actions, the `MailTo` attribute is updated to include the file server administrator, as well as the identified owner of the files.

When completed, we can review the settings in the File Server Resource Manager and confirm that both the administrator, as well as the user checkboxes are selected. Open File Server Resource Manager and go to **Quota Management | Quota Templates**. Right-click on the quota and select **Edit Template Properties**. Select the **Warning (100%)** threshold and click on **Edit** to view the properties as shown in the following screenshot:

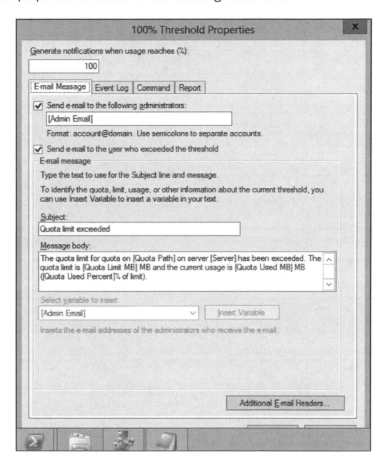

6

Managing Network Shares with PowerShell

In this chapter, we will cover the following recipes:

- ▶ Creating and securing CIFS shares
- ▶ Accessing CIFS shares from PowerShell
- ▶ Creating iSCSI target and virtual disk
- ▶ Using a iSCSI disk
- ▶ Configuring and using iSNS
- ▶ Creating an NFS export
- ▶ Mounting NFS exports
- ▶ Making CIFS shares highly available
- ▶ Configuring DFS and DFSR replication
- ▶ Configuring BranchCache

Introduction

This chapter covers creating, managing, securing, and using CIFS, NFS, and iSCSI shares. This chapter will also cover how to use server clustering to create highly available network shares, managing replication, and configuring BranchCache.

Creating and securing CIFS shares

Common Internet File Services, or **CIFS**, is the traditional method for sharing files and folders between Windows computers. These file shares are normally referenced with a **Universal Naming Convention** (**UNC**) in the form of \\server\share.

Occasionally referred to as **Server Message Block** (**SMB**), CIFS shares have been the primary method for sharing files, print jobs, and information. These shares can be created to provide access to files and folders on a system, and then secured to restrict which users have access to read, update, or manage permissions on the contents.

Windows Server automatically includes the necessary features to enable file sharing over CIFS. As such, there is no need to install or configure the feature, instead we can begin creating and managing shares.

In this recipe we will create two file shares. The first share will provide Read Only access to the Everyone group, and later we will provide Full Control access for a domain user. The second share will provide Read Only access to the Everyone group and Full Control access to the Administrator account.

Getting ready

For this recipe we will be working with a Windows Server 2012 server joined to a domain. This server will operate as a file server and contain a separate drive, E:\, to hold the file shares.

How to do it...

Carry out the following steps in order to create and secure CIFS shares:

1. View the current shares on your server:

    ```
    Get-SmbShare
    ```

    When executed, a list of the current shares will be returned as shown in the following screenshot:

```
PS C:\> Get-SmbShare

Name            ScopeName        Path            Description
----            ---------        ----            -----------
ADMIN$          *                C:\Windows      Remote Admin
C$              *                C:\             Default share
IPC$            *                                Remote IPC
```

Notice that a server will contain CIFS shares even if the administrator hasn't created them. These are known as administrative shares and are hidden from most users.

2. Create the first basic file share:

```
New-Item -Path E:\Share1 -ItemType Directory
New-SmbShare -Name Share1 -Path E:\share1
```

When executed, PowerShell will return a window confirming the success as shown in the following screenshot:

```
PS C:\> New-SmbShare -Name Share1 -Path E:\share1

Name              ScopeName            Path              Description
----              ---------            ----              -----------
Share1            *                    E:\share1
```

3. Create a second share granting everyone read access:

```
New-Item -Path E:\Share2 -ItemType Directory
New-SmbShare -Name Share2 -Path E:\share2 -ReadAccess Everyone `
-FullAccess Administrator -Description "Test share"
```

When executed, PowerShell will create the share and return a confirmation screen:

```
PS C:\> New-SmbShare -Name Share2 -Path E:\share2 -ReadAccess Everyone -FullAcce
ss Administrator -Description "Test share"

Name              ScopeName            Path              Description
----              ---------            ----              -----------
Share2            *                    E:\share2         Test share
```

4. To confirm the shares and permissions from the prior steps, list the share permissions:

```
Get-SmbShare | Get-SmbShareAccess
```

When executed, PowerShell will return all shares and the assigned permissions as shown in the following screenshot:

```
PS C:\> Get-SmbShare | Get-SmbShareAccess

Name           ScopeName      AccountName      AccessControlTy AccessRight
                                               pe
----           ---------      -----------      --------------- -----------
ADMIN$         *              BUILTIN\Admi...  Allow           Full
ADMIN$         *              BUILTIN\Back...  Allow           Full
ADMIN$         *              NT AUTHORITY...  Allow           Full
IPC$           *              BUILTIN\Admi...  Allow           Full
IPC$           *              BUILTIN\Back...  Allow           Full
IPC$           *              NT AUTHORITY...  Allow           Full
C$             *              BUILTIN\Admi...  Allow           Full
C$             *              BUILTIN\Back...  Allow           Full
C$             *              NT AUTHORITY...  Allow           Full
Share2         *              SERVER1\Admi...  Allow           Full
Share2         *              Everyone         Allow           Read
Share1         *              Everyone         Allow           Read
E$             *              BUILTIN\Admi...  Allow           Full
E$             *              BUILTIN\Back...  Allow           Full
E$             *              NT AUTHORITY...  Allow           Full
```

5. Grant `Full Control` access to the first share for user `Joe Smith`:

```
Grant-SmbShareAccess -Name Share1 -AccountName CORP\Joe.Smith `
-AccessRight Full -Confirm:$false
```

When completed, the new permissions for the share will be returned:

```
PS C:\> Grant-SmbShareAccess -Name Share1 -AccountName CORP\Joe.Smith -AccessRig
ht Full -Confirm:$false

Name           ScopeName      AccountName      AccessControlTy AccessRight
                                               pe
----           ---------      -----------      --------------- -----------
Share1         *              Everyone         Allow           Read
Share1         *              CORP\Joe.Smith   Allow           Full
```

How it works...

We start off by calling `Get-SmbShare` to view the shares already on the server. This is a new server, so only the administrative shares exist. These administrative shares are hidden from normal users because they end in a dollar sign ($).

 By default, Windows Server 2012 includes the **Storage Services** feature that provides basic file sharing. No additional feature is needed to support CIFS shares.

Next, in step 2, we use `New-SmbShare` to create a new file share on `E:\share1`. When executed without any additional switches, PowerShell creates the share with the default permissions of the `Everyone` group having read access.

In step 3, we use `New-SmbShare` to create another share at `E:\share2`. This time we the use additional `-ReadAccess` and `-FullAccess` switches to define permissions on the share. Additionally, we include the `-Description` switch to assign a description to the share. This description is seen by users when browsing shares on a server and are normally used to help identify the purpose of the share.

Next, in step 4, we call `Get-SmbShareAccess` to report on the current permissions for each share. As we can see in the results, PowerShell returns the shares, the user/group, if they are allowed access, and the level of access granted.

Lastly, in step 5, we update the permissions on the first share that we created. Here we are using `Grant-SmbShareAccess` in order to allow the domain user `CORP\Joe.Smith` access to the share. We use the `-AccessRight` switch to define the access rights we want to grant the target user or group. Once complete, PowerShell returns the new access list for the share.

> In addition to share permissions, Windows also utilizes NTFS permissions to determine a user's total access. When granting access to a share, we also need to review the file permissions to ensure access is appropriate.

There's more...

In addition to granting access to Windows shares, PowerShell can also deny access. Often referred to as an explicit deny, this revokes access for a user or group to the designated share, regardless of other permissions. To manage this, PowerShell has two built in commands: `Block-SmbShareAccess` and `Unblock-SmbShareAccess`.

For instance, if we need to block access for a user to a share, we can use the `Block-SmbShareAccess` cmdlet.

```
Block-SmbShareAccess -Name Share2 -AccountName CORP\joe.smith `
-Confirm:$false
```

When executed, PowerShell returns the updated access list. Notice the first line for `CORP\Joe.Smith` now has an `AccessControlType` of Deny:

```
PS C:\> Block-SmbShareAccess -Name Share2 -AccountName CORP\joe.smith -Confirm:$
false

Name          ScopeName      AccountName        AccessControlTy AccessRight
                                                pe
----          ---------      -----------        --------------- -----------
Share2        *              CORP\Joe.Smith     Deny            Full
Share2        *              SERVER1\Admi...    Allow           Full
Share2        *              Everyone           Allow           Read
```

See also

For more information about CIFS shares and PowerShell, see `http://blogs.technet.com/b/josebda/archive/2012/06/27/the-basics-of-smb-powershell-a-feature-of-windows-server-2012-and-smb-3-0.aspx`.

Accessing CIFS shares from PowerShell

Once CIFS shares are provided by a server, we can access them remotely. We can access these shares by using different methods to in order to access them temporarily or permanently and to connect to them using different credentials.

Getting ready

For this recipe we will be using a Windows Server 2012 system to remotely access the file shares created in the *Creating and securing CIFS shares* recipe.

How to do it...

Carry out the following steps to access a CIFS share:

1. Use `Get-ChildItem` to view the contents of a share:

   ```
   Get-ChildItem \\server1\share2
   ```

   When completed, a listing of the contents of the share is returned as shown in the following screenshot:

   ```
   PS C:\> Get-ChildItem \\server1\Share2


       Directory: \\server1\Share2


   Mode                LastWriteTime     Length Name
   ----                -------------     ------ ----
   d----          2/15/2013   4:47 PM           users
   ```

2. Map the share as persistent:

   ```
   New-PSDrive -Name S -Root \\server1\share1 -Persist -PSProvider
   FileSystem
   ```

When completed, the share will appear in Windows File Explorer as a mapped drive:

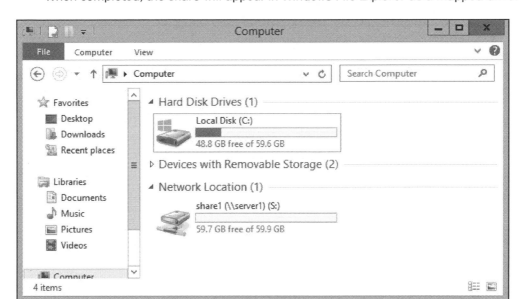

3. Map the share using alternative credentials:

```
$secPass = ConvertTo-SecureString 'P@$$w0rd11' -AsPlainText -Force
$myCred = New-Object -TypeName PSCredential `
-ArgumentList "CORP\Administrator",$secPass
New-PSDrive -Name S -Root \\server1\share1 -Persist `
-PSProvider FileSystem -Credential $myCred
```

How it works...

We start by accessing the CIFS share directly by using `Get-ChildItem`. This process passes the credentials of the currently logged on user to the target file server and returns the contents of the share. If the user has limited permissions to the share, the results will be limited appropriately.

In step 2, we use `New-PSDrive` to map the remote share to the current user session. The `-Name` switch specifies how to reference the remote drive, in this case as `S:\`. The `-Persist` switch instructs PowerShell to create a persistent connection for the current user, and re-establish the connection the next time the user logs in.

In step 3, we are connecting to the remote share by using different credentials. We start by creating a `PSCredential` object that contains the the username and password of a user. We then use the same command as in step 2, but we include the `-Credential` argument to pass the `PSCredential` object.

Creating iSCSI target and virtual disk

Internet Small Computer System Interface, or **iSCSI**, is a storage technology that uses TCP/IP to link storage with computers. iSCSI is based on the proven SCSI technology that is used in many servers and storage arrays, but is transmitted over TCP/IP instead of specialized cables or interfaces.

A basic iSCSI connection consists of an iSCSI target and an iSCSI initiator. The target contains the storage resources that are presented to clients. This can be a dedicated storage array, a Windows 2012 Server, or another resource, such as a tape library. The initiator is the iSCSI client that accesses data on the remote target.

Because iSCSI utilizes TCP/IP as a transport medium, it can be implemented wherever there is an existing IP network with little to no cost. iSCSI can be used to transmit data within a datacenter, within a **Local Area Network** (**LAN**), across a **Wide Area Network** (**WAN**), or even across the Internet. Different layers of security can be implemented between the target and initiator in order to secure and encrypt the connections depending on the needs of the environment.

Getting ready

In this recipe we will be installing the iSCSI target on our file server. We will then create a virtual disk on the E:\ and share it to a client with the IP address of 10.10.10.10.

How to do it...

Perform the following steps to create an iSCSI target:

1. Install the iSCSI target feature as follows:

    ```
    Install-WindowsFeature -Name FS-iSCSITarget-Server
    ```

2. Identify the iSCSI initiators that are allowed access:

    ```
    New-iSCSIServerTarget -Targetname ContosoServers `
    -InitiatorID IPAddress:10.10.10.10
    ```

3. Create a new virtual disk for iSCSI:

    ```
    New-iSCSIVirtualDisk "E:\iSCSIVirtualDisks\Drive1.vhd" -Size 20GB
    ```

4. Map the virtual disk to the iSCSI initiators:

    ```
    Add-iSCSIVirtualDiskTargetMapping -Targetname ContosoServers `
    -DevicePath "E:\iSCSIVirtualDisks\Drive1.vhd"
    ```

5. Review the iSCSI mappings:

    ```
    Get-IscsiServerTarget | `
    Select-Object TargetName, Status, InitiatorIds, LunMappings
    ```

When completed, we will see the current iSCSI mappings presented by the server, as shown in the following screenshot:

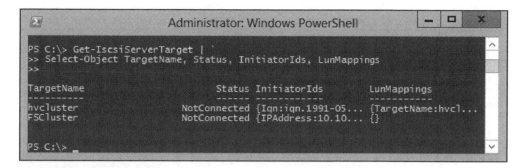

How it works...

In step 1, we install the `FS-iSCSITarget-Server` feature on our file server. This is the feature that allows our server to operate as an iSCSI target and present virtual disks to clients.

In step 2, we call `New-iSCSIServerTarget` to create a new client group named `ContosoServers` on the server. This allows us to add one or more initiator IDs to the group to define which clients will be able to see the resources presented.

> In this instance we are configuring the `InitiatorID` based on the IP address of the initiator. Alternatively, we can use the DNS name, MAC address of the adapter, or **iSCSI Qualified Name** (**IQN**) to identify the client.

Next, we use `New-iSCSIVirtualDisk` to create a virtual hard disk (VHD) file.

In step 4 and step 5, we call `Add-iSCSIVirtualDiskTargetMapping` to map the virtual disk to the iSCSI client group. This process links the recently created virtual disk to the client group. When a system in the client group `ContosoServers` queries the iSCSI target for available resources, the newly-created virtual disk will be presented.

Lastly, we use `Get-IscsiServerTarget` to query our server for all iSCSI targets. This returns a list of all target groups, their connectivity status, initiator addresses and presented disks. This is useful to review your configuration and quickly view or report on the status.

There's more...

While iSCSI has the flexibility of being implemented over existing IP networks using existing adapters, in busy environments it may be beneficial to dedicate resources to improve iSCSI performance. For instance, using network cards with a **TCP/IP Offload Engine** (**TOE**) or a dedicated iSCSI **Host Bus Adapter** (**HBA**) in the servers and clients will lessen the CPU requirements on the systems and improve performance. Additionally, segmenting the traffic onto a separate network with dedicated HBAs, cabling, and switches can also improve performance.

See also

For more information about the iSCSI target feature in Windows Server 2012, see `http://blogs.technet.com/b/filecab/archive/2012/05/21/introduction-of-iscsi-target-in-windows-server-2012.aspx`.

Using a iSCSI disk

Once an iSCSI target has been configured and a virtual disk presented, we can configure clients to access the storage presented. Unlike CIFS or NFS shares, which share files and objects, iSCSI presents disks from a block level. This means that most applications and services can utilize the iSCSI disks as if they are physically installed on the system.

Microsoft includes a software iSCSI initiator built into Windows Server 2012 that is capable of connecting to the iSCSI target. To utilize this initiator, we enable the service, search for available resources, and connect to the resources.

Getting ready

In this recipe, we are connecting a Windows Server 2012 system to the storage presented in the *Creating iSCSI target and virtual disk* recipe.

How to do it...

Complete the following steps to access a remote iSCSI disk:

1. Start the iSCSI initiator and set it to automatic:

    ```
    Start-Service MSiSCSI
    Set-Service MSiSCSI -StartupType Automatic
    ```

2. Connect to the iSCSI portal:

    ```
    New-IscsiTargetPortal -TargetPortalAddress 10.10.10.100
    ```

3. Identify the available targets:

```
$tar = Get-IscsiTarget
```

4. Connect to the target:

```
Connect-IscsiTarget -NodeAddress $tar.NodeAddress
```

5. Review the connection information:

```
Get-IscsiSession
```

When executed, we will see connection information for our iSCSI target:

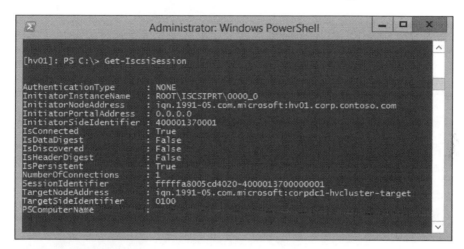

How it works...

By default, Windows comes with the iSCSI initiator service installed, but the service is set to manual start. We start the process of accessing the iSCSI disk by starting the `Microsoft iSCSI Initiator Service` and setting it to start up automatically. This will allow any drives presented to remain persistent between reboots.

In step 2, we connect the initiator to the iSCSI portal on the target server. The iSCSI portal provides mapping and security between the client computers and the iSCSI disks. This command adds the address of the iSCSI portal to the local iSCSI initiator to be used in the future.

Next, we use `Get-IscsiTarget` to query the portal and return all targets accessible to the client. The portal returns a list of resources available to the client based on the initiator ID and stores the information in the variable `$tar`.

Lastly, we use `Connect-IscsiTarget` to connect to our available targets. At this point, all iSCSI disks returned by the iSCSI server will be presented to the local system.

There's more...

If this is the first time the client has connected to the iSCSI drive, it will appear as a new drive—unformatted and unpartitioned. We can confirm this by opening **Computer Management (Start | compmgmt.msc)** and viewing the **Disk Management** node as shown in the next screenshot. Once the new disk has been partitioned, future connections will use the drive as normal.

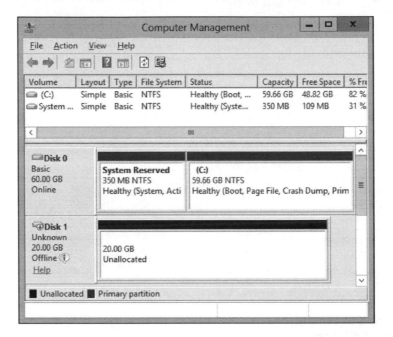

Configuring and using iSNS

The **Internet Storage Name Service** (**iSNS**) is a central directory of iSCSI targets and iSCSI initiators. Similar to the idea of a DNS, clients and servers register to the iSNS server, and then perform a lookup for resources available on the network. Once the list of resources is returned, the clients can then log into the resources as needed.

In a small or highly-centralized environment, this type of configuration may not be needed. If your environment has only one or two iSCSI targets, then the built-in target portals will provide the required information. However, if your environment contains multiple iSCSI targets, or will eventually grow to include multiple iSCSI targets, the iSNS server provides a central lookup and registration tool.

Getting ready

In this example, we will be setting up the simple configuration as shown in the next figure, with three different systems: iSNS Server, iSCSI Target, and iSCSI Initiator. The iSCSI target and initiators will both be configured to register with the iSNS server and automatically access the directory information.

An iSCSI disk has already been created on the target computer and exported to the initiator. However, no configuration has occurred on the initiator, and it currently does not have access to the iSCSI LUN.

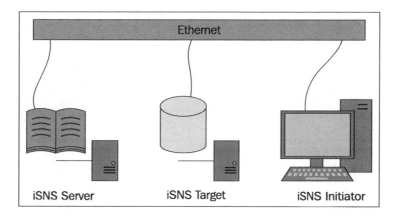

How to do it...

Carry out the following steps to configure and use iSNS:

1. Install the iSNS server:

   ```
   Add-WindowsFeature iSNS
   ```

2. Configure the iSCSI targets to register with the iSNS server:

   ```
   Set-WmiInstance -Namespace root\wmi -Class WT_iSNSServer `
   -Arguments @{ServerName="corpdc1.corp.contoso.com"}
   ```

3. Configure iSCSI initiators to register with the iSNS server:

   ```
   Set-WmiInstance -Namespace root\wmi `
   -Class MSiSCSIInitiator_iSNSServerClass `
   -Arguments @{iSNSServerAddress="corpdc1.corp.contoso.com"}
   ```

4. Discover and register the targets:

```
Start-Service MSiSCSI
Set-Service MSiSCSI -StartupType Automatic
$tar = Get-IscsiTarget
$tar | ForEach-Object{ Connect-IscsiTarget -NodeAddress `
$_.NodeAddress -IsPersistent $true }
```

How it works...

We start on the iSNS server and install the `iSNS` feature. In addition to the service, this feature also includes a tool for managing the iSNS zones. The tool can be accessed from **Server Manager | Tools | iSNS Server**.

In step 2, we use PowerShell to configure the Windows iSCSI targets to register with the iSNS server. To accomplish this we access WMI on the server and add an instance in the `WT_iSNSServer` WMI class. For large or complicated environments, this command can be repeated to register multiple iSNS servers simultaneously.

We then repeat the registration process on the iSCSI initiators. This time we are adding an instance to the `MSiSCSIInitiator_iSNSServerClass` WMI class. Unlike when configuring the target, this step can also be done manually by using the Microsoft iSCSI initiator console.

In step 4, we start up and register the iSCSI initiator. This step is similar to the prior recipe; however, when using iSNS we are executing `Get-IscsiTarget` against the iSNS server, potentially returning results from multiple iSCSI targets. Once the targets are returned, the script will cycle through the nodes and call `Connect-IscsiTarget` to attempt to connect to them persistently.

iSNS will return all available nodes in the current zone, including nodes that the client isn't authorized to access. When this `Connect-IscsiTarget` command is executed, it is normal for some errors to be returned.

There's more...

As your iSCSI environment grows, the number of targets, LUNs, and initiators may become difficult to manage. Additionally, attempting to connect to the targets may become slow due to the large number of resource connections being attempted.

To resolve this issue, the Microsoft iSNS server supports multiple `Discovery Domains`. A discovery domain is a group that contains iSCSI targets and initiators. When a member of a specific domain requests the available resources, only the resources included in the member's domain are returned. Similar to Active Directory groups, both targets and initiators can be included in multiple groups.

To manage the discovery domains, use the iSNS management tool from **Server Manager | Tools | iSNS Server**, or call `isnsui.exe`. Using this tool, shown in the next screenshot, we can create additional discovery domains and discovery domain sets that can be enabled as needed:

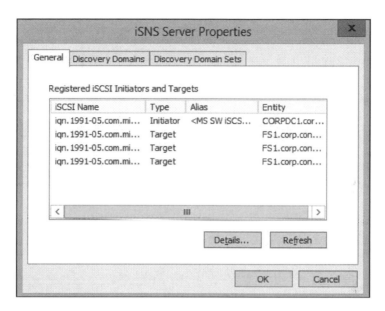

See also

For more information about the iSNS feature in Server 2012 see `http://technet.microsoft.com/en-us/library/cc772568.aspx`.

Creating an NFS export

Network File System, or **NFS**, is file sharing technology that is very common in Unix/Linux environments. Initially used for sharing files similar to CIFS, the use of NFS has grown to include high-performance environments such as Oracle databases and virtualization. Features such as connection resiliency and the ability to use either UDP or TCP make NFS versatile and powerful.

For Unix/Linux environments, basic share access was traditionally based on IP addressing; file level security was then used to further restrict access. Microsoft has expanded share security in NFS to include Kerberos authentication. This allows clients to be fully authenticated and access granted or restricted by using Active Directory.

NFS exports in Windows can still utilize IP-based security. This is useful when working in heterogeneous environments with non-Windows systems.

Getting ready

In this recipe, we will be working in a simple Active Directory environment for authentication. Our file server will create a share by using NFS and provide access to our clients.

How to do it...

Carry out the following steps to create an NFS export:

1. Install the NFS server service:

   ```
   Add-WindowsFeature FS-NFS-Service –IncludeManagementTools
   ```

2. Create a new NFS share:

   ```
   New-Item C:\shares\NFS1 -ItemType Directory
   New-NfsShare -Name NFS1 -Path C:\shares\NFS1
   ```

   When executed, PowerShell will display the new share information as shown in the following screenshot:

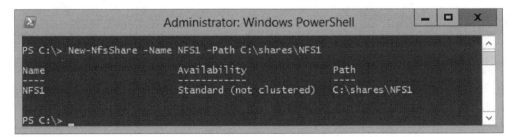

3. Grant access to a remote computer:

   ```
   Grant-NfsSharePermission -Name NFS1 -ClientName Server1 `
   -ClientType host -Permission readwrite -AllowRootAccess $true
   ```

How it works...

We start on our file server by installing the `FS-NFS-Service` feature service. This feature includes everything necessary to present and secure NFS shares to clients.

Once installed, we use `New-NfsShare` to create the new NFS share. At its simplest, this command requires a share path and a name. This command can also be used to identify the type of authentication being used: Kerberos, IP address, or anonymous.

To view the authentication information, execute `Get-NfsShare` and PowerShell will return the available authentication types as shown in the following screenshot:

```
Get-NfsShare -Name NFS1 | Format-List
```

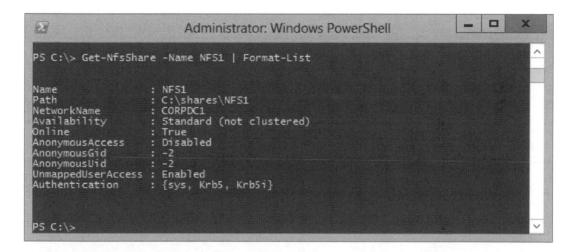

Once the share is created, we call `Grant-NfsSharePermission` to provide access to the share. By default, Windows creates a rule for the share of `ALL MACHINES` with `No Access`. If no additional rules exist, access to the share will be restricted. To grant access, we add the machine or network group and the appropriate type of access.

To review the permissions for an NFS share, execute `Get-NfsSharePremission`. The permissions assigned will be returned to the console as shown in the following screenshot:

```
Get-NfsSharePermission -Name NFS1
```

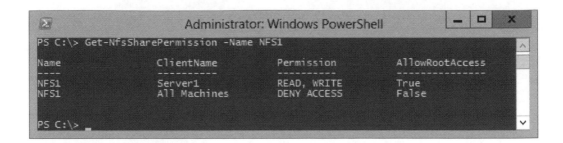

There's more...

In addition to the PowerShell commands for creating shares and granting access, Windows also includes a built-in tool named `Nfsadmin`. This tool exposes the dozens of advanced settings and options in NFS such as configuring to use UDP or TCP, using hard or soft mounts, timeout periods, and so on.

See also

For more information about NFS in Server 2012 and interoperability with Linux, see `http://blogs.technet.com/b/filecab/archive/2012/10/09/how-to-nfs-kerberos-configuration-with-linux-client.aspx`.

Mounting NFS exports

In addition to exporting shares using NFS, Windows can also mount NFS exports. Windows can access NFS exports from other Windows servers, as well as from Unix/Linux systems, making this an ideal technology for sharing files and data in heterogeneous environments.

Getting ready

In this recipe, we will be accessing the NFS export shared in the prior *Creating an NFS export* recipe. We will be utilizing the default Kerberos authentication included with NFS.

How to do it...

Carry out the following steps to mount the NFS export:

1. Install the NFS client:

    ```
    Install-WindowsFeature NFS-Client
    ```

2. Mount the NFS share using the `\\server\share` naming scheme:

    ```
    New-PSDrive N -PSProvider FileSystem -Root \\corpdc1\NFS1
    ```

When executed, PowerShell confirms the connection was successful as shown in the following screenshot:

```
PS E:\> New-PSDrive N -PSProvider FileSystem -Root \\corpdc1\NFS1

Name          Used (GB)      Free (GB) Provider      Root
----          ---------      --------- --------      ----
N                                      FileSystem    \\corpdc1\NFS1
```

How it works...

In this recipe we start by installing the `NFS-Client` feature on the client computer. By default, this feature is not installed in Windows Server and must be installed in order to use NFS mounts.

Next, we use `New-PSDrive` to map to the network share. This command is similar to the command used when mounting remote CIFS shares on a system. When connecting to the remote shares, PowerShell intelligently determines whether the connection is CIFS or NFS and connects appropriately.

There's more...

In addition to the PowerShell commands, there is a built-in tool, `C:\Windows\System32\Mount.exe`, that can also be used to connect and manage NFS drives. In addition to mounting NFS shares, it also allows for more advanced settings such as buffer sizes, locking, and file access. For general use, the default options are sufficient; however, specialized technologies often suggest changing these advanced options.

Making CIFS shares highly available

Prior to Windows Server 2012, the only solutions for making file servers redundant was to use Clustering Services. In that case, if the primary server went offline, the backup server would take ownership of the cluster resources. This active/passive configuration provided redundancy during a failure, but forced the connections to be reestablished and caused issues with some applications. Additionally, the time necessary to identify the failure and perform the failover could cause data loss or other problems.

In Windows Server 2012, we can now use **Cluster Shared Volumes** (**CSV**) to present highly available file shares. CSV was originally created for hosting virtual machines and allows for multiple nodes in a Windows cluster to access the same file system simultaneously. This allows us to present a file share in an active/active configuration with multiple servers providing the file share. If a server is taken offline for any reason, the client connections will automatically reconnect to the alternate cluster node without data loss.

Getting ready

For this recipe, we will be using an iSCSI server to host the source drive. Two file servers will then attach to the same iSCSI virtual disk, and present the clustered share to clients.

We will be using the environment shown in the next with the following addresses:

Role	Address
iSCSI target	10.10.10.102
File server—FS1	10.10.10.103
File server—FS2	10.10.10.104
Cluster—CIFS1	10.10.10.106

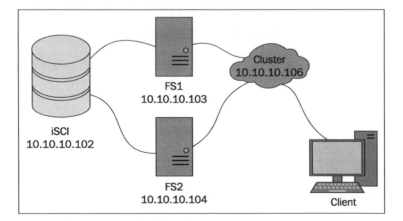

How to do it...

Carry out the following steps:

1. Set up iSCSI on the backend server:

```
Install-WindowsFeature -Name FS-iSCSITarget-Server, iSCSITarget-
VSS-VDS
New-iSCSIServerTarget -Targetname "FSCluster" `
-InitiatorID "IPAddress:10.10.10.103","IPAddress:10.10.10.104"
New-Item e:\iSCSIVirtualDisks -ItemType Directory
New-iSCSIVirtualDisk "e:\iSCSIVirtualDisks\Drive1.vhd" -Size 20GB
Add-iSCSIVirtualDiskTargetMapping -Targetname "FSCluster" `
-DevicePath "e:\iSCSIVirtualDisks\Drive1.vhd"
```

 This is the same process as used in the *Creating iSCSI target and virtual disk* recipe.

2. Set up iSCSI clients on the file servers:

```
Invoke-Command -ComputerName FS1, FS2 -ScriptBlock{
Install-WindowsFeature -Name Failover-Clustering
-IncludeManagementTools
Start-service msiscsi
Set-service msiscsi -StartupType Automatic
New-IscsiTargetPortal -TargetPortalAddress 10.10.10.102
$tar = Get-iscsitarget
Connect-iscsitarget -NodeAddress $tar.NodeAddress
}
```

 This is the same process as used in the *Using a iSCSI disk* recipe.

3. Create the failover cluster:

```
New-Cluster -Name FSCluster -Node "FS1","FS2" `
-StaticAddress 10.10.10.106
```

4. Add the `Cluster Scale Out File Server` role:

```
Get-Cluster FSCluster | Add-ClusterScaleOutFileServerRole -name
CIFS1
```

5. Run the validation tests:

    ```
    Get-Cluster FSCluster | Test-Cluster
    ```

6. List the available disks:

    ```
    Get-Cluster FSCluster | Get-ClusterAvailableDisk
    ```

7. Add disks to the cluster:

    ```
    Get-Cluster FSCluster | Get-ClusterAvailableDisk | Add-ClusterDisk
    ```

8. Convert disks to CSV:

    ```
    Get-Cluster FSCluster | Add-ClusterSharedVolume -Name "Cluster
    Disk 1"
    ```

9. Create the clustered share:

    ```
    Invoke-Command -ComputerName FS1 -ScriptBlock{
    New-Item "c:\clusterstorage\volume1\Share1" -ItemType Directory
    New-SmbShare -Name Share1 -Path "c:\clusterstorage\volume1\Share1"
    }
    ```

10. Connect to the cluster share the same as if it was a standard server share:

    ```
    \\cifs1\Share1
    ```

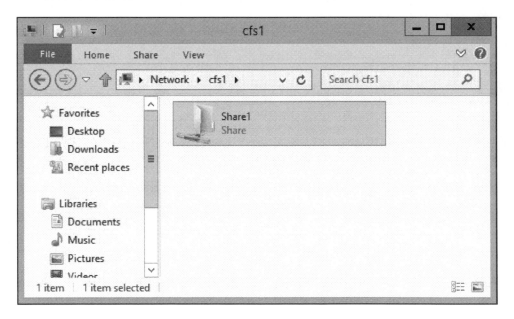

How it works...

In step 1, we start the process by creating an iSCSI target for our file server clients. We install the iSCSI features on the server and then create a new target group named FSCluster that is zoned with the IP addresses of our file servers. We then create a new iSCSI disk and map the disk to the cluster.

 In this example, we are using Windows iSCSI target and initiators. Instead of hosting the storage on a Windows server, we can also use an iSCSI or Fibre Channel SAN instead.

In step 2, we set up the file servers. We start by installing the Failover-Clustering feature on both of the servers. We then start the iSCSI initiators and configure them to connect to the target configured in step 1. Finally, both file servers connect to the iSCSI target.

Next, we create the failover cluster. First, we create the cluster named FSCluster and assign it a static IP address. We then add the Scale Out File Server role to this cluster. This role enables the servers to use Cluster Shared Volumes across the nodes and present file shares from the volumes.

Next, we call Test-Cluster to run validation tests on the cluster. The validation tests check that the networking, shared storage, unshared storage, performance, and failover capabilities are suitable for clustering. This process tests the cluster for all clustering features and some errors will be expected. Review the generated report and specifically confirm that the CSV tests completed successfully. In order to proceed, the test process must succeed.

In step 6, we query the cluster and return the available disks for clustering. In this example, the command will return only one result. If no disks are returned, something is wrong with the iSCSI or clustering configuration and needs to be resolved.

In step 7 we use Add-ClusterDisk to add the available disks into the cluster. Then in step 8, we call Add-ClsuterSharedVolume to add the disk as a CSV resource. This command will mount the disk on our file servers under C:\ClusterStorage\Volume1.

Lastly, we create the clustered share and connect to the cluster name. We connect to the first file server and create a directory in our ClusterStorage folder named Share1. We then use New-SmbShare to create a new CIFS share for the new folder; this share is automatically included as a cluster resource.

See also

More information about using failover clustering for highly available file shares can be found at `http://blogs.technet.com/b/clausjor/archive/2012/06/07/smb-transparent-failover-making-file-shares-continuously-available.aspx`.

Configuring DFS and DFSR replication

Distributed File System (**DFS**) and **Distributed File System Replication** (**DFSR**) allow for information to be replicated and accessed using a common namespace. This namespace can contain resources from multiple different systems and in different locations, yet users are able to access the information using a common name.

The most common usage of these technologies is Windows Active Directory, which stores and replicates user information among domain controllers.

Getting ready

In this recipe, we will be using our two file servers, namely FS1 and FS2, to configure a DFS namespace. We will add folders to the DFS namespace and configure replication between the servers.

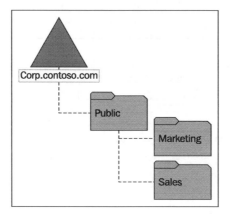

How to do it...

Carry out the following steps to configure DFS and DFSR replication:

1. Create the shares for the DFS root:

    ```
    Invoke-Command -ComputerName FS1, FS2 -scriptblock{
    New-Item C:\Shares\Public -ItemType Directory
    New-SmbShare -Name Public -Path C:\Shares\Public -FullAccess
    ```

```
Everyone
}
```

2. Create the DFS root on both servers:

```
New-DfsnRoot -TargetPath \\FS1\Public -Type DomainV2
New-DfsnRootTarget -TargetPath \\FS2\Public
```

3. Create the shares for `Marketing` and `Sales`:

```
Invoke-Command -ComputerName FS1, FS2 -ScriptBlock{
New-Item C:\Shares\Marketing -ItemType Directory
New-Item C:\Shares\Sales -ItemType Directory
New-SmbShare -Name Marketing -Path C:\Shares\Marketing -FullAccess
Everyone
New-SmbShare -Name Sales -Path C:\Shares\Sales -FullAccess
Everyone
}
```

4. Add the new shares to the DFS root:

```
New-DfsnFolder -Path \\corp\Public\Marketing -TargetPath \\FS1\
Marketing
New-DfsnFolder -Path \\corp\Public\Sales -TargetPath \\FS1\Sales
New-DfsnFolderTarget -Path \\corp\Public\Marketing -TargetPath \\
FS2\Marketing
New-DfsnFolderTarget -Path \\corp\Public\Sales -TargetPath \\FS2\
Sales
```

5. Create a DFSR replication group:

```
DfsrAdmin RG New /RgName:Public /Domain:corp.contoso.com
```

6. Add the file servers to the replication group:

```
DfsrAdmin Mem New /RgName:Public /MemName:FS1 /Domain:corp.
contoso.com
DfsrAdmin Mem New /RgName:Public /MemName:FS2 /Domain:corp.
contoso.com
```

7. Create replication folders:

```
DfsrAdmin Rf New /RgName:Public /RfName:Marketing /RfDfspath:\\
corp.contoso.com\Public\Marketing /force
DfsrAdmin Rf New /RgName:Public /RfName:Sales /RfDfspath:\\corp.
contoso.com\Public\Sales /force
```

8. Configure the replication folder paths:

```
DfsrAdmin Membership Set /RgName:Public /RfName:Marketing /
MemName:FS1 /LocalPath:C:\Shares\Marketing /MembershipEnabled:true
/IsPrimary:true /force
DfsrAdmin Membership Set /RgName:Public /RfName:Marketing /
MemName:FS2 /LocalPath:C:\Shares\Marketing /MembershipEnabled:true
/IsPrimary:false /force
DfsrAdmin Membership Set /RgName:Public /RfName:Sales /MemName:FS1
/LocalPath:C:\Shares\Sales /MembershipEnabled:true /IsPrimary:true
/force
DfsrAdmin Membership Set /RgName:Public /RfName:Sales /
MemName:FS2 /LocalPath:C:\Shares\Sales /MembershipEnabled:true /
IsPrimary:false /force
```

9. Create connections between the servers:

```
DfsrAdmin Conn New /RgName:Public /SendMem:corp\FS1 /Recvmem:corp\
FS2 /ConnEnabled:true
DfsrAdmin Conn New /RgName:Public /SendMem:corp\FS2 /Recvmem:corp\
FS1 /ConnEnabled:true
```

How it works...

We start by configuring folders and CIFS shares for the DFS root. We use `Invoke-Command` to execute the commands on both servers simultaneously.

In step 2, we create the DFS root. We start by creating the DFS root on server `FS1` at `\\FS1\Public` and configure it as a domain DFS root. This type of DFS root is more flexible and allows for replication and other location-aware features. We then add `\\FS2\Public` as an additional target for the root.

Now that the root is configured, in step 3 we set up additional shares to be added to the DFS root. In this case, we are creating two folders and two CIFS shares: `Marketing` and `Sales`. We default the permissions for these shares to full access for everyone, which is not a preferred configuration in a production environment.

 It is possible to create folders directly inside the DFS root. This type of configuration limits the scalability and functions of DFS. Instead, it is best practice to create additional file shares and add them to the DFS tree.

In step 4, we add our new shares to the DFS tree. We first use `New-DfsnFolder` to add the share in the DFS, and then use `New-DfsnFolderTarget` to add additional targets to the DFS object. Here, we are only configuring two targets; however multiple targets can be configured for each share across multiple servers. At this point our DFS configuration is complete.

Once our DFS hierarchy is created, we can create our replication policies. To manage replication we use the `DfsrAdmin.exe` tool found in the Windows directory. `DfsrAdmin` includes built-in help that can be viewed by calling `DfsrAdmin.exe /?`.

In step 5, we use `dfsradmin rg` to create a new replication group named `Public` in our `corp.contoso.com` domain. A replication group is used to contain the servers, shares, and replication policies.

Next, we call `dfsradmin mem` to add our file servers as members to the new replication group.

In step 7, we use `dfsradmin rf` to add our DFS folders to the new replication group. This command creates a replication folder that links the newly-created replication group to the DFS folders on the file servers.

In step 8, we configure the replication folders. We call `dfsradmin membership set` for each server/share included in the replication group. This configures the replication folder with the local folder on the file server. Additionally, the `/IsPrimary:true` switch configures FS1 as the primary source of information for both shares. When replication begins, the primary source will overwrite any conflicting items on the target servers.

Finally, we use `dfsradmin conn new` to create replication connections between the file servers. Here, we create two connections: the first from `FS1` to `FS2`, and the second from `FS2` to `FS1`. Additional servers and links can be configured, including cross-site links in order to replicate data to other locations.

Configuring BranchCache

BranchCache is a technology designed by Microsoft to ease file and website access in remote branch offices. These sites traditionally utilize slow WAN links, resulting in slow access to centralized services.

Similar to a proxy server, BranchCache intelligently caches information requests across a WAN link. Once in the cache, subsequent requests are fulfilled by the cache instead of resending the information across the network.

There are two types of BranchCache: file servers and web servers. As the names suggest BranchCache for file servers caches information accessed from CIFS shares, while BranchCache for web servers caches information accessed from web sites. Windows clients utilize group policies to define if they should use BranchCache and how to discover the BranchCache resources.

Getting ready

In this recipe, we will be working in an Active Directory environment with a remote site similar to the one shown in the next figure. In the corporate office, there is a file server FS1, and at the remote office, there is a BranchCache server named BC1. The two sites are joined by a WAN link.

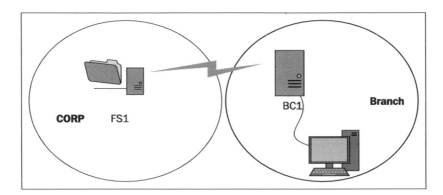

We will also create a **Group Policy (GPO)** for the servers and clients in the branch office. This group policy will set the following registry keys on the client:

Location	Setting	Value
HKLM\Software\Policies\Microsoft\ PeerDisk\Service	Enable	1
HKLM\Software\Policies\Microsoft\ PeerDisk\CooperativeCaching	Enable	1
HKLM\Software\Policies\Microsoft\ PeerDisk\HostedCache\Discovery	SCPDiscoveryEnabled	1

How to do it...

Carry out the following steps to configure BranchCache:

1. Create a Group Policy (GPO) for the clients in the remote office:

    ```
    New-GPO -Name "BranchCache Client"
    ```

2. Add the appropriate registry values to the GPO:

    ```
    Set-GPRegistryValue -Name "BranchCache Client" `
    -Key HKLM\SOFTWARE\Policies\Microsoft\PeerDist\Service `
    -Valuename Enable -Value 1 -Type DWord
    Set-GPRegistryValue -Name "BranchCache Client" `
    ```

```
-Key HKLM\SOFTWARE\Policies\Microsoft\PeerDist\CooperativeCaching
`

-Valuename Enable -Value 1 -Type DWord
Set-GPRegistryValue -Name "BranchCache Client" `
-Key HKLM\SOFTWARE\Policies\Microsoft\PeerDist\HostedCache\
Discovery `
-ValueName SCPDiscoveryEnabled -Value 1 -Type DWord
```

3. Apply GPO to the branch site as follows:

```
New-GPLink -Name "BranchCache Client" -Target Branch
```

4. Install BranchCache on all participating systems in the following way:

```
Invoke-Command -ComputerName FS1, BC1, Client1 -ScriptBlock {
Install-WindowsFeature BranchCache, FS-BranchCache
-IncludeManagementTools
}
```

 This step is only needed if the client computers are running Windows Server 2012. Windows 8 has the BranchCache client installed automatically and it just needs to be enabled.

5. Publish the BranchCache web server:

```
Publish-BCWebContent -Path C:\InetPub\WWWRoot
```

6. Publish the BranchCache file server:

```
Publish-BCFileContent -Path C:\Shares\Sales
```

7. Configure the BranchCache host:

```
Enable-BCHostedServer -RegisterSCP
```

8. Update BranchCache clients:

```
GPUpdate /force
Restart-Service peerdistsvc
```

How it works...

We start by creating a group policy named BranchCache Client for our clients and servers in the remote branch. In this GPO, we add three settings: Service—which enables the BranchCache server, CooperativeCaching—which specifies the caching type, and Discovery—which enables discovery of the BranchCache servers via DNS. We then link the new GPO to our remote branch site.

In step 4, we install the BranchCache feature on all participating systems. This is performed on the file and web servers that host the content, the BranchCache server, and the client systems. In this scenario, there are three systems included: `FS1`—the file server hosting the content, `BC1`—the remote BranchCache server, and `Client1`—our first BranchCache client.

In steps 5 and 6, we use `PublishBCWebContent` and `PublishBCFileContent` to publish the content to be cached. This process configures the necessary information for the BranchCache clients to identify when content has changed and the cached content is out of date.

Lastly, we update the BranchCache clients. First, we execute `GPUpdate` to ensure the client has the latest caching policies. Then; we restart the `peerdistsvc` service, which performs the caching process on the clients and servers. This ensures that the clients have the updated policy from the GPO.

There's more...

When a file or web content is accessed from the remote site, it will be intelligently cached by the BranchCache server. When a second client in the site accesses the same content, instead of being accessed across the WAN link, the content will be provided by the caching server.

To confirm that the data is being cached, you can execute `Get-BCStatus` from the BranchCache server `BC1`. The result will be similar to that shown in the following screenshot:

```
DataCache:

    CacheFileDirectoryPath                :
    C:\Windows\ServiceProfiles\NetworkService\AppData\Local\PeerDistRepub
    MaxCacheSizeAsPercentageOfDiskVolume : 5
    MaxCacheSizeAsNumberOfBytes          : 3202770325
    CurrentSizeOnDiskAsNumberOfBytes     : 311566336
    CurrentActiveCacheSize               : 8734912

    DataCacheExtensions:
```

The `CurrentActiveCacheSize` shows how much data is currently in the cache and ready to service additional clients.

See also

For more information about using BranchCache see `http://technet.microsoft.com/en-us/library/jj862369.aspx` and `http://www.microsoft.com/en-us/download/details.aspx?id=30418`.

7
Managing Windows Updates with PowerShell

In this chapter, we will cover the following recipes:

- ▶ Installing Windows Server Update Services
- ▶ Configuring WSUS update synchronization
- ▶ Configuring the Windows update client
- ▶ Creating computer groups
- ▶ Configuring WSUS auto-approvals
- ▶ Reporting missing updates
- ▶ Installing updates
- ▶ Uninstalling updates
- ▶ Configuring WSUS to inventory clients
- ▶ Creating an update report
- ▶ Exporting WSUS data to Excel

Introduction

Windows Server Update Services (**WSUS**) is a feature included in Windows Server 2012 that allows administrators to manage the distribution of updates, hotfixes, and service packs to clients. WSUS downloads updates from the public Microsoft Update servers, and clients then connect to the WSUS server to download and install the updates. WSUS allows administrators to control which updates are installed in their environment, enforce their installation, and report on compliance.

This chapter details the installation and configuration of WSUS as well as the Windows Update client. Additionally, this chapter will include methods to automate update installation, report on installed updates, and report on hardware and software inventory.

Installing Windows Server Update Services

Microsoft Windows Server Update Services is a built-in feature of Server 2012 that can be installed in any Server 2012 edition. The update service provides simplified, centralized management of updates in your environment. This feature inventories the updates installed on computers, downloads the updates, and then distributes them to clients as defined by the administrator.

For WSUS to function, two steps are needed: install the Update Services feature, and perform the initial configuration, which is referred to as the **postinstall** phase. This postinstall phase finalizes the WSUS installation by configuring the database and location to store the updates.

Getting ready

To perform this recipe, we will be using a domain-joined server with access to the Internet. Once the Update Services feature is installed, we will perform the initial configuration of the system and perform the initial update synchronization. All of the tasks shown will be performed locally on the update server.

 Windows Server Update Services can be deployed in many different configurations, for example, a secure environment without Internet access, or a large corporation with multiple sites. In this recipe, we will be deploying a simple, single server configuration.

How to do it...

Carry out the following steps in order to install Windows Server Update Services:

1. Install the `UpdateServices` feature:

   ```
   Install-WindowsFeature UpdateServices -IncludeManagementTools
   ```

2. Perform the initial configuration:

   ```
   New-Item E:\MyContent -ItemType Directory
   & 'C:\Program Files\Update Services\Tools\WsusUtil.exe'
   postinstall contentdir=e:\Mycontent
   ```

3. Review the current synhronization settings:

   ```
   $myWsus = Get-WsuscServer
   $myWsus.GetSubscription()
   ```

   When executed, we will see the current configuration as shown in the following screenshot:

   ```
   PS C:\> $mywsus = Get-WsusServer
   PS C:\> $mywsus.GetSubscription()


   UpdateServer                      : Microsoft.UpdateServices.Internal.BaseApi.U
                                       pdateServer
   SynchronizeAutomatically          : False
   SynchronizeAutomaticallyTimeOfDay : 00:00:44
   LastModifiedTime                  : 11/15/2012 8:17:24 PM
   LastModifiedBy                    : CORP\administrator
   LastSynchronizationTime           : 1/1/0001 12:00:00 AM
   Anchor                            : 0,2000-01-01 00:00:01.000
   DeploymentAnchor                  :
   NumberOfSynchronizationsPerDay    : 1
   IsCategoryOnlySync                : False
   ```

4. If you are using a proxy server to access the internet, then configure for using a proxy (optional) as follows:

   ```
   $wuConfig = $myWsus.GetConfiguration()
   $wuConfig.ProxyName = "proxy.corp.contoso.com"
   $wuConfig.ProxyServerPort = 8080
   $wuConfig.UseProxy = $true
   $wuConfig.Save()
   ```

5. Perform the initial synchronization (only syncs categories):

   ```
   $mySubs = $myWsus.GetSubscription()
   $mySubs.StartSynchronizationForCategoryOnly()
   ```

6. Get a report on the synchronization status as follows:

```
$mySubs.GetSynchronizationProgress()
$mySubs.GetSynchronizationStatus()
$mySubs.GetLastSynchronizationInfo()
```

When completed, we will see the synchronization results as shown in the following screenshot:

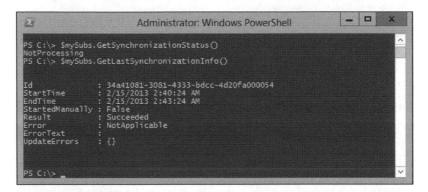

How it works...

We start by installing and configuring the `UpdateServices` feature on our server. To install, we simply use `Install-WindowsFeature`. Once installed, there is an initial configuration that needs to take place. At its simplest, we use the `contentdir` switch to define the directory for the downloaded content to be placed. Additionally, if you have an existing SQL server on which you would like to host the WSUS database, you can specify it by using the `SQL_Instance_Name` switch.

 The & symbol used in step 2 at the beginning of the `postinstall` command signals PowerShell to execute a remote command and not return to the Command Prompt until the command is finished. We then use this as a signal the system is ready to continue with the configuration.

Next, we create a connection to the WSUS server and review the current synchronization settings. By default, `SynchronizeAutomatically` is set to `False`. This tells us that the system is configured to not synchronize automatically. In addition, the `LastSynchronizationTime` shows `1/1/0001 12:00:00 AM` because no synchronization has occurred yet. In step 4, if a proxy server is used to access the Internet, we configure Windows Update to use the proxy server. This is accomplished by first retrieving the WSUS server configuration. Then, we update the configuration with the `ProxyName`, `ProxyServerPort`, and `UseProxy` values. Finally, we call the `Save()` method to save the configuration to the server. If no proxy server is required in your environment, this step can be skipped.

In order to further configure WSUS, we need to perform an initial synchronization. We start by calling the `GetSubscription()` method to load the current subscription information. We then call `StartSynchronizationForCategoryOnly()` method to perform the initial synchronization. The initial synchronization does not download any updates; however, it contacts Microsoft's update servers and downloads the update category information. This includes information about the currently supported products and types of updates available for download.

Finally, we report on the synchronization status. Depending on the speed of your network connection and the number of updates being synchronized, the synchronization process can take a while to complete. Here we are executing three different commands: the first command, `Get-SynchronizationProgres()`, returns the current synchronization progress including the number of items to process and items currently processed. The second command, `GetSynchronizationStatus()`, returns the current status (`Processing` or `NotProcessing`) of the synchronization process. The last command, `GetLastSynchronizationInfo()`, returns information about the last synchronization that occurred.

There's more...

As Windows Update uses the HTTP and BITS protocols, it is possible to load balance clients among multiple update servers. To accomplish this, we can configure Network Load Balancing among the update servers, similar to balancing an IIS site. Information on configuring a web server for load balancing can be found in the *Monitoring load balancing across NLB nodes* recipe in *Chapter 3, Managing IIS with PowerShell.*

See also

For more information on the available PowerShell cmdlets for WSUS, see `http://technet.microsoft.com/en-us/library/hh826166.aspx`.

Configuring WSUS update synchronization

Once the initial synchronization is finished, we can configure what applications and types of updates we want WSUS to scan and patch. Once identified, during the next synchronization process, the server will download the scanning criteria for those updates. Additionally, we can configure the synchronization process to occur automatically throughout the day, and without intervention.

Getting ready

For this recipe, we will be using our server that has just finished the initial synchronization, similar to the prior recipe. In this recipe, we will only be synchronizing the information for the following products:

- ▸ Forefront Client Security
- ▸ SQL Server 2008 R2
- ▸ Office
- ▸ Windows

Additionally, we will specify the following update types, or classifications, to synchronize:

- ▸ Update Rollups
- ▸ Security Updates
- ▸ Critical Updates
- ▸ Definition Updates
- ▸ Service Packs
- ▸ Updates

These steps can also be performed on an existing update server, but care should be taken as this process will overwrite any existing configurations.

How to do it...

Carry out the following steps to configure WSUS update synchronization:

1. Define the product categories to include, as follows:

```
$myProducts = Get-WsusProduct | `
Where-Object {$_.Product.Title -in ('Forefront Client Security', `
'SQL Server 2008 R2', 'Office', 'Windows')}
$myProducts | Set-WsusProduct
```

2. Define the update classifications to include, as follows:

```
$myClass = Get-WsusClassification | `
Where-Object { $_.Classification.Title -in ('Update Rollups', `
'Security Updates', 'Critical Updates', 'Definition Updates', `
'Service Packs', 'Updates')}
$myClass | Set-WsusClassification
```

3. Initiate synchronization:

    ```
    $mySubs = $myWsus.GetSubscription()
    $mySubs.StartSynchronization()
    ```

4. Configure automatic synchronization:

    ```
    $mysubs = $myWsus.GetSubscription()
    $mysubs.SynchronizeAutomatically = $true
    $mysubs.NumberOfSynchronizationsPerDay = 1
    $mysubs.Save()
    ```

How it works...

We start our process by identifying the products that we want WSUS to patch. We do this by calling `Get-WsusProduct` to return all available products and filtering based on the title. The filtered contents are then piped into `Set-WsusProduct` to set the products to synchronize in the future. In this instance, we are including in only four products: Forefront Client Security, SQL Server 2008 R2, Office, and Windows. Different environments will include different products.

In most environments, not all products updated by WSUS exist, so this step helps to limit the downloading and testing that is necessary. Additionally, there may be some products in your environment that business requirements mandate that you patch manually. An example of this is a mail server or other critical component that requires manually shutting down and restarting of services when patching.

In step 2, we identify the types of updates to include. This time we call `Get-WsusClassification` to return the available classifications, and filter based on the title of the classification. The filtered list is then piped into `Set-WsusClassification` to set the classification types to include in the synchronization.

In step 3, we call `StartSynchronization()` to initiate the update synchronization. This downloads details about the updates and information on how WSUS will identify whether the updates are needed or are already installed.

Lastly, we configure the synchronization to occur automatically during the day so that manual effort is not required to update the WSUS server. First, we set `SynchronizeAutomatically` to `$true` to enable automatic synchronization, then we set `NumberOfSynchronizationsPerDay` to `1`. WSUS can be configured to synchronize up to 24 times a day; however, normally one or two times per day is sufficient.

There's more...

A full list of available products and update types can be viewed by executing the following commands in PowerShell. This will help identify which products and categories are available to include in steps 1 and 2 before .

▶ To list all available products for WSUS, use the `Get-WsusProduct` command.

▶ To list all available classifications, use the `Get-WsusClassification` command.

Configuring the Windows update client

The Windows update client on servers and workstations default to downloading updates from Microsoft's public update servers. In a business environment, this is not always desirable due to unpredictable installation schedules and potentially varied patch revisions.

Once the update server is configured, we can configure the Windows update client. At its most simplistic configuration, the client configuration includes the address of the update server and a setting instructing the client to use the update server.

Getting ready

The simplest way to configure the clients is to create one or more group policies that define the address of the local update servers. This group policy can then be deployed to the entire **Active Directory** (**AD**) environment, specific sites, or only a subset of computers.

Our group policy will define the following registry setting on our clients:

Path	Name	Value
HKLM\Software\Policies\ Microsoft\Windows\ WindowsUpdate\AU	UseWUServer	1
HKLM\Software\Policies\ Microsoft\Windows\ WindowsUpdate\AU	AUOptions	2
HKLM\Software\Policies\ Microsoft\Windows\ WindowsUpdate	WUServer	http://update.corp. contoso.com:8530
HKLM\Software\Policies\ Microsoft\Windows\ WindowsUpdate	WUStatusServer	http://update.corp. contoso.com:8530

How to do it...

Carry out the following steps in order to configure the Windows Update client:

1. On the update server, confirm the WSUS address and port:

```
Get-WsusServer | Format-List *
```

2. Create the group policy:

```
New-GPO -Name "WSUS Client"
```

3. Link the group policy to a site:

```
New-GPLink -Name "WSUS Client" -Target "DC=Corp,DC=Contoso,DC=Com"
```

4. Add registry key settings to the group policy to assign the WSUS server:

```
$wuServer = "http://update.corp.contoso.com:8530"
Set-GPRegistryValue -Name "WSUS Client" `
-Key "HKLM\Software\Policies\Microsoft\Windows\WindowsUpdate\AU" `
-ValueName "UseWUServer" -Type DWORD -Value 1
Set-GPRegistryValue -Name "WSUS Client" `
-Key "HKLM\Software\Policies\Microsoft\Windows\WindowsUpdate\AU" `
-ValueName "AUOptions" -Type DWORD -Value 2
Set-GPRegistryValue -Name "WSUS Client" `
 Key "HKLM\Software\Policies\Microsoft\Windows\WindowsUpdate" `
-ValueName "WUServer" -Type String -Value $wuServer
Set-GPRegistryValue -Name "WSUS Client" `
-Key "HKLM\Software\Policies\Microsoft\Windows\WindowsUpdate" `
-ValueName "WUStatusServer" -Type String -Value $wuServer
```

5. On the client, update the group policy to load the new settings (optional):

```
Gpupdate /force
```

6. Initiate a update scan on the client (optional):

```
Wuauclt /detectnow
```

How it works...

We start by using `Get-WsusServer` to review the Windows update server configuration. Specifically, we are looking for the values on the lines labeled `PortNumber` and `UseSecureConnection`. This defines how clients will connect to the update server. The results of these values will help define the connection in our group policy.

In the second step, we use `New-GPO` to create a new group policy named WSUS Client. This policy will house all the settings necessary for our clients to access our WSUS server. A best practice for group policies is to create a new policy for each setting. By creating a separate policy for the update server, we can easily change this or other settings in the future.

Next, in step 3, we use `New-GPLink` to link our new group policy to the root of our domain. Because we are placing this policy at the root of the domain, all domain clients will receive the policy. If instead we want to target a specific OU, we can change the `-Target` switch to a specific OU such as `ou=desktops`, `dc=corp`, `dc=contoso`, or `dc=com`.

In step 4, we then add the appropriate values to the group policy. Here, we start by defining our update server address by using HTTP or HTTPS and the port number identified in step 1. We then call `Set-GPRegistryValue` to assign the attributes needed to use the update server.

Finally, we update the client and scan for updates. We can manually initiate the client update by executing `GPUpdate /force`, which tells the client to download the latest group policies and apply them. Then, we initiate a scan by executing `Wuaclt /detectnow`. These steps are not necessary for the clients to function properly as they will occur automatically during the next GPO refresh and scanning cycle. However, it is useful to manually initiate the scanning to confirm the systems are reporting properly.

There's more...

In a non-domain environment, or with non-domain joined computers, you can configure clients to use the update server directly. To accomplish this, we can either use a local computer policy or assign the registry keys directly. Following is an example of configuring the local registry keys of the local client to use the update server:

```
New-ItemProperty -PropertyType String `
-Path HKLM:\Software\Policies\Microsoft\Windows\WindowsUpdate `
-Name WUServer -Value "http://update.corp.contoso.com:8530"
New-ItemProperty -PropertyType String `
-Path HKLM:\Software\Policies\Microsoft\Windows\WindowsUpdate `
-Name WUStatusServer -Value "http://update.corp.contoso.com:8530"
New-ItemProperty -PropertyType DWord `
-Path HKLM:\Software\Policies\Microsoft\Windows\WindowsUpdate\AU `
-Name UseWUServer -Value 1
```

Here, we are calling `New-ItemProperty` to create/update registry values on the local computer. These commands are setting the `WUServer`, `WUStatusServer`, and `UseWUServer` values; these are the minimum settings needed to use a WSUS server.

- ▶ More information about the Group Policy PowerShell cmdlets can be found at `http://technet.microsoft.com/en-us/library/ee461027.aspx`

- ▶ More information about the available WSUS client registry keys can be found at `http://technet.microsoft.com/en-us/library/dd939844(v=ws.10).aspx`

Creating computer groups

One of the great features of Windows Server Update Services is its ability to group computers. Once a group is created, updates can be deployed and reporting can be performed on a group-by-group basis. This allows for servers and clients to be grouped by application, criticality, or business unit, each with different update policies applied to them.

In this recipe, we will be using an update server with multiple clients. We will be creating a group for the domain controllers in our environment in order to maintain a consistent patch level on the systems.

Getting ready

For this recipe we will be using a WSUS server configured as shown in the *Configuring WSUS update synchronization* recipe with one or more clients configured as shown in the *Configuring the Windows update client* recipe.

How to do it...

In order to create computer groups, carry out the following steps:

1. Create the computer group:

   ```
   $myWsus = Get-WsusServer
   $myWsus.CreateComputerTargetGroup("Domain Controllers")
   ```

2. Add clients to the computer group:

   ```
   Get-WsusComputer -NameIncludes corpdc | `
   Add-WsusComputer -TargetGroupName "Domain Controllers"
   ```

3. List the clients in the computer group:

   ```
   $myGroup = $myWsus.GetComputerTargetGroups() | `
   Where-Object Name -eq "Domain Controllers"
   Get-WsusComputer | `
   Where-Object ComputerTargetGroupIDs -Contains $myGroup.Id
   ```

When executed, the contents of the new computer group will be displayed as shown in the following screenshot:

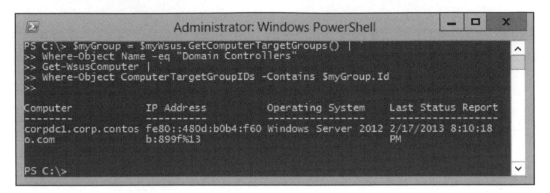

How it works...

We start by connecting to the WSUS server and calling `CreateComputerTargetGroup` to create a computer group named `Domain Controllers`.

In step 2, we add our domain controller to the new group. We do this by first calling `Get-WsusComputer` to search for clients of the update server with a name like `corpdc`. This command allows us to search using the NetBIOS name of the server and return the object even if it has been identified by using its fully-qualified name. The result is piped into `Add-WsusComputer` to add the computers to our new group as shown in the preceding screenshot.

Lastly, we can use PowerShell to return the list of clients in the group. We start by calling `GetComputerTargetGroups` to search for computer groups and filtering for our `Domain Controllers` group. We then use `Get-WsusComputer` to return all of the computers, and then filter this list based on the group membership to return the members of our group.

Configuring WSUS auto-approvals

Another great feature of Windows Server Update Services is the ability to automatically approve updates. This allows the administrator to define specific application updates or types of update to be automatically downloaded and installed on client computers.

Getting ready

It is not uncommon in some environments to create a rule that automatically approves all critical security updates and enforces the automatic installation. In this recipe, we will create a rule to automatically install all `Critical Updates` and all `Definition Updates` to our newly created `Domain Controllers` group.

How to do it...

WSUS auto-approvals can be configured by using the following steps:

1. Create the auto-approval rule:

```
$myWsus = Get-WsusServer
$myRule = $myWsus.CreateInstallApprovalRule("Critical Updates")
```

2. Define a deadline:

```
$myDeadline = New-Object `
Microsoft.UpdateServices.Administration.
AutomaticUpdateApprovalDeadline
$myDeadline.DayOffset = 3
$myDeadline.MinutesAfterMidnight = 180
$myRule.Deadline = $myDeadline
```

3. Add update classifications to the rule:

```
$myClass = $myRule.GetUpdateClassifications()
$myClass.Add(($myWsus.GetUpdateClassifications() | `
Where-Object Title -eq 'Critical Updates'))
$myClass.Add(($myWsus.GetUpdateClassifications() | `
Where-Object Title -eq 'Definition Updates'))
$myRule.SetUpdateClassifications($myClass)
```

4. Assign the rule to a computer group:

```
$myGroups = New-Object `
Microsoft.UpdateServices.Administration.
ComputerTargetGroupCollection
$myGroups.Add(($myWsus.GetComputerTargetGroups() | `
Where-Object Name -eq "Domain Controllers"))
$myRule.SetComputerTargetGroups($myGroups)
```

5. Enable and save the rule:

```
$myRule.Enabled = $true
$myRule.Save()
```

6. Review the rules and classifications to confirm the settings:

```
$myWsus.GetInstallApprovalRules()
$myApproval = $myWsus.GetInstallApprovalRules() | `
Where-Object Name -eq 'Critical Updates'
$myApproval.GetUpdateClassifications() | Select-Object Title
$myApproval.GetComputerTargetGroups()
```

When completed, we will see the current rules and target groups as shown in the following screenshot:

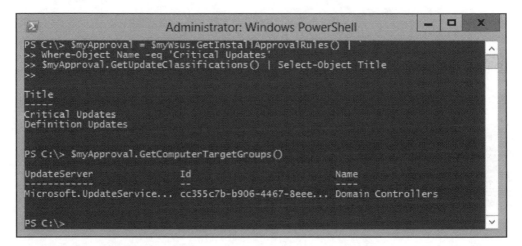

How it works...

We start off by connecting to the update server and calling `CreateInstallApprovalRule` to create our approval rule. In this situation, we name the rule `Critical Updates` because we are creating a rule that will automatically apply all updates classified as critical to a set of computers.

In step 2, we create an installation deadline. The deadline provides a grace period for users and administrators to install the updates manually. If the updates are not installed by the deadline, they will be automatically installed. First, we create an `AutomaticUpdateApprovalDeadline` object. Next, we define the `DayOffset` to identify how many days (3) after the update approval that the update will be forced. Then, we define `MinutesAfterMidnight`, which identifies what time during the day (3 a.m. in our case) the updates will be installed. Then, we apply our new deadline to our approval rule.

Next, we identify what update types we want to be included in our deadline. First we call `GetUpdateClassifications` to get a list of the current update types in our rule and place them into the `$myClass` object. Next, we call `$myClass.Add` in order to add all `Critical Updates` and `Definition Updates` to the classifications. Finally, we use `SetUpdateClassifications` to apply the update classifications to our approval rule.

In step 4, we assign our rule to our computer group. First, we create a `ComputerTargetGroupCollection` object. Then, we use `GetComputerTargetGroups` to list the computer groups and filter on the group name. Finally, we call `SetComputerTargetGroups` to apply the computer groups to our approval rule.

Finally, we call `Enable` and `Save()` to enable and save the rule. Enabling the rule activates it and allows computers to apply the included updates. Saving the rule commits the configurations that we have applied.

When finished, we call `GetInstallApprovalRules` and `GetComputerTargetGroups` to review the new automatic approval rule that we have created and the appropriate configuration.

Reporting missing updates

When managing updates, the first step Windows performs is scanning for reporting on the applicable updates. This is performed automatically by the Windows update client randomly during the day and reported to the update server. However, this process can be manually initiated and the results viewed at the local client.

Getting ready

In this recipe, we will be working with a client that has already been configured with a local update server.

How to do it...

Complete the following steps to report on missing updates:

1. Create the searcher object:

    ```
    $searcher = New-Object -ComObject Microsoft.Update.Searcher
    $searcher.Online = $true
    $searcher.ServerSelection = 1
    ```

2. Define the search criteria:

    ```
    $results = $searcher.Search('IsInstalled=0')
    ```

3. Display the results:

```
$results.Updates | `
Select-Object @{Name="UpdateID"; `
Expression={$_.Identity.UpdateID}}, Title
```

When executed, the list of available updates will be returned as shown in the following screenshot:

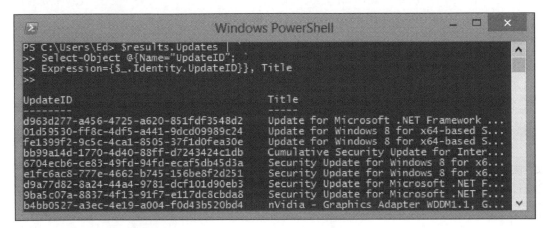

How it works...

PowerShell uses `ComObject` to access the local update client. For the most part, this functions exactly the same way as the managed code objects used for the update server. However, as shown here, they are accessed slightly differently. Once we create the `Microsoft.Update.Searcher` object, we configure the object settings.

 In this example, we are configuring `ServerSelection = 1`, which tells the update client to use the local update server. If we change this to `ServerSelection = 2`, the update client will search against Microsoft's public update servers.

Next, we define our search criteria and begin scanning by calling `$searcher.Search`. In this example we use the simple criteria of `IsInstalled=0`, to show updates that are applicable to the system. The results of the searcher are saved to a `$results` variable. This criteria can be modified to scan for specific updates, certain types of updates, or updates for specific products.

Lastly, we call `$results.Updates` to return a report of all applicable updates for the system. Here we are returning the basic information about the updates; however, more information can be returned, depending upon your needs.

There's more...

All update client activity for a system is tracked in a central log file at `C:\Windows\WindowsUpdate.log`. This log file is useful for viewing the activity of the update client and confirming the functionality of the system.

There are several utilities that will allow you to view the log file live as it is updated. An example of one such utility is shown in the following screenshot:

Log Text
2012-11-2014:50:38:83810049ccAU##############
2012-11-2014:55:16:73210046e0EPGot WSUS Client/Server URL: "http://update.corp.contoso.com:8530/ClientWebService/client.asmx"
2012-11-2014:55:16:73210046e0PTWARNING: Cached cookie has expired or new PID is available
2012-11-2014:55:16:73210046e0EPGot WSUS SimpleTargeting URL: "http://update.corp.contoso.com:8530"
2012-11-2014:55:16:73210046e0PTInitializing simple targeting cookie, clientId = 0e4ef7d9-96a2-4d12-9d14-eb0804c0d1cf, target group = , DNS
2012-11-2014:55:16:73210046e0PT Server URL = http://update.corp.contoso.com:8530/SimpleAuthWebService/SimpleAuth.asmx
2012-11-2014:55:17:07010046e0EPGot WSUS Reporting URL: "http://update.corp.contoso.com:8530/ReportingWebService/ReportingWebS
2012-11-2014:55:17:07010046e0Report Uploading 6 events using cached cookie, reporting URL = http://update.corp.contoso.com:8530/Repoi
2012-11-2014:55:17:61710046e0Report Reporter successfully uploaded 6 events.
2012-11-2015:06:24:79610046e0ReportWARNING: CSerializationHelper:: InitSerialize failed : 0x80070002
2012-11-2015:08:25:78410049ccAU############## AU: Uninitializing Automatic Updates ###############
2012-11-2015:08:26:82110049ccWuTaskUninit WU Task Manager
2012-11-2015:08:27:08610049ccAgentSending shutdown notification to client
2012-11-2015:08:27:0863360584COMAPIWARNING: Received service shutdown/self-update notification.
2012-11-2015:08:27:11710049ccService*********
2012-11-2015:08:27:11710049ccService** END ** Service: Service exit [Exit code = 0x240001]
2012-11-2015:08:27:11710049ccService**************

Installing updates

Once the applicable updates are identified, the next step for managing updates on the client is to install the updates themselves. This process involves confirming the updates are necessary, downloading the updates, and installing the updates.

Getting ready

This recipe is similar to the prior recipe in that it starts by searching for missing updates on the local system. This list of missing updates is then used to initiate the download and installation of these updates.

How to do it...

The updates can be installed through the following steps:

1. Set up the necessary update client objects:

    ```
    $searcher = New-Object -ComObject Microsoft.Update.Searcher
    $updateCollection = New-Object -ComObject Microsoft.Update.
    UpdateColl
    $session = New-Object -ComObject Microsoft.Update.Session
    $installer = New-Object -ComObject Microsoft.Update.Installer
    ```

2. Search for missing updates:

    ```
    $searcher.online=$true
    $searcher.ServerSelection=1
    $results = $searcher.Search("IsInstalled=0")
    ```

3. Create a collection of applicable updates:

    ```
    $updates=$results.Updates
    ForEach($update in $updates){ $updateCollection.Add($update) }
    ```

4. Download the updates:

    ```
    $downloader = $session.CreateUpdateDownloader()
    $downloader.Updates = $updateCollection
    $downloader.Download()
    ```

5. Install the updates:

    ```
    $installer.Updates = $updateCollection
    $installer.Install()
    ```

How it works...

We start by creating four objects to be used by the update client. The $searcher object is the same as in the prior recipe and is responsible for searching for applicable updates. The $updateCollection object will hold information about the applicable updates and their install information. The $session object will handle the downloading of updates. And the $installer object performs the installation of the updates.

In step 2, we search for the applicable updates. The search command is the same as in the prior recipe.

> Sometimes it is only desired to install a specific update on a system. To accomplish this, we can use the *Reporting missing updates* recipe to identify the appropriate `UpdateID`. We then change the search command to the following using appropriate `UpdateID` as shown:
>
> ```
> $Results = $Searcher.Search("UpdateID='6965f95b-2b79-
> 4a6e-b4d1-d500c30e8c8e'")
> ```

We then use a `ForEach` loop to cycle through each applicable update. These updates are then added to the `$updateCollection` object in preparation for download and installation.

In step 4, we download all applicable updates to the system. We start by calling `$session.CreateUpdateDownloader` to create our downloader. We then add `$updateCollection` to our downloader to identify which updates to include. Lastly, we call `Download()` to begin downloading the updates. This uses the same download process as the native update client, and automatically utilizes the included bandwidth protection and dynamic downloads provided by the client.

Lastly, we install the updates. This starts by loading `$upateCollection` into `$installer` object to identify the updates to install. We then call `Install()` to begin the update installation. This will automatically install the updates in the appropriate order necessary to ensure any dependencies are met. When finished installing, a return code and notification of a pending reboot will be reported, as shown in the following screenshot:

```
HResult                      RebootRequired                      ResultCode
-------                      --------------                      ----------
2359299                                True                               3
```

In this result, we see that the update installation completed with `RebootRequired` set to `True`. In order for the updates to complete the installation, we need to reboot our server. Additionally, the installation returned a `ResultCode` of 3, meaning the installation succeeded with errors. Following are the possible `ResultCodes` and their meanings:

Result Code	Description
0	Not started
1	In progress
2	Succeeded
3	Succeeded with errors
4	Failed
5	Aborted

There's more...

Sometimes Microsoft releases updates, such as Service Packs, that cannot be installed at the same time as other updates. Because of this, the first set of updates must be installed, the system rebooted, and then additional updates can be installed.

If you are unsure of the updates applicable to a system, and you are installing all applicable updates, it is suggested that you run the install multiple times. The multiple executions, with reboots in between, will ensure that all applicable updates are installed.

Uninstalling updates

In addition to installing updates, PowerShell and the Windows update client can also uninstall updates. This is occasionally necessary when an installed update causes an unexpected result or compatibility issue.

The uninstall process for updates is similar to the installation process. The main difference here is that we are searching for only one update or a subset of updates, and then calling the `UnInstall` command.

Getting ready

In this recipe, we are working with a Windows client that has installed updates. We have already identified that we wish to uninstall the update titled **Update for Office File Validation 2010 (KB2553065), 64-bit Edition**.

How to do it...

Carry out the following steps to uninstall the updates:

1. List the installed updates to identify which update will be removed:

```
$searcher = New-Object -ComObject Microsoft.Update.Searcher
$searcher.Online = $true
$searcher.ServerSelection = 1
$results = $searcher.Search('IsInstalled=1')
$results.Updates | `
Select-Object @{Name="UpdateID"; `
Expression={$_.Identity.UpdateID}}, Title
```

When executed, the currently installed updates and update IDs are returned as shown in the following screenshot:

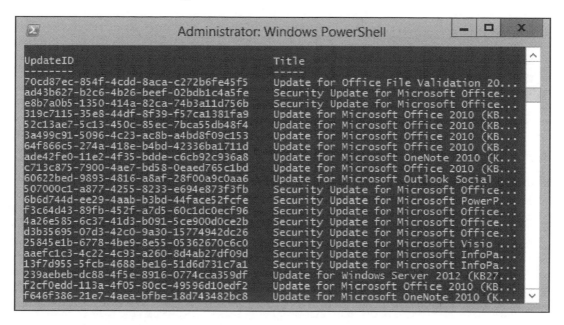

2. Setup the necessary update client objects:

```
$updateCollection = New-Object -ComObject Microsoft.Update.
UpdateColl
$installer = New-Object -ComObject Microsoft.Update.Installer
```

3. Search for the appropriate update by UpdateID:

```
$searcher.online = $true
$searcher.ServerSelection = 1
$results = $searcher.Search("UpdateID='70cd87ec-854f-4cdd-8aca-
c272b6fe45f5'")
```

4. Create a collection of applicable updates:

```
$updates = $results.Updates
ForEach($update in $updates){ $updateCollection.Add($update) }
```

5. Uninstall the updates:

```
$installer.Updates = $updateCollection
$installer.UnInstall()
```

How it works...

We start by searching for the installed updates on our system. This is the same process as the *Reporting missing updates* recipe, except this time the $searcher.Search string is changed to 'IsInstalled = 1' to return the updates already installed. We then search the results for Update ID matching the update "Update for Office File Validation 2010 (KB2553065), 64-bit Edition". In this case the first result in the list is the update that we are interested in with UpdateID of 70cd87ec-854f-4cdd-8aca-c272b6fe45f5.

We next create the additional objects to be used by the update client to uninstall the update. The $UpdateCollection object will hold information about the applicable updates and their install information. The $Installer object performs the uninstallation of the updates.

In step 3, we perform the search again, this time limiting our query to the appropriate Update ID. We save the results of the search into our $results variable.

Lastly, we create a collection for the updates and initiate the installer with the Uninstall() command. This performs the uninstall of the update.

There's more...

In addition to the PowerShell commands shown here, we can also use the **Windows Update Standalone Installer** command-line tool WUSA.exe included with Windows. The Windows Update Standalone Installer is a stand-alone tool that can be used to install and uninstall updates on a client.

To uninstall an update, open a command prompt with administrative credentials and execute WUSA /Uninstall /KB:<kb number>. For example:

```
wusa /uninstall /kb:2553065
```

Configuring WSUS to inventory clients

In addition to scanning and reporting on client updates, Windows Server Update Services can also report on the hardware and software inventory included in a system. While this won't provide a complete asset inventory of your environment, it does provide up-to-date information of your systems.

The Windows update client uses multiple methods (WMI queries, registry keys, file versions) to scan for applicable updates. Once scanned, the results are reported to the update server for reporting purposes.

The Windows update server includes a set of additional WMI queries that can be enabled to report on the hardware and software on client computers. This information is scanned by the client and reported back to the server. There are no built-in reports to display this information, but once enabled, we can query the database directly.

Getting ready

In this recipe we will be using a WSUS server that is configured with one or more clients.

How to do it...

Perform the following to begin collecting the client inventory:

1. Configure the update server to collect the inventory:

```
$wuConfig = $myWsus.GetConfiguration()
$wuConfig.CollectClientInventory = $true
$wuConfig.Save()
```

2. Initiate a scan on a client:

```
Wuauclt /detectnow
```

How it works...

We start on the update server and configure it to collect the client inventory. We start by getting the current server configuration and placing it in the $wuConfig variable. Then, we set the CollectClientInventory attribute to $true. Lastly, we commit the configuration back to the server.

During a client's next polling cycle, it will automatically detect the updated configuration. However, we can manually force a client to update by using Wuauclt.exe, in order to confirm that the process is working properly.

WSUS instructs clients to inventory the following WMI classes:

- ▶ Win32_Processor
- ▶ Win32_BIOS
- ▶ Win32_PCMCIAController
- ▶ Win32_OperatingSystem
- ▶ Win32_DiskDrive
- ▶ Win32_LogicalDisk
- ▶ Win32_NetworkAdapterConfiguration
- ▶ Win32_NetworkAdapter
- ▶ Win32_SoundDevice
- ▶ Win32_VideoController
- ▶ Win32_DesktopMonitor

- ▶ `Win32_ComputerSystem`
- ▶ `Win32_Printer`
- ▶ `WsusInternal_ARP`

There's more...

Troubleshooting this inventory process can be difficult as it involves the Windows update server, the update client, HTTP, WMI, and the system's registry. Following is an excerpt of the `WindowsUpdate.log` file on a client, showing the start of the inventory collection process:

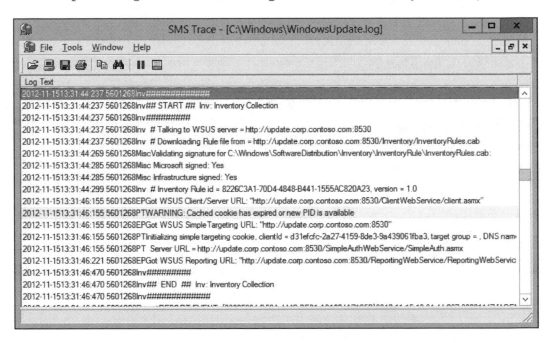

As we can see from the screenshot, we can confirm that the inventory process started and completed successfully. The client has contacted the server and downloaded the `InventoryRules.cab` file, which contains the instructions on what to inventory. The client performs the inventory process and identifies the WSUS reporting URL to send the results. Later in the log file, we can see the results being sent to the WSUS system.

See also

- ▶ The *Exporting WSUS data to Excel* recipe
- ▶ The *Creating an update report* recipe

Creating an update report

Windows update server contains multiple built-in reports that provide administrators with many of the details needed to perform their jobs. However, rare cases do exist where the built-in reports don't fit your specific needs and a custom report must be created.

One example of needing a custom report is searching for systems missing a certain update. This report could then be automatically processed by a script that would initiate installation of the updates on the clients. Using PowerShell, this process can be done in a single step.

In this recipe, we will be directly querying the WSUS database on the update server by using PowerShell. We will be using a SQL query to generate our custom report and then returning the information back to PowerShell as `DataSet`.

Getting ready

In this recipe, we will be working with a WSUS server with one or more clients. Specifically, we will be querying the **Windows Internal Database** which is used by the default installation of WSUS.

How to do it...

An update report can be created by using the following steps:

1. Define the server and database:

   ```
   $serverInstance = '\\.\pipe\MICROSOFT##WID\tsql\query'
   $database = "SUSDB"
   $connectionTimeout = 30
   $queryTimeout = 120
   ```

    In this step, `$serverInstance` is referring to the Windows Internal Database location used by WSUS by default. If you chose to use a separate SQL database during installation of WSUS, change the variable to the necessary connect string.

2. Define the query:

   ```
   $query= "select ct.FullDomainName, ct.IPAddress
   , ic.Name, ici.KeyValue, ip.Name, ipi.Value
   FROM tbComputerTarget ct
   INNER JOIN tbInventoryClassInstance ici on ici.TargetID=ct.
   TargetID
   INNER JOIN tbInventoryClass ic on ic.ClassID=ici.ClassID
   INNER JOIN tbInventoryPropertyInstance ipi on
   ```

```
ipi.ClassInstanceID=ici.ClassInstanceID
INNER JOIN tbInventoryProperty ip on ip.PropertyID=ipi.PropertyID"
```

3. Connect to the server:

```
$conn = New-Object System.Data.SqlClient.SQLConnection
$connectionString = "Server={0};Database={1};Integrated
Security=True;Connect Timeout={2}" `
-f $serverInstance, $database, $connectionTimeout
$conn.ConnectionString = $connectionString
$conn.Open()
```

4. Query the database:

```
$cmd = New-Object System.Data.SqlClient.SqlCommand($query,$conn)
$cmd.CommandTimeout=$queryTimeout
$da = New-Object System.Data.SqlClient.SqlDataAdapter($cmd)
```

5. Display the results:

```
$ds = New-Object system.Data.DataSet
[void]$da.fill($ds)
$conn.Close()
$ds.Tables | Format-Table
```

When executed, the client inventory will be displayed as shown in the following screenshot:

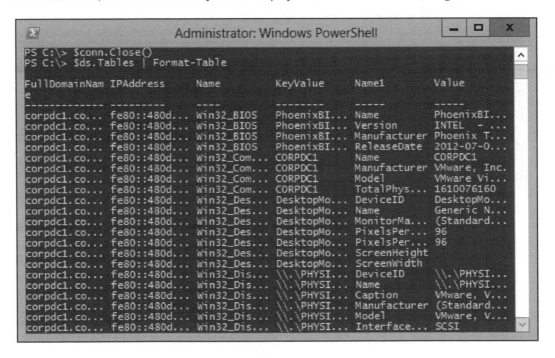

How it works...

We start by logging on to the update server and defining our database connection. If you used the default update server installation, then you are using the Windows Internal Database. This database can only be accessed from the local server and it requires a specially-crafted connection string as shown.

 If you are using a full version of SQL, then the connection can be performed remotely and you don't have to log on locally. Your DBA should be able to help with the necessary connection string.

Next, we define our SQL query. The query shown is somewhat complex, but will return all of the inventory information in the database (updates, hardware, and software) for all systems managed by the update server. This is a good starting point to see what information is available in your system.

In step 3, we connect to the SQL database. We start by creating a SQLConnection object named $conn that is capable of accessing a SQL server. We then define the $connectionString, which is used to select which server, which database, and how to authenticate to the system. We add $connectionString to our $conn object and call Open() to open our connection.

Next, we execute our query in the database. We create a SQLCommand object named $cmd that contains the SQL query that we had defined and connection object previously created. Then, we create a SqlDataAdapter object, $da, and execute the SQL query.

Finally, we return the results. First we create a DataSet object, $ds, and fill it with the results from the SqlDataAdapter object. The SQL connection is closed, and then the contents of $ds is displayed on the screen.

There's more...

One request that administrators often receive is for a report of the software installed in the environment. If the update server is configured to inventory the clients, as shown in the *Configuring WSUS to inventory clients* recipe, then this information can easily be retrieved.

To report on the installed software, we update the SQL query to the following:

```
$query= "Select DISTINCT ct.FullDomainName
, (Select TOP 1 i2.Value FROM tbInventoryPropertyInstance i2 WHERE
i2.ClassInstanceID = i1.ClassInstanceID AND i2.PropertyID = 98)
'DisplayName'
, (Select TOP 1 i2.Value FROM tbInventoryPropertyInstance i2 WHERE
i2.ClassInstanceID = i1.ClassInstanceID AND i2.PropertyID = 99)
'DisplayVersion'
, (Select TOP 1 i2.Value FROM tbInventoryPropertyInstance i2 WHERE
i2.ClassInstanceID = i1.ClassInstanceID AND i2.PropertyID = 101)
'Publisher'
FROM tbInventoryPropertyInstance i1
INNER JOIN tbInventoryClassInstance ici on i1.ClassInstanceID =
ici.ClassInstanceID
INNER JOIN tbComputerTarget ct on ici.TargetID = ct.TargetID
WHERE (Select TOP 1 i2.Value FROM tbInventoryPropertyInstance i2
WHERE i2.ClassInstanceID = i1.ClassInstanceID AND i2.PropertyID =
98) is not null"
```

The following screenshot is an example of the query in my test lab:

```
PS C:\> $ds.Tables | ft

FullDomainName      DisplayName       DisplayVersion    Publisher
--------------      -----------       --------------    ---------
corpdc1.corp.con... Microsoft Visual... 9.0.30729.4148  Microsoft Corpor...
corpdc1.corp.con... Microsoft Visual... 9.0.30729.4148  Microsoft Corpor...
corpdc1.corp.con... VMware Tools        9.2.0.15626     VMware, Inc.
update.corp.cont... Microsoft Visio ... 15.0.4420.1017  Microsoft Corpor...
update.corp.cont... Microsoft Visual... 9.0.30729.4148  Microsoft Corpor...
update.corp.cont... Microsoft Visual... 9.0.30729.4148  Microsoft Corpor...
update.corp.cont... VMware Tools        9.2.0.15626     VMware, Inc.
```

See also

For more information about accessing the WSUS Windows Internal Database, see `http://blogs.technet.com/b/gborger/archive/2009/02/27/exploring-the-wsus-windows-internal-database.aspx`.

Exporting WSUS data to Excel

In addition to generating update reports in PowerShell, the results can also be exported into Excel or other tools. By exporting the update or inventory reports to Excel, we can use a familiar tool to view, filter, and display the information in ways that are useful to us.

Getting ready

In this recipe, we will be using the process in the prior recipe to query the update server database. We will then return the resulting dataset and export it into a format that Excel can utilize.

How to do it...

Carry out the following steps to export WSUS data to Excel:

1. Create the dataset object. This is the same process as the *Creating an update report* recipe.

2. Export the dataset to an XML file:

   ```
   $ds.Tables[0].WriteXml("C:\temp\inventory.xml")
   ```

3. Open the XML file with Excel:

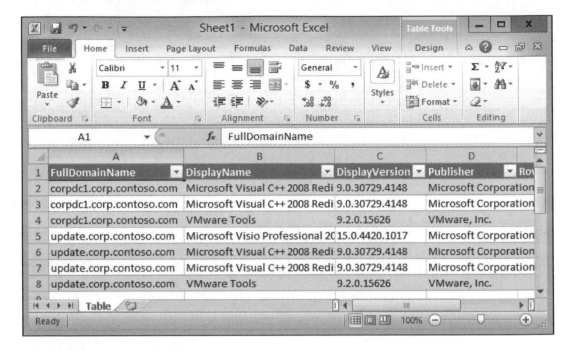

How it works...

We start by collecting the inventory information as in the prior recipe. Once the database has been queried, it returns a dataset object, which is capable of hosting multiple tables. We instruct PowerShell to return only the first table ($ds.Tables[0]) and then convert the contents to an XML file.

Next, we open the XML file in Microsoft Excel. We can accomplish this by using **File | Open** on the menu bar or simply drag-and-drop the XML file into Excel. You may be prompted regarding how to open the XML file (shown in the following screenshot). Select **As an XML table** and click on **OK**. Once opened, you can save the file as a standard Excel document.

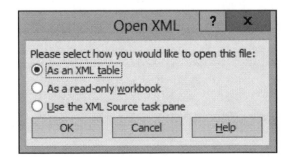

There's more...

Another method of exporting the data to Excel is to use the `Export-Excel.ps1` PowerShell script from `http://www.powershellcommunity.org/Forums/tabid/54/aft/8420/Default.aspx`. This script accepts a dataset object as a parameter and creates an Excel document. Unlike the `WriteXML` method, this script is capable of handling datasets with multiple tables. Each table in the dataset will be displayed as a separate sheet in Excel.

To use this script, download the script on the page and save it as a PS1 file. Query the database and reference the dataset object as shown in the following command:

```
Export-Excel.ps1 $ds
```

This command functions similar to the XML method; however, it interacts directly with Excel. Because of this, the script requires Excel to be installed on the local computer, which may not be ideal in a production environment.

8

Managing Printers with PowerShell

This chapter covers the following recipes:

- ▸ Setting up and sharing printers
- ▸ Changing printer drivers
- ▸ Reporting on printer security
- ▸ Adding and removing printer security
- ▸ Mapping clients to printers
- ▸ Enabling Branch Office Direct Printing
- ▸ Reporting on printer usage

Introduction

From an architectural standpoint, there have been major changes in Server 2012. New in Server 2012 is the inclusion of Version 4 drivers, which greatly improves the installation and support of printers and removes the need for cross-platform drivers. There are now two types of printer drivers available: printer class and model-specific. Printer class drivers support a wide range of devices with a single driver. Model-specific drivers are often distributed by the printer manufacturer and support features specific to the printer.

Additionally in Server 2012, the print server no longer is used to distribute print drivers to clients. Instead, clients use a point and print feature to send print jobs to the server. If print drivers are desired on the clients, administrators can use software distribution methods to install the driver on these clients.

This chapter covers installing, managing, and updating printers on print servers. This includes using PowerShell to map clients to printers, and generating usage reports for the printers.

Setting up and sharing printers

When setting up a print environment, often one of the first steps is to set up a print server. The print server allows for a centralized location to configure and manage printers, change configurations, and distribute print drivers. Additionally, a print server provides end users with a single location in which to look for available printers, and automatically apply drivers and administrative changes.

In this recipe, we will be setting up a print server to manage several network-based printers. We will configure the server to share the printers to clients.

Getting ready

In this recipe, we will be using a Windows Server 2012 server to function as our print server. Additionally, we will be accessing and sharing an HP LaserJet 9000 printer. The printer is already assigned the IP of `10.0.0.200`.

How to do it...

Carry out the following steps to install and share a printer:

1. Install the print server:

    ```
    Add-WindowsFeature Print-Server -IncludeManagementTools
    ```

2. Create the printer port:

    ```
    Add-PrinterPort -Name Accounting_HP -PrinterHostAddress
    "10.0.0.200"
    ```

3. Add the print driver:

    ```
    Add-PrinterDriver -Name "HP LaserJet 9000 PCL6 Class Driver"
    ```

4. Add the printer:

    ```
    Add-Printer -Name "Accounting HP" -DriverName "HP LaserJet 9000
    PCL6 Class Driver" -PortName Accounting_HP
    ```

5. Share the printer:

    ```
    Set-Printer -Name "Accounting HP" -Shared $true -Published $true
    ```

6. Review the printers to confirm the process:

```
Get-Printer | Format-Table -AutoSize
```

When executed, the currently installed printers will be displayed as shown in the following screenshot:

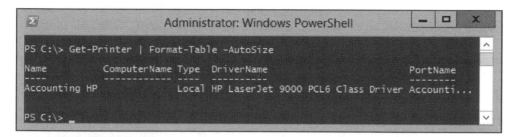

How it works...

We start by adding the `Print-Server` feature to our print server. Along with the print server role, this includes the Print Management tool and PowerShell cmdlets.

In step 2, we use `Add-PrinterPort` to create a port for the printer. Here, we are targeting an IP-based network printer at `10.0.0.200`. We provide the name `Accounting_HP` as an easily recognizable name so that we can easily find it later.

Next, we call `Add-PrinterDriver` to install the driver. This process installs the driver onto the server, however, the driver won't be used until it is configured for a printer.

 It is best practice to only use the print drivers built-in to Windows or provided via Windows Update. Custom drivers provided by vendors may provide more functionality, but in environments with many different types of printers they can cause conflicts.

In step 4, we use `Add-Printer` to add the printer to the print server. This process pairs the printer port, `Accounting_HP`, with the print driver, and defines the printer name of `Accounting HP`. At this point, the printer is functional; however, print jobs can only be sent from the print server.

Lastly, we use `Set-Printer` in order to share the printer. By setting the `-Shared` switch to `$true`, the other users on the network will be able to send print jobs to the printer. By setting the `-Published` switch to `$true`, the printer is published in Active Directory for clients to more easily find the printer.

Changing printer drivers

Occasionally, print drivers need to be upgraded or changed for some reason. When using a print server, this is significantly simpler because the print server holds the printer driver, which means that we do not need to install the driver on all of the client machines.

In this example, we will be changing the print driver from a `PCL6` driver to a `PS` driver for the same model printer as used in the previous recipe.

Getting ready

In this recipe, we will update the driver of the printer created in the preceding *Setting up and sharing printers* recipe.

How to do it...

To change the print driver, perform the following steps.

1. Install the print driver:

   ```
   Add-PrinterDriver -name "HP LaserJet 9000 PS Class Driver"
   ```

2. List the installed printers to determine the name needed:

   ```
   Get-Printer
   ```

When executed, the currently installed printers will be displayed as shown in the following screenshot:

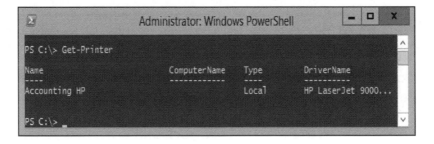

1. Change the driver:

   ```
   Get-Printer -Name "Accounting HP" | Set-Printer -DriverName "HP
   LaserJet 9000 PS Class Driver"
   ```

2. Confirm the printer is using the new driver:

   ```
   Get-Printer | Format-Table –AutoSize
   ```

When executed, the currently installed printers will be displayed as shown in the following screenshot:

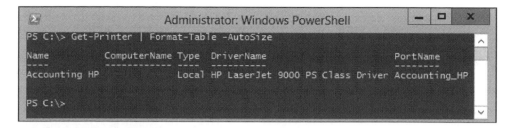

How it works...

We start by using `Add-PrinterDriver` to install our new print driver. This process is the same as we used in the *Setting up and sharing printers* recipe when installing the printer and simply adds the printer driver to the print server.

In step 2, we use `Get-Printer` to find our target printer and change the driver. This command lists all of the installed printers on the system and helps confirm the name of the printer that we need to change to change.

Next, we call `Get-Printer` and select our printer by name. We then use the `Set-Printer` command with the `-DriverName` switch to define the new driver for our printer.

Lastly, we call `Get-Printer` again to review the new configuration. As we can see in the image, the printer is now using the "HP LaserJet 9000 PS Class" driver.

The next time clients connect to the print server, the printer configuration on the client will be updated and the clients will utilize the features of the new driver.

Reporting on printer security

When sharing printers, the default configuration is to allow all domain users to print to all printers. Occasionally this is not a desired configuration as there may be special-purpose printers or printers in restricted areas.

To manage this need, we can apply security on the printers themselves to limit which users can perform various functions. We can use permissions to restrict who can print to specific printers, or delegate administrative permissions to certain users.

In this recipe we will report on the printer security on the print server. This will iterate through each printer on the server and return the security attributes assigned to each user.

Getting ready

For this recipe we will be accessing a Server 2012 print server with one or more printers installed and shared.

How to do it...

Perform the following steps to view the printer security:

1. Create a hash table containing printer permissions:

```
$pace = DATA {
ConvertFrom-StringData -StringData @'
131072 = ReadPermissions
131080 = Print
262144 = ChangePermissions
524288 = TakeOwnership
983052 = ManagePrinters
983088 = ManageDocuments
'@
}
```

2. Create an array of available permissions:

```
$flags = @(131072,131080,262144,524288,983052,983088)
```

3. Return a list of all printers:

```
$myPrinters = Get-WmiObject -Class Win32_Printer
ForEach ($printer in $myPrinters){
Write-Host "`nPrinter: $($printer.DeviceId)"
```

4. Get the **Security Descriptor** and **Discretionary Access Control Lists** (**DACL**) for each printer:

```
$sd = $printer.GetSecurityDescriptor()
$myDACLs = $sd.Descriptor.DACL
ForEach ($dacl in $myDACLs) {
```

5. Iterate through each DACL and return:

```
Write-Host "`n$($dacl.Trustee.Domain)\$($dacl.Trustee.Name)"
ForEach ($flag in $flags){
If ($dacl.AccessMask -cge $flag){
Write-Host $pace["$($flag)"]
```

```
            }
        }
    }
}
```

When executed, the security permissions will be returned as shown in the following screenshot:

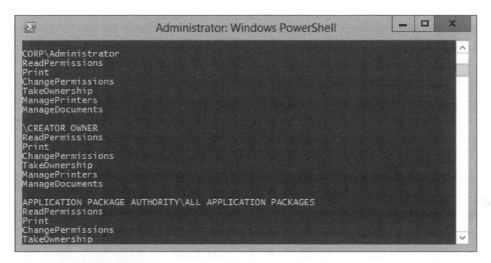

How it works...

We start in the first two steps by creating a hash table and array. The $pace hash table allows us to perform lookups between the decimal permissions used by the server and the human-readable text. The $flags array provides a lookup method to compare permissions.

In step 3, we call Get-WmiObject to query WMI and return a list of all printers on the local system. We store the printers into the $myPrinters variable and use a ForEach loop to cycle through each printer. We start the loop by calling Write-Host to write the printer name to the console.

Next, we retrieve the security objects from each printer. We start by executing the GetSecurityDescriptor on the printer object and store the security descriptor in the variable $sd. We then extract the DACLs from the descriptor and use a ForEach loop to cycle through them.

Lastly, in step 5, we return the assigned permissions. We start by writing out the user domain and name from the DACL. We then use another ForEach loop to iterate through our $flags array and perform a binary comparison between the DACL permissions and the values in the array. If a comparison is successful, we return the human-readable permission to the console.

Adding and removing printer security

Printer security allows for access to a printer to be restricted or for management of the printer to be delegated. By restricting access, only specific users or groups can be allowed to view or print to a specific printer. By delegating access, management of the printer can be provied to local administrators or power users to manage the printer and print jobs.

For applying permissions to a shared printer on a print server, Server 2012 uses the **Security Definition Description Language (SDDL)**. The SDDL allows an administrator to define or review the **Access Control Lists (ACL)** placed on an object in the form of a string, instead of different objects.

In this recipe we will update the security for a previously created printer. In this situation we will be restricting access to the printer to only the Domain Administrators and the users included in a specific security group. The Domain Admins will retain Full Control of the printer object, while the security group Accounting Users will only be allowed Print permission to the printer.

Getting ready

In this recipe, we will be working with the print server and printer created in the *Setting up and sharing printers* recipe.

How to do it...

Perform the following steps to change the security on a printer:

1. Retrieve the SID for the user/group being granted permissions:

    ```
    $User = "CORP\Accounting Users"

    $UserSID = (new-object security.principal.ntaccount $User).
    Translate([security.principal.securityidentifier]).Value
    ```

2. Construct the Security Descriptor Definition Language (SDDL):

    ```
    $SDDL = "O:BAG:DUD:PAI(A;OICI;FA;;;DA)(A;OICI;0x3D8F8;;;$UserSID)"
    ```

3. Retrieve the printer object:

    ```
    $myPrinter = Get-Printer -Name "Accounting HP"
    ```

4. Set the permissions:

    ```
    $myPrinter | Set-Printer -PermissionSDDL $SDDL
    ```

5. Use the script in the recipe *Reporting on printer security* to confirm the new printer permissions.

When executed, the new permissions will be displayed as shown in the following screenshot:

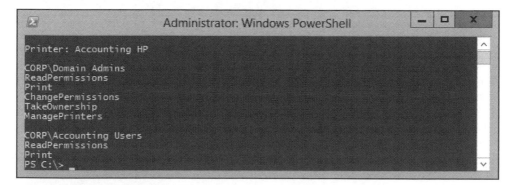

```
Printer: Accounting HP

CORP\Domain Admins
ReadPermissions
Print
ChangePermissions
TakeOwnership
ManagePrinters

CORP\Accounting Users
ReadPermissions
Print
PS C:\>
```

How it works...

We start by retrieving the Security ID, or SID, of the user or group being granted permissions. We first create a `Security.Principal.NtAccount` object for our target user. We then translate the account object into a `Security.Principal.SecurityIdentifier` object. Lastly, we return the `SID` value and store it in the `$userSID` variable.

Next, we construct our SDDL. An SDDL is a Security Descriptor Definition Language that allows us to describe our security settings in a string form. The permissions are stored inside the braces –"(" and ")" –and in this instance we are defining two sets of permissions: the first provides `full control` to the `Domain Administrators`, and the second provides `Print` and `Read` permissions to our group `CORP\Accounting Users`.

Next we get our printer object. Finally, we use `Set-Printer` to apply the permissions.

> This method replaces all existing permissions on the printer. Care should be taken whenever using this script in a production environment.

There's more...

More information about the makeup of SDDLs can be found at `http://blogs.technet.com/b/askds/archive/2008/05/07/the-security-descriptor-definition-language-of-love-part-2.aspx`.

Mapping clients to printers

With Server 2012, there are two automated methods of mapping clients to printers: logon script and Group Policy. Logon scripts are the traditional deployment method for printers and have been used since the early days of Windows NT. The scripts can be customized based on users, groups, AD sites, and more. Group Policies are a newer method of configuring printers and utilize the existing OU infrastructure in your organization.

In this recipe, we will cover the various built-in methods of configuring printers via a logon script. Each method has benefits and drawbacks, and your choice will likely depend on your environment. We will show how to map printers using the following methods:

- `Printui.dll`
- WMI
- WScript

Getting ready

For this recipe we will be working on a client system, mapping to a shared printer on our print server. In this recipe we will be referencing the print server `PrntSrv` and the printer `Accounting HP`.

How to do it...

Perform the following steps to begin mapping printers:

1. Map a printer by using `Printui.dll`:

   ```
   $PrinterPath = "\\PrntSrv\Accounting HP"
   rundll32.exe printui.dll,PrintUIEntry /q /in /n$PrinterPath
   ```

2. Set the default printer by using `Printui.dll`:

   ```
   $PrinterPath = "\\PrntSrv\Accounting HP"
   rundll32 printui.dll,PrintUIEntry /y /n$PrinterPath
   ```

3. Delete a printer by using `Printui.dll`:

   ```
   $PrinterPath = "\\PrntSrv\Accounting HP"
   rundll32.exe printui.dll,PrintUIEntry /q /dn /n$PrinterPath
   ```

4. Map a printer by using WMI:

   ```
   $PrinterPath = "\\PrntSrv\Accounting HP"
   ([wmiclass]"Win32_Printer").AddPrinterConnection($PrinterPath)
   ```

5. Set the default printer by using WMI:

```
$PrinterPath = "\\PrntSrv\Accounting HP"
$filter = "DeviceID='$($PrinterPath.Replace('\','\\'))'"
(Get-WmiObject -Class Win32_Printer -Filter $filter).
SetDefaultPrinter()
```

6. Remove a printer by using WMI:

```
$PrinterPath = "\\PrntSrv\Accounting HP"
$filter = "DeviceID='$($PrinterPath.Replace('\','\\'))'"
(Get-WmiObject -Class Win32_Printer -Filter $filter).Delete()
```

7. Map a printer by using WScript

```
$PrinterPath = "\\PrntSrv\Accounting HP"
(New-Object -ComObject WScript.Network).AddWindowsPrinterConnectio
n($PrinterPath)
```

8. Set the default printer by using WScript:

```
$PrinterPath = "\\PrntSrv\Accounting HP"
(New-Object -ComObject WScript.Network).
SetDefaultPrinter($PrinterPath)
```

9. Remove a printer by using WScript:

```
$PrinterPath = "\\PrntSrv\Accounting HP"
(New-Object -ComObject WScript.Network).RemovePrinterConnection($P
rinterPath)
```

How it works...

We start by using `Printui.dll` to map and manage network printers. `Printui.dll` is the library used by Windows to manage printers and view the print server properties; with this dll we can view the printers and drivers, add and remove printers, start the add printer wizard, and do many other tasks. We access the dll functions by using `rundll32.exe`.

In step 1, we map a network printer. We start by defining the UNC path to the target printer as `\\PrntSrv\Accounting HP`. Next we call `rundll32.exe printui.dll` with the `/q`, `/in`, and `/n` switches. The `/q` switch tells the system to perform the task quietly and not to show an interface. The `/in` switch tells the system to add a network printer. And the `/n` switch identifies the UNC path of the target printer.

Next, we define our printer as the default printer. Again we call `rundll32.exe printui.dll`, but this time using the `/y` and `/n` switches. The `/y` switch tells the system to define a printer as the default, and the `/n` switch identifies the UNC path of the target printer.

In step 3, we delete a network printer. We call `rundll32.exe printui.dll` with the /q, /dn, and /n switches. The /q switch tells the system to perform the task quietly and not to show an interface. The /dn switch tells the system to delete a network printer. The /n switch identifies the UNC path of the target printer.

> There are many additional options for using `PrintUI.dll` that can be found by opening a Command Prompt and executing `rundll32.exe printui.dll,PrintUIEntry`.

Next, starting with step 4, we perform the same tasks, but this time using WMI. We map a new printer by first defining the UNC path to the target printer. Next, we create a `wmiclass` reference to the `Win32_Printer` class. With the WMI reference, we can execute the `AddPrinterConnection` method and pass the printer UNC path as a parameter.

In step 5, we define our printer as the default printer. We start by defining the UNC path to the target printer. Next, we create a WMI filter based on the `DeviceID` of the WMI object. The `DeviceID` is essentially the same as the UNC path. However, because WMI uses the \ character as an escape character, we have to replace every backslash with two backslashes. We then call `Get-WmiObject` to query the `Win32_Printer` class using our filter to return the printer object. Lastly, we execute the `SetDefaultPrinter` method to set our printer as the default.

In step 6, we delete the printer. This process starts the same as when we set a printer as the default printer. However, in this case, we execute the `Delete` method to remove the network printer from our client.

In steps 7 through 9 we perform the same tasks again, but this time using WScript. In step 7 we start mapping a printer by defining the UNC path of the target printer. Next we create a `WScript.Network` ComObject. Using this object, we execute the `AddWindowsPrinterConnection` method and pass the printer UNC path as an attribute.

In steps 8 and 9, we set our printer as the default printer and remove printers. These methods are the same as mapping a printer except they use the `SetDefaultPrinter` and `RemovePrinterConnection` methods respectively.

There's more...

Printers can also be mapped to users and computers by using Group Policies. Depending on your environment this may be a preferred method for deploying printers; however, much of the deployment process is manual and cannot currently be managed via PowerShell.

1. Create a new group policy and link it to the domain, site, or appropriate OU:

```
New-GPO -Name "Accounting Print"
New-GPLink -Name "Accounting Print" -Target corp
```

2. Open the **Print Management** console.

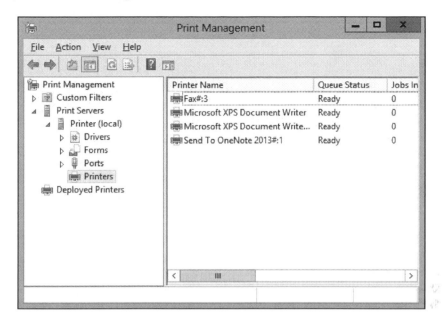

3. Right-click on the printer and select **Deploy with Group Policy...** as shown in the following screenshot:

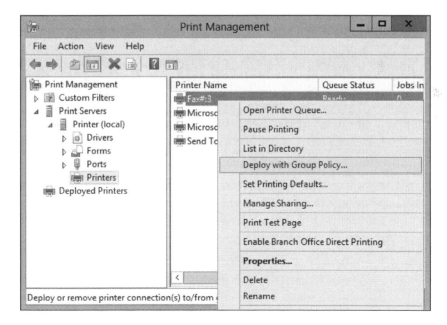

4. Click **Browse** and select the target GPO.

5. Select **per User** and/or **per Machine** as appropriate for the environment, and then click on **Add**.

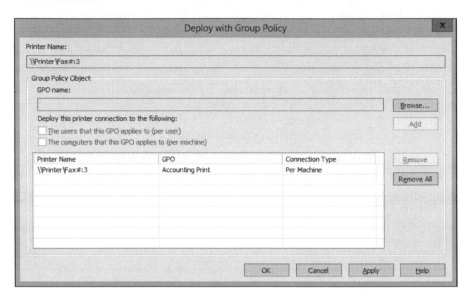

6. Click on **OK**.

The next time the group policy is refreshed for the user or target computer, the new printer will be mapped.

Enabling Branch Office Direct Printing

Prior to Windows Server 2012, for clients to print, they would send all print traffic to the print server, which then sent the data to the appropriate printer. In main office environments, or environments with local print servers, this worked well since the print server was readily accessible to the clients and printers via high speed connections.

However, this model caused problems in branch offices, which traditionally utilized slower WAN links to the main office. When printing, the client would often send a print job to the print server at the main office, which would then process and send the job to the printer back at the branch office.

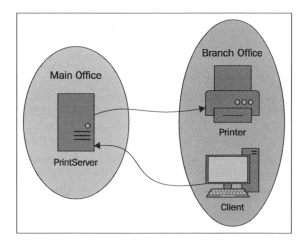

To resolve the bandwidth issues in branch offices, many solutions could be implemented. For example, the WAN links between the offices could be improved. Or a separate print server could be installed in the branch office itself. Alternatively, clients could bypass the print server and print directly to the local printer.

A new feature with Server 2012 known as **Branch Office Direct Printing** resolves these problems. While still using a centralized print server for printer and driver configuration, clients are configured to print directly to the printer. This bypasses the problems caused by printing across the WAN link, while still maintaining management and monitoring of the print environments.

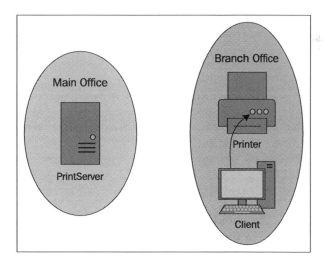

In this recipe, we will be configuring Branch Office Direct Printing for a specific printer. Once enabled, we will confirm that the print jobs are going directly from the client to the printer, leaving the WAN link available for other uses.

Getting ready

For this recipe we will be using a print server with one or more printers attached to it and shared. Additionally, we will need a client to print to the printer.

How to do it...

Perform the following steps in order to enable Branch Office Direct Printing:

1. Define a printer to use for direct printing:

```
Set-Printer -Name "Accounting HP" -ComputerName Printer1 `
-RenderingMode BranchOffice
```

2. Pause printing on the printer:

```
(Get-WmiObject -Class Win32_Printer | `
Where-Object Name -eq "Accounting HP").Pause()
```

3. Send a print job to the printer:

```
(Get-WmiObject -Class Win32_Printer | `
Where-Object Name -eq "Accounting HP").PrintTestPage()
```

4. Review the print queues on the client and printer, confirm that the print job only exists on the client:

```
Get-PrintJob -PrinterName "Accounting HP"
```

5. Resume printing:

```
(Get-WmiObject -Class Win32_Printer | `
Where-Object Name -eq "Accounting HP").Resume()
```

How it works...

We start by using `Set-Printer` with the `-RenderingMode BranchOffice` setting to configure our target printer on the print server to use Branch Office mode. This configuration is defined at the print server, and all clients using this printer will receive the new configuration to bypass the print server and print directly to the printer.

In step 2, we pause printing on the printer. First, we pause the printer by querying WMI for the printers and filtering by the nam; we then call the `Pause` command on the printer object. By pausing doing this, we can review the print queues on the clients and on the print server.

Next, we send a print job from our client to the printer. Same as the previous step, we start by querying WMI for our printers and filtering on the printer name. We then call the PrintTestPage command to send a print job. The print job should appear only on the client, confirming that the client is sending the print job directly to the printer.

In step 4, we use Get-PrintJob to view the print queues on the client and on the print server. This command will return all jobs in the print queues. When the configuration is operating correctly, we will see the print job on the local client, but not on the print server. This confirms the job is going directly from the client to the printer.

Lastly, we call the Resume command on the printer object to resume the printer and allow other print jobs to continue.

Reporting on printer usage

In many environments, it is desirable to ensure that all resources are being used as efficiently as possible. With printers, this often comes down to knowing which printers are being used the most or least, and which users are most active. With this information, an administrator can best determine locations that need printer upgrades, and locations that can be downsized.

In this recipe, we will review how to monitor the print jobs through our print server.

Getting ready

For this recipe, we need a print server with one or more shared printers attached to it. Additionally, we need one or more clients to print to the print server.

How to do it...

1. Enable logging on the print server by using the wevutil.exe utility:

   ```
   wevtutil.exe sl "Microsoft-Windows-PrintService/Operational" /
   enabled:true
   ```

2. Query the event log for successful print jobs:

   ```
   Get-WinEvent -LogName Microsoft-Windows-PrintService/Operational |
   `

   Where-Object ID -eq 307
   ```

How it works...

We start by enabling logging of the print service. To do this we use the command-line tool `Wevtutil.exe`. This is a command-line utility that allows us to view and change the configuration of the event logs on our server. In this instance, we are enabling the `Microsoft-Windows-PrintService/Operational` log on our print server. This log exists by default, but does not track any printing events until it is enabled.

Once logging is enabled, we can view the log for events by opening **Event Viewer** and browsing to **Application and Services log | Microsoft | Windows | PrintService | Operational**, as shown in the following screenshot:

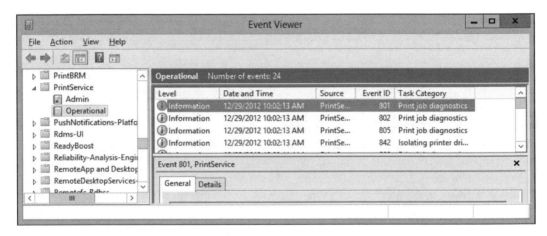

Next, we use `Get-WinEvent` to query our event log for successful print jobs. Successfully-printed jobs are recorded as event ID `307`. This simple query will return sufficient information to be able to create a report on how much each printer is being used, and by which users. Additional filters can be applied to restrict the report to a specific timeframe or other event log attributes.

There's more...

In addition to the basic report, we can also drill into the details of the event logs and report on them individually. Each event log entry contains a `Properties` object, which contains many of the event details. By querying specifically for these properties, we can return the details we are specifically looking for as follows:

```
Get-WinEvent -LogName Microsoft-Windows-PrintService/Operational |
`
Where-Object ID -eq 307 | `
Select-Object TimeCreated, `
@{Name="User";Expression={$_.Properties[2].Value}}, `
@{Name="Source";Expression={$_.Properties[3].Value}}, `
@{Name="Printer";Expression={$_.Properties[4].Value}}, `
@{Name="Pages";Expression={$_.Properties[7].Value}}
```

The preceding query returns a more concise report of who printed documents when, and how large the print files were, as shown in the following screenshot:

```
TimeCreated                User            Source          Printer    Pages
-----------                ----            ------          -------    -----
12/29/2012 9:40:45 AM Administrator \\10.10.10.10 Accounting 1
12/29/2012 9:39:48 AM Administrator \\10.10.10.10 Accounting 1
```

9
Troubleshooting Servers with PowerShell

This chapter covers the following topics:

- Testing if a server is responding
- Using troubleshooting packs
- Using Best Practices Analyzers
- Searching event logs for specific events
- Forwarding event logs to a central log server

Introduction

This chapter covers utilization of PowerShell troubleshooting packs, Windows Best Practices Analyzers, and using Windows event logs. This includes basic monitoring and the configuration of services, as well as creating a central event log server.

Testing if a server is responding

Often, when troubleshooting availability issues, one of the first steps is to test if the server is online. Prior to PowerShell, the tool of choice for testing if a system or device was online was `Ping`. For only a few systems, this worked well, however problems arose whenever attempting to use the command on a large scale or in a automated fashion.

PowerShell includes a new feature called `Test-Connection` that allows us to perform the same type of test, but that is more useful for automation. This command returns a `Win32_PingStatus` object that can be utilized by PowerShell.

In this recipe, we will be executing an ICMP ping against one or more target devices. PowerShell then returns a managed object that can be interpreted by PowerShell to determine the success or failure. PowerShell can then execute tasks based on the success or failure.

For this command to work, we must target a device that is configured to respond to ICMP ping requests. By default, Windows firewall blocks ICMP traffic, and many network devices can be configured to block ICMP as well. Prior to testing the connection, the target device must be configured to allow the ping request/response. For Windows devices, this can be configured locally or via a Group Policy.

Getting started

For this recipe, we will need two or more systems. The first system will be used to test connectivity with other systems on the network.

How to do it...

Carry out the following steps in order to test whether a server is responding or not:

1. Ping a single host.

   ```
   Test-Connection -ComputerName corpdc1
   ```

   When executed, we will see the response similar to the following screenshot:

   ```
   PS C:\> Test-Connection corpdc1

   Source          Destination       IPV4Address          IPV6Address
   ------          -----------       -----------          -----------
   PRINTER         corpdc1           10.10.10.10
   PRINTER         corpdc1           10.10.10.10
   PRINTER         corpdc1           10.10.10.10
   PRINTER         corpdc1           10.10.10.10
   ```

2. Ping multiple hosts.

   ```
   Workflow Ping-Host ([string[]] $targets)
   {
       ForEach -Parallel ($target in $targets)
       {
           If (Test-Connection -ComputerName $target -Count 2 -Quiet)
               {
   ```

```
            "$target is alive"
        } Else {
            "$target is down"
        }
    }
}
Ping-Host 10.10.10.10, 10.10.10.11
```

When executed, we will see a response similar to the following screenshot:

```
PS C:\> Ping-Host 10.10.10.10, 10.10.10.11
10.10.10.10 is down
10.10.10.11 is down
```

How it works...

We start the first step by calling Test-Connection against a single host. By default, this sends four sets of 32 bit ICMP echo requests (pings) to the target system. If the target is online and the firewall allows the traffic, the system will return a response. The target system can be referenced by its name, or by its IPv4 or IPV6 address.

In the second step, we create a workflow named Ping-Host. Workflows appear and operate similar to functions, except they provide additional capabilities. In this case, we are using a workflow to provide us with the ability to perform tasks in parallel.

This workflow accepts an array of names or addresses and initiates a separate task for each of them. The workflow then executes Test-Connection, and based on the output returns a message stating if the target is responding or not.

There's more...

In addition to pinging only one or two hosts on the network, it is possible to ping an entire network and return a list of available targets. This can be useful if you are attempting to find a resource, or trying to determine which addresses in your network are currently being used.

To accomplish this, we can use a loop to cycle through a range of possible addresses and call our Ping-Host workflow.

```
Ping-Host -Targets (1..254 | ForEach-Object{"10.10.10.$_"})
```

In this case we are searching for all available nodes in the 10.10.10.X network. We start by creating a loop for the numbers 1 through 254 and append this value to our network address. This value is passed into our Ping-Host workflow which then creates parallel tasks for the Test-Connection command.

Using the traditional ping command, this process can take between several minutes and several hours to ping the same network. However, because we are executing the tasks in parallel, the results are returned within a few moments, as shown in the following screenshot:

```
PS C:\> Ping-Host -targets (1..254 | %{"10.10.10.$_"})
10.10.10.252 is down
10.10.10.254 is down
10.10.10.253 is down
10.10.10.251 is down
10.10.10.250 is down
10.10.10.249 is down
10.10.10.248 is down
10.10.10.247 is down
10.10.10.246 is down
10.10.10.243 is down
```

 Note that because the workflow processes in parallel, the results are returned in a random order.

Using troubleshooting packs

Microsoft includes several in-built troubleshooting packs with Windows Server 2012. These troubleshooting packs perform many of the troubleshooting steps necessary for common errors. Additionally, they provide suggestions and steps for the resolution of common errors.

Depending on the system and applications, the troubleshooting packs available will vary. A basic Windows Server 2012 system only includes two packs: Networking and PCW (Program Compatibility Wizard). In this recipe, we will be using the Networking pack to test connectivity and Internet access.

Getting ready

For this recipe we will be using a basic Windows Server 2012 system.

How to do it

Complete the following steps to execute the troubleshooting pack:

1. List the available packs.

   ```
   Get-ChildItem C:\Windows\diagnostics\system
   ```

2. Start the troubleshooting pack.

   ```
   Invoke-TroubleshootingPack `
   (Get-TroubleshootingPack C:\Windows\diagnostics\system\networking)
   ```

3. Answer the prompts as necessary.

```
Select entry point
Please select the entry point for Network Diagnostics.

[1] Web Connectivity
[2] File Sharing
[3] Network Adapter
[4] Winsock Connectivity
[5] Grouping
[6] Inbound
[7] DirectAccess
[8] DefaultConnectivity
[9] Reserved

[?] Help
[x] Exit
:1
```

4. Create an answer file for the troubleshooting pack.

```
Get-TroubleshootingPack C:\Windows\diagnostics\system\networking `
-AnswerFile c:\temp\answer.xml
```

5. Execute the troubleshooting pack using the answer file.

```
Invoke-TroubleshootingPack `
(Get-TroubleshootingPack C:\Windows\diagnostics\system\Networking)
`
-AnswerFile c:\temp\answer.xml
```

How it works...

In the first step, we start by viewing the available troubleshooting packs on our system. These troubleshooting packs are collections of scripts, DLLs, and reference information contained in a folder.

Next, once we have identified which packs are available, we can execute the desired one. First, we use `Get-TroubleshootingPack` to retrieve a reference to the pack, and then use `Invoke-TroubleshootingPack` to start it.

In the third step, we walk through the troubleshooting pack. In this case, we are executing the `Networking` pack in order to troubleshoot `Web Connectivity`. In order to begin testing, we enter the number *1* and press *Enter*. The script prompts for more information before performing tests, suggesting resolutions, and performing any automated resolutions necessary.

In addition to executing the troubleshooting packs manually, we can automate them using an answer file. The answer file allows an administrator to automate the troubleshooting process for potentially common problems.

In step 4, to create the answer file, we use `Get-TroubleshootingPack` with the `-AnswerFile` switch. This switch instructs PowerShell to build the answer file at the target location. When prompted, provide the appropriate responses to be saved in the file.

In the fifth step, to use the answer file, we reference it when starting the troubleshooting pack. This is similar to the second step, except we use the `-AnswerFile` switch. The system will proceed through the troubleshooting as instructed.

When using answer files on remote systems, the file must be accessible to the remote system. Normally, this is performed by copying the file to the remote system before performing the troubleshooting tasks.

There's more...

In addition to the troubleshooting packs included with Windows Server, additional packs can be installed by various applications.

Additionally, by using the Windows SDK, it is possible to create custom troubleshooting packs. These can be used to troubleshoot specific applications or common errors in your environment.

Using Best Practices Analyzers

The Windows Best Practices Analyzer is a system management tool included with Server 2012. These analyzers contain the best practices defined for several server roles and features. These best practices include multiple aspects of the system, including performance, reliability, and security. The analyzer scans the system for these best practices and generates a report on the system's compliance level.

In this recipe, we will be scanning a system using the `FileServices` Best Practices Analyzer. Multiple analyzers are included with Windows by default, however they will only return results if the appropriate feature is installed. The basic storage services role is included by default with Windows Server and should run for all environments.

Getting started

For this recipe, we will be using a basic Windows Server 2012 system.

How to do it...

Complete the following steps to initiate the Best Practices Analyzers:

1. List the available analyzers.

   ```
   Get-BpaModel | Format-Table Id, Name, LastScanTime -AutoSize
   ```

   When executed, the results will be shown similar to the following screenshot:

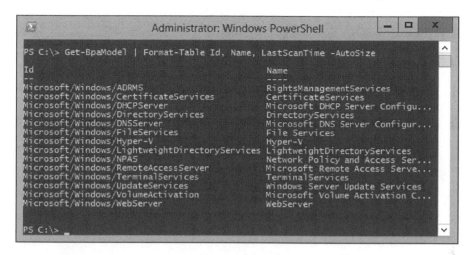

2. Initiate a scan on the local system.

   ```
   Invoke-BpaModel -ModelId Microsoft/Windows/FileServices
   ```

3. Get the analyzer results.

   ```
   Get-BpaResult -ModelId Microsoft/Windows/FileServices | `
   Where-Object Severity -NE Information
   ```

   When executed, the results should be displayed as shown in the following screenshot:

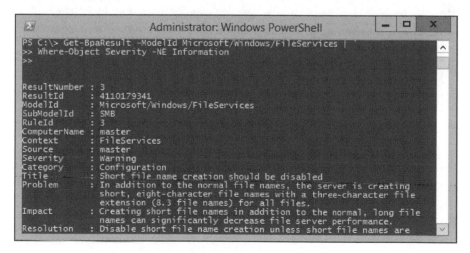

4. Execute the analyzer on multiple systems and store the results centrally.

```
Invoke-BpaModel -ModelId Microsoft/Windows/WebServer `
-RepositoryPath \\corpdc1\BPA -ComputerName Web1, Web2
```

5. Review the analyzer results.

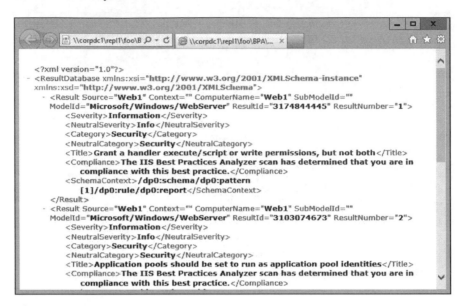

How it works...

We start off by calling `Get-BpaModel` to list the available analyzers on our system. Here we are returning the `ID`, `Name`, and `LastScanTime` to show the last time that the analyzer was executed. Microsoft includes several analyzers in Windows by default, and many more are available for download online from Microsoft or third-party vendors.

In the second step, we call `Invoke-BpaModel` to initiate a scan on the local system. In this situation, we are calling the `Microsoft/Windows/FileServices` model to scan the system for the `FileServices` role. This initiates multiple checks against the system for both file and print features. The results are saved as an XML file in `C:\Windows\Logs\BPA\Reports`.

Next, we use `Get-BpaResult` to review the results. We can return all of the available results, or use filtering to return only information we are interested in. In the example shown, we are using a filter based on the `Severity` being something other than `Information`. This filter limits the results to only a warning about a short name file creation. In addition to the problems found, the best practice report includes information about the impact of the best practice, and resolution steps.

In the fourth step, we call `Invoke-BpaModel` again, but this time with the `-ComputerName` switch. Using this switch, we can execute the analyzer on multiple remote systems simultaneously. In this example, we are also using the `-RepositoryPath` switch, which instructs the analyzer to store the results in a specific location. In this case, we are using a network share on a server.

Finally, we can review the results by using Internet Explorer or other tools capable of viewing XML files.

There's more...

In addition to viewing the raw XML content, it is possible to convert the results into an HTML report. This can be done by creating the necessary `XSL` file, or by using a script such as the one created by Cristian Edwards at `http://blogs.technet.com/b/cedward/archive/2011/01/11/hyper-v-bpa-html-report.aspx`. This script executes the analyzer, saves the XML output, and using an embedded XSL, saves the output as an HTML file. The results can then be viewed in Internet Explorer.

An example report is shown as follows:

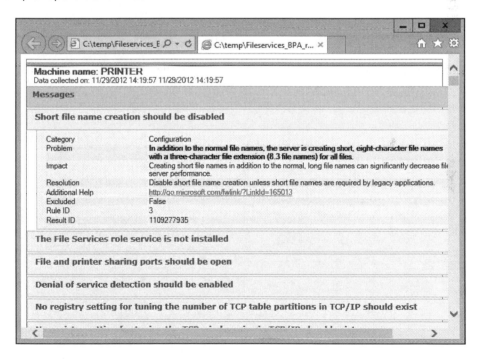

Searching event logs for specific events

Several times after discovering a problem, the first question asked is: *How often has this occurred?* If the problem is logged in the Windows event log, the answer to that question is only a matter of looking in the logs for the specific error.

However, this can also be problematic. If the event is logged on multiple systems, or in a busy event log, or has been occurring for a long time, searching for the error events can be difficult. Searching for a needle in a large haystack can be next to impossible.

In this recipe, we will cover multiple methods to query the Windows event log.

Getting started

For this recipe, we will be using a basic Windows Server 2012 system.

How to do it...

Complete the following steps to query the event log:

1. Show the recent events that have been recorded in a specific log.

   ```
   Get-WinEvent -LogName System -MaxEvents 10
   ```

   When executed, the last ten events will be displayed, as shown in the following screenshot:

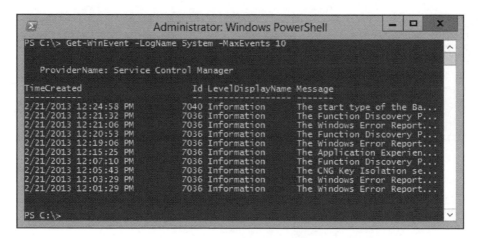

2. Show the recent events from the `Service Control Manager` event provider.

   ```
   Get-WinEvent -ProviderName "Service Control Manager" -MaxEvents 10
   ```

3. Search for specific events in a log.

```
Get-WinEvent -FilterHashtable @{LogName='System';ID=17} -MaxEvents
10
```

4. Show the specific events in a log for last ten minutes.

```
Get-WinEvent -FilterHashtable `
@{LogName='System';ID=17;StartTime=$(Get-Date).AddMinutes((-10)}
```

5. Search multiple computers.

```
"Server1", "Server2" | `
ForEach-Object{ Get-WinEvent -ComputerName $_ -FilterHashtable `
@{LogName='System';ID=17;StartTime=$(Get-Date).AddMinutes((-10)} }
```

How it works...

We start by using Get-WinEvent to query the local System event log. This first example simply returns the 10 most recent events in the event log. This can be helpful in restricting the number of results displayed, or to display only the most recent events.

In the second step, we are using Get-WinEvent with the -ProviderName switch to query all event logs on a system for events from a specific provider. Most applications, services, or types of services that write to the event log tag their events with a unique provider name. In this way, we are able to search all event logs for events from the defined provider. In this case, we are returning events from the Service Control Manager, or events regarding the starting and stopping of services.

In the third step, we use the -FilterHastable switch to create a complex filter. In this case, we are querying the System event log for a specific event ID. In this case, we are returning the last 10 events with either event ID 17, or for WindowsUpdateClient or Installation Ready events.

Next, we query the event log for specific events that have occurred in the last 10 minutes. This builds off the prior query and adds the starttime attribute to limit the results, based on time. This query is particularly useful when you need to find specific events that have occurred in the last hour, day, week, or month.

Lastly, we search for events on multiple computers. We are using the same query as defined in the previous step and passing a collection of computer names. These names are used in the -ComputerName switch to tell PowerShell to query the remote system.

There's more...

By using this method, it is possible to set up a rudimentary monitoring and alert system. Instead of returning the results to the screen, PowerShell can be scripted to generate an e-mail or initiate tasks to generate an alert or automatically remediate problems.

We can create an active monitoring tool by creating a scheduled task to query a remote system every 10 minutes for a specific event ID. If an event is returned, then the defined issue has occurred and we can initiate a task. This task can be the sending of an alert to an Administrator, or the initiation of a script to automatically remediate the issue.

Forwarding event logs to a central log server

In Windows Server, it is possible to configure the forwarding of event logs to remote servers. By forwarding events to another system, the centralized server can be configured with different retention options, reporting, and potentially performing actions based on the forwarded events.

This event forwarding uses a standard-based communication method using SOAP over HTTP.

There are two types of event log subscriptions: client-initiated and collector-initiated. For client-initiated subscriptions, we use a Group Policy and configure clients to push events to the collector. For collector-initiated, we configure the collector to pull events from each of the clients.

In this recipe, we will be creating a client-initiated subscription. We will use a Group Policy to distribute the configuration to our event sources. We will only be configuring one client, but the process can be extended to include dozens or even hundreds of clients.

Getting ready

For this recipe we need a minimum of two Server 2012 systems in an Active Directory environment. Here, we will be using `Server1` as our event collector system, and `Server2` will forward events to our collector as shown in the following diagram:

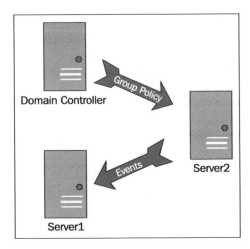

How to do it...

Complete the following steps to configure event forwarding:

1. Create the collector security group.

   ```
   New-ADGroup -Name "Event Collector" -GroupScope Global
   Add-ADGroupMember -Identity "Event Collector" -Members Server1$
   ```

2. Create the GPO for the collector system.

   ```
   New-GPO -Name "Event Collector"
   New-GPLink -Name "Event Collector" `
   -Target "DC=Corp,DC=Contoso,DC=Com"
   Set-GPPermission -Name "Event Collector" `
   -TargetName "Event Collector" -TargetType Group `
   -PermissionLevel GpoApply
   Set-GPPermission -Name "Event Collector" `
   -TargetName "Authenticated Users" -TargetType Group `
   -PermissionLevel None
   ```

3. Apply the settings to the collector GPO.

   ```
   $WinRMKey="HKLM\Software\Policies\Microsoft\Windows\WinRM\Service"
   Set-GPRegistryValue -Name "Event Collector" -Key $WinRMKey `
   -ValueName "AllowAutoConfig" -Type DWORD -Value 1
   Set-GPRegistryValue -Name "Event Collector" -Key $WinRMKey `
   -ValueName "IPv4Filter" -Type STRING -Value "*"
   Set-GPRegistryValue -Name "Event Collector" -Key $WinRMKey `
   -ValueName "IPv6Filter" -Type STRING -Value "*"
   ```

4. Enable and configure `Windows Event Collector` on the collector system.

   ```
   echo y | wecutil qc
   ```

5. Create the XML file for the subscription, and save the file.

   Following is an example of the `subscription.xml` file used in this example:

   ```
   <?xml version="1.0" encoding="UTF-8"?>
   <Subscription xmlns="http://schemas.microsoft.com/2006/03/windows/
   events/subscription">
           <SubscriptionId>Collect security</SubscriptionId>
           <SubscriptionType>SourceInitiated</SubscriptionType>
   ```

```
<Description></Description>

<Enabled>true</Enabled>

<Uri>http://schemas.microsoft.com/wbem/wsman/1/windows/
EventLog</Uri>

<ConfigurationMode>Normal</ConfigurationMode>

<Query>

    <![CDATA[

<QueryList><Query Id="0"><Select Path="Security">*[System[(Level=1
or Level=2 or Level=3)]]</Select></Query></QueryList>

    ]]>

</Query>

<ReadExistingEvents>false</ReadExistingEvents>

<TransportName>HTTP</TransportName>

<ContentFormat>RenderedText</ContentFormat>

<Locale Language="en-US"/>

<LogFile>ForwardedEvents</LogFile>

<PublisherName>Microsoft-Windows-EventCollector</
PublisherName>

<AllowedSourceNonDomainComputers>

    <AllowedIssuerCAList>

    </AllowedIssuerCAList>

</AllowedSourceNonDomainComputers>

<AllowedSourceDomainComputers>O:NSG:BAD:P(A;;GA;;;DC)S:</
AllowedSourceDomainComputers>

</Subscription>
```

A sample XML file can be viewed by executing `wecutil cs /?`.

 You can export an existing subscription to XML by executing `wecutil gs <name> /f:XML`.

6. Create a subscription.

```
wecutil cs subscription.xml
```

7. Create the source security group.

```
New-ADGroup -Name "Event Source" -GroupScope Global

Add-ADGroupMember -Identity "Event Source" -Members Server2$
```

8. Create the GPO for the source systems.

```
New-GPO -Name "Event Source"

New-GPLink -Name "Event Source" -Target
"DC=Corp,DC=Contoso,DC=Com"

Set-GPPermission -Name "Event Source" -TargetName "Event Source" `
-TargetType Group -PermissionLevel GpoApply

Set-GPPermission -Name "Event Source" `
-TargetName "Authenticated Users" -TargetType Group `
-PermissionLevel None
```

9. Apply the settings for the source GPO.

```
$EventKey="HKLM\Software\Policies\Microsoft\Windows\EventLog\
EventForwarding\SubscriptionManager"

$TargetAddress="Server=http://server1.corp.contoso.com:5985/wsman/
SubscriptionManager/WEC"

Set-GPRegistryValue -Name "Event Source" -Key $EventKey `
-ValueName "1" -Type STRING -Value $TargetAddress
```

 If using HTTPS or an alternative port, the `$TargetAddress` string needs to be updated to reflect the connection type and port.

10. Open the **Group Policy Management Editor** and update the GPO to add `Network Service` to the `Event Log Readers` group.

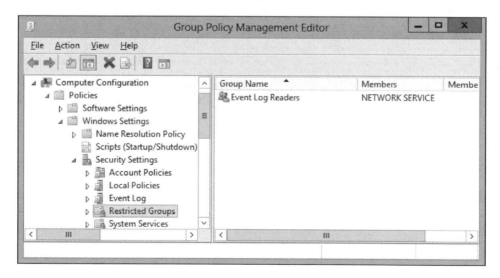

11. Reboot the source computer.

12. Open **Event Viewer** on the collector computer and view the **Forwarded Events**.

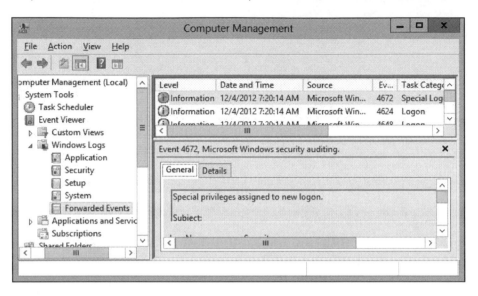

How it works...

We start by creating an AD security group named `Event Collector` to host our collector computer. This security group will be used to limit which computers the collector Group Policy is applied to.

In the second step, we use `New-GPO` to create the Group Policy for our collector computer. We first create the Group Policy and call `New-GPLink` to link it to the domain. We use `Set-GPPermission` to modify the permissions of the GPO to limit access to our `Event Collector` security group.

Next, we configure the GPO settings. The first setting, `AlowAutoConfig`, instructs Windows to start the `WinRM` service and listen for events from remote sources. The `IPv4Filter` and `IPv6Filter` values specify which systems to accept connections from. In this scenario we have entered *, meaning any source.

In the fourth step, we configure the `Windows Event Collector`. Executing `wecutil qc` applies the basic configuration for the collector and configures the service to start automatically.

Next, we create the `subscription.xml` file. This sample XML file instructs the collector system to request all events from the `Security` event log that have a `Critical`, `Error` or `Warning` status.

In the sixth step, we create our subscription using our XML file. To create the subscription, we use `wecutil.exe` with the `cs` parameter and reference our XML file. The collector configuration is complete and we now configure the source computers.

In the seventh step, we begin configuring our source systems by creating an AD security group to house our source computers. First, we call `New-ADGroup` to create a group named `Event Source`. We then call `Add-ADGroupMember` to add the systems that will be forwarding events. In this instance, we are only adding one system-`Server2`-to the group, but multiple systems can be included at this step.

Next, we use `New-GPO` to create the Group Policy for our source computers. We first create the Group Policy and use `New-GPLink` to link it to the domain. We then use `Set-GPPermission` in order to modify the permissions to limit access to our `Event Source` security group.

In the ninth step, we configure the GPO settings. We start by defining `$EventKey` to identify the registry key location that we will be configuring. We then define the `$TargetAddress` to define the location to which the clients will forward the events. Lastly, we configure the `SubscriptionManager` key with the target server address.

In the tenth step, we open the **Group Policy Management Editor** screen to update our Event Source GPO. This step cannot be performed by using PowerShell and must be completed using the editor. Edit the Event Source GPO and browse to **Computer Configuration | Policies | Windows Settings | Security Settings | Restricted Groups**. We add the `Network Service` role to the local `Event Log Readers` group. This permission is necessary for the source system to send event log messages.

Finally, for the security permissions to apply, the source computers need to be rebooted. Once rebooted, the event logs should start to be forwarded to the target system.

There's more...

In addition to the simple forwarding shown here, it is also possible to configure multi-tier forwarding. For example, if your environment contains multiple sites, it is possible to configure a collector computer at each site, and then forward events from the remote sites' collectors to a central collector in your datacenter.

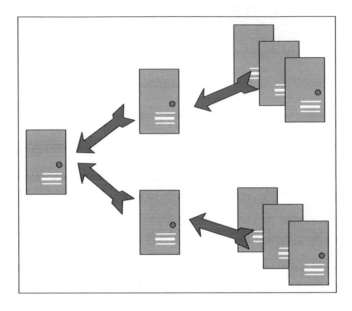

In this configuration, each level of forwarding can have different retention and forwarding rules applied. For example, it may be desirable to retain all application logs at the remote sites, but only critical security events at the central site.

10
Managing Performance with PowerShell

This chapter covers the following recipes:

- ▶ Reading performance counters
- ▶ Configuring Data Collector Sets
- ▶ Reporting on performance data
- ▶ Generating graphs
- ▶ Creating server performance reports

Introduction

This chapter shows how to use PowerShell to track and report on historical performance and identify bottlenecks. This chapter will also show how to integrate PowerShell objects with Excel to create usable performance reports and graphs.

Reading performance counters

Often the best method of identifying how a system is performing is by viewing the performance counters. Microsoft has included PerfMon in Server 2012 for collecting and viewing performance information graphically; however this has been problematic to automate across multiple systems. Several system management tools have been created to enable enterprise-wide monitoring, however they are normally very expensive, difficult to maintain, and are designed to do more than most people need.

In this recipe, we will review various methods of gathering performance data using PowerShell.

Getting ready

For this recipe, we will be using a basic Windows Server 2012 system. Additionally, we will export the performance statistics for viewing in Microsoft Excel.

How to do it...

Carry out the following steps to read the performance data using PowerShell:

1. Read the basic performance counters.

    ```
    Get-Counter
    ```

    When executed, performance metrics will be displayed, as shown in the following screenshot:

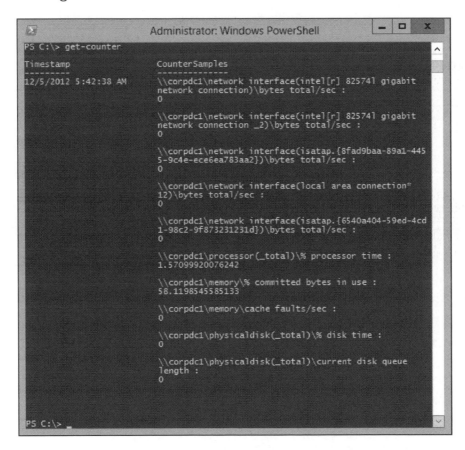

2. Retrieve the multiple performance counter samples.

```
Get-Counter -Counter "\Processor(_Total)\% Processor Time" `
-MaxSamples 4 -SampleInterval 10
```

When completed, the results will be displayed, as shown in the following screenshot:

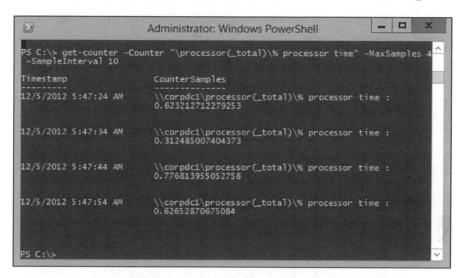

3. Read the counters on multiple computers.

```
$myNodes = "server1","server2"
$myCounter = $myNodes | ForEach-Object {
    "\\$_\Memory\% Committed Bytes In Use"
    "\\$_\PhysicalDisk(_Total)\% Disk Time"
}
Get-Counter -Counter $myCounter
```

4. Save the counter results to a file.

```
$results = Get-Counter -Counter $myCounter -MaxSamples 4 `
-SampleInterval 10
$results | Export-Counter -Path "c:\temp\perfcounter.csv" `
-FileFormat CSV
```

How it works...

We start by executing the in-built PowerShell Cmdlet `Get-Counter`. This command is used to query performance counters and return the results. Without any additional switches, the command returns a point-in-time snapshot of the environment, including network, CPU, memory, and disk counters.

In the second step, we use `Get-Counter` to retrieve multiple counter samples over a period of time. Here, we are collecting the `\Processor(_Total)\% Processor Time` of our system every `10` seconds. We specify the `–SampleInterval` switch to tell PowerShell to collect data every `10` seconds, and the `–MaxSamples` switch tells PowerShell how many intervals to collect.

Next, we collect multiple performance counters from multiple systems simultaneously. We start by creating an array object named `$myNodes` that contains the names of the systems to query. This array is then piped into a `ForEach-Object` loop that adds multiple performance counters to the `$myCounter` array. Finally, we call `Get-Counter` with our array. The system will then return the values for each counter on each system.

To access performance counters remotely, the `Remote Event Log Management` firewall exception must be enabled on the target system. This can be applied locally to the server, or via a Group Policy.

In the fourth step, we save our results so that they can be viewed in Excel, PowerShell, or other tools. We use the same `$myCounter` object as used in the previous step, except this time we call `Get-Counter` with the `–MaxSamples` and `–SampleInterval` switches to retrieve multiple samples. The results are saved to a variable named $results. $results is then piped to `Export-Counter` with the `–Path` and `–FileFormat` switches, which saves the results into a comma separated value (CSV) file. The CSV file can then be opened in Excel or used by PowerShell as the source for other processes.

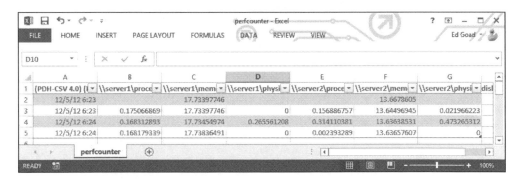

Configuring Data Collector Sets

When reviewing the performance of a server, I normally include a large set of performance counters. I configure the counters to collect multiple times every minute for an entire day. When finished, I have a complete picture of the performance of every aspect of the system for the day.

Windows includes a feature known as Data Collector Sets that allows us to define this configuration. Once defined, we can execute it locally or remotely, and it will run automatically for the predefined time frame.

In this recipe, we will be creating a basic Data Collector Set that will collect performance data from a system every 10 seconds for 24 hours. This data will be saved to the local filesystem in a format that can be accessed by PowerShell, Excel, and other reporting tools. We will then export this configuration and use it to configure remote systems.

Getting ready

For this recipe, we will need two Server 2012 systems. Additionally, we will need a manually created Data Collector Set to act as a template for deploying to other systems.

Complete the following steps to create the Data Collector Set manually:

1. Open Performance Monitor and right-click on **User Defined** under **Data Collector Sets**, and then select **New | Data Collector Set**.

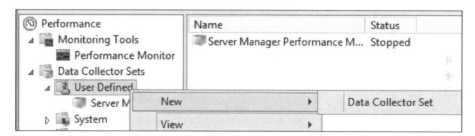

2. In the **Create new Data Collector Set** wizard, enter a name, select **Create manually (Advanced)**, and then click on **Next**.

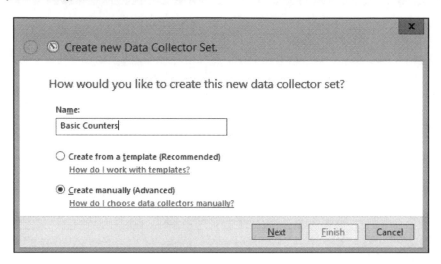

3. Select **Performance counter**, and then click on **Next**.

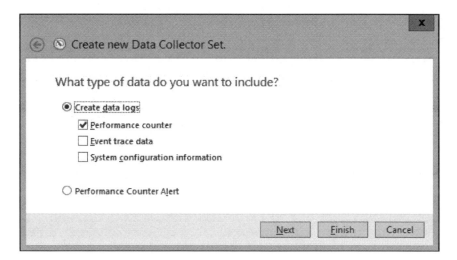

4. Add the performance counters that you wish to collect and specify the **Sample interval**, and then click on **Finish**.

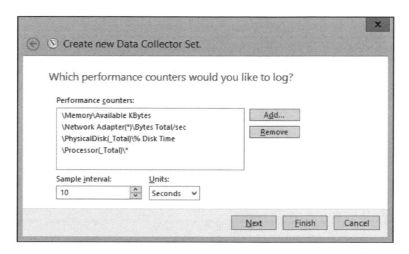

5. In **Performance Monitor** edit the properties of the new collector and select the **Stop Condition** tab.

    ❏   Specify a **Duration** of **24** and **Units** as **Hours,** and then click on **OK**.

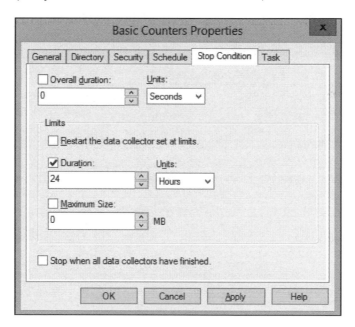

❑ Edit the properties of **DataCollector01** and change **Log format** to **Comma Separated**. Click on **OK**.

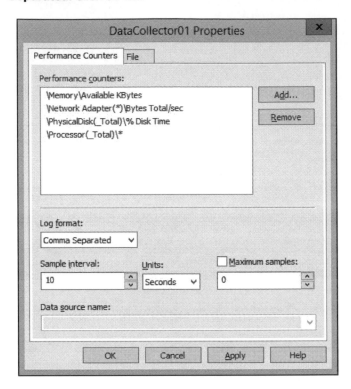

We start by creating a template Data Collector Set. We are using the graphical interface to quickly and easily define the settings, and will later export them to an XML file. In addition to the few counters shown here, we can add dozens, or even hundreds, more.

How to do it...

Complete the following steps to use PowerShell to manage Data Collector Sets:

1. On the primary system, export the data collector as XML.

   ```
   $dataCollectorSet = New-Object -ComObject Pla.DataCollectorSet
   $dataCollectorSet.Query("Basic Counters",$null)
   $dataCollectorSet.Xml | Out-File C:\PerfLogs\BasicCounters.xml
   ```

2. Import the data collector on a remote system.

```
Copy-Item c:\PerfLogs\BasicCounters.xml '\\server1\c$\PerfLogs'
Enter-PSSession server1
$dataCollectorSet = New-Object -ComObject Pla.DataCollectorSet
$xmlCounters = Get-Content "c:\perflogs\BasicCounters.xml"
$dataCollectorSet.SetXml($xmlCounters)
$dataCollectorSet.Commit("Basic Counters",$null,1)
$dataCollectorSet.Start($true)
```

3. After you have finished collecting data, delete the data collector.

```
$dataCollectorSet = New-Object -ComObject Pla.DataCollectorSet
$dataCollectorSet.Query("Basic Counters",$null)
$dataCollectorSet.Stop($true)
Sleep 2
$dataCollectorSet.Delete()
```

How it works...

In the first step, we export the data collector as an XML file. We start by creating a COM object reference to the Performance Logs and Alerts (PLA.DataCollectorSet) object to access our data collector. We query the DataCollectorSet object for our Data Collector Set by name, and then export it to an XML file named BasicCounters.xml.

In the second step, now that we have the Data Collector Set in XML format, we can execute it on remote computers. First, we use Copy-Item to copy the XML file to the remote computer, and then use Enter-PSSession to connect to the system. We create a PLA.DataCollectorSet COM object to allow us to access the local data collectors. We use the SetXml command to import the XML file on the system and call Commit to save the collector on the remote system. Lastly, we call Start in order to start the Data Collector on the remote computer. Based on our predefined settings, the collector will gather information for 24 hours and then automatically stop. When finished, the results will be saved as a CSV file on the remote system.

When we have finished collecting data, in the third step we delete the data collector. We create our PLA.DataCollectorSet COM object and query for the data collector by name. We call Stop to stop the collector in case it is currently running and then call Sleep for 2 seconds to allow any data collector processes to close. Finally, we Delete the data collector from the computer.

It isn't necessary to delete the Data Collector Sets after being used to collect performance information. If you have a set that will be used frequently, it can be deployed once and stay on the remote system for as long as it is needed.

There's more...

In addition to the few data points defined in this example, we can add dozens or hundreds of additional data points. One example of a large Data Collector Set can be found at `http://flippingbits.typepad.com/blog/perfcollect.html`. This tool automates the collection of performance data for nearly 600 data points. Although it was designed specifically for use with systems connected to EMC equipment, it is a great example of a data collector that contains most of the data points needed to troubleshoot performance on most systems.

Reporting on performance data

Once performance data has been collected, the next challenge is to organize the information into a usable format. There are basic statistics that can be gathered easily through PowerShell—minimum, maximum, and average, however, these only tell a part of the story.

In addition to these basic statistics, it is often useful to identify the 95th percentile. The 95th percentile identifies how many resources are consumed, or how much performance is needed, 95 percent of the time. The remaining 5 percent can often be regarded as a statistical anomaly, and excluded from most performance or sizing practices.

Getting ready

In this recipe, we will be using the performance data collected in the previous recipe, *Configuring Data Collector Sets*, to generate a performance report. This report will include only one aspect of the computer utilization, but it can be easily expanded to include additional counters.

How to do it...

Complete the following steps to analyze the performance data:

1. Import the performance counters.

   ```
   $counters = Import-Csv "C:\PerfLogs\Admin\Basic Counters\
   CORPDC1_20121205-000002\DataCollector01.csv"

   $counters[0] = $counters[1]
   ```

2. Report on the basic CPU stats.

```
$stats = $counters | Measure-Object `
"*Processor(_Total)\% Processor Time" -Average -Minimum -Maximum
```

3. Report on the 95th percent of the CPU stats:

```
$row = [int]($counters.Count * .95 )
$cpu = ([double[]](`
$counters."\\CORPDC1\Processor(_Total)\% Processor Time") | `
Sort-Object)
$cpu95 = $CPU[$row]
```

4. Combine the results into a single report:

```
Add-Member -InputObject $stats -Name 95thPerc `
-MemberType NoteProperty -Value $cpu95
$stats
```

When executed, the results will be displayed, as shown in the following screenshot:

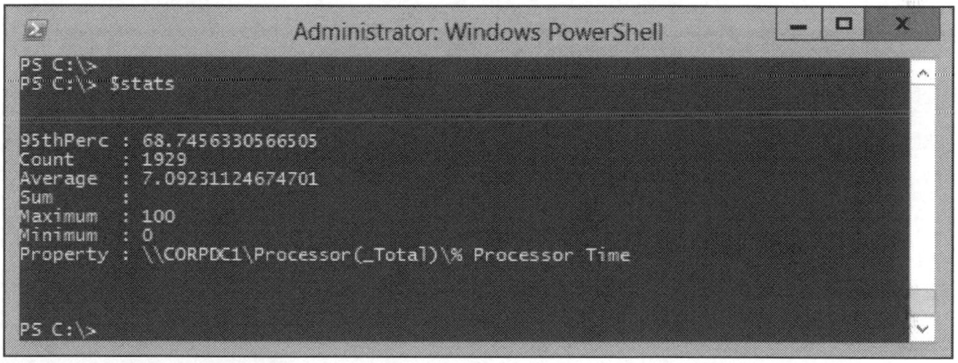

How it works...

We start by accessing the performance data saved from the prior recipe. We use Import-CSV to import the data and save it into a variable named $counters. We then set $counters[0] equal to $counters[1] in order to overwrite the first row of information with the contents of the second because PerfMon often doesn't populate this row entirely. Otherwise, this missing data can cause problems with our scripts.

In the second step, we use Measure-Object to collect basic information on our Processor(_Total) performance. Here we are using the –Average, -Minimum, and –Maximum switches. We then save the results into the variable $stats.

In the third step, we identify the 95th percentile of our CPU utilization. To calculate this value, we call `$counters.Count` to count the total number of rows in our dataset and multiply this by `.95`. This returns the row number that contains the 95th percentile value. Next, we sort our counters based on the CPU utilization and place them in an array named `$CPU`. Lastly, we call `$CPU[$row]` to return the value in the target row.

Lastly, we use `Add-Member` to add our 95th percentile value to the `$stats` object. Once added, we return the results.

As we can see from the results, the system averaged only 7 percent utilization during our polling period, but occasionally spiked to 100 percent. However, the 95th percentile tells us that for most of the sample time, the system rarely utilized more than 68 percent of the CPU.

In other words, in a 24 hour period, nearly 23 hours used less than 68 percent of the CPU and the system only spiked higher than 68 percent for a little more than an hour. For normal operation, this suggests the system has more than sufficient CPU capacity to satisfy most needs.

There's more...

There are many methods available for calculating the utilization percentile for performance numbers. For more details on the various methods, you can review the Wikipedia article at `http://en.wikipedia.org/wiki/Percentile`.

Generating graphs

There is an old saying that a picture is worth a thousand words, and when reporting on performance numbers, pictures can be significantly more useful than raw numbers. With a performance graph, you can quickly show the utilization of a system, any performance spikes, and when they occur during the day.

To generate our graphs we will be using the `System.Windows.Forms.DataVisualization.Charting.Chart` class that is included in `.NET Framework 4` and greater on Windows 7 and greater.

Getting ready

In this recipe, we will be using the performance data previously collected in the *Configuring Data Collector Sets* recipe to generate a graph showing the CPU utilization. The graph will be saved as a PNG file that can be printed, attached to a report, or e-mailed along with the performance report.

How to do it...

Carry out the following steps to generate a graph:

1. Create a chart object.

    ```
    $myChart = New-Object `
    System.Windows.Forms.DataVisualization.Charting.Chart
    $myChart.Width = 600
    $myChart.Height = 400
    ```

2. Define the chart.

    ```
    [void]$myChart.Titles.Add("CPU Utilization")
    $chartarea = New-Object `
    System.Windows.Forms.DataVisualization.Charting.ChartArea
    $chartarea.Name = "CPU"
    $chartarea.AxisY.Title = "% CPU"
    $myChart.ChartAreas.Add($chartarea)
    ```

3. Import the CSV data.

    ```
    $counters = Import-Csv "C:\PerfLogs\Admin\Basic Counters\
    CORPDC1_20121205-000002\DataCollector01.csv"
    $counters[0]=$counters[1]
    ```

4. Identify the date/time column.

    ```
    $name = ($counters[0] | Get-Member | `
    Where-Object MemberType -eq "NoteProperty")[0].Name
    ```

5. Add the data points to the chart.

    ```
    [void]$myChart.Series.Add("CPUPerc")
    $myChart.Series["CPUPerc"].ChartType = "Line"
    $counters | ForEach-Object{
    [void]$myChart.Series["CPUPerc"].Points.AddXY($_.$name, `
    $_."\\corpdc1\Processor(_Total)\% Processor Time")
    }
    ```

6. Save the chart image.

    ```
    $myChart.SaveImage("c:\temp\CPUUtil.png","png")
    ```

How it works...

In the first step, we start by creating our chart object. The chart object is a container that holds all of the applicable chart resources. Because PowerShell is based on the .NET framework, and the charting objects are built into Windows Server 2012, we can easily create a chart object. Once we have created the chart, we configure the desired `Width` and `Height`.

Next, we create the chart area. The chart area defines the chart and is used to contain the data series. First, we add a `Title` to the chart and then create the `ChartArea` object. On the `ChartArea`, we define the `Name` and axis `Title`, and add it to the chart object `$myChart`.

In the third step, we load the performance data that we previously collected. Here, we call `Import-CSV` to import the CSV export of the performance data. We overwrite the first row of results because they are normally invalid and can cause problems with scripts.

Next, we identify the name of the date/time column in our CSV file. This is needed because PerfMon names the first column based on the time zone of the client, for example, on my test client the column is named `(PDH-CSV 4.0) (Pacific Standard Time)(480)`. We need to identify the column name so that we can later access the values. To find the name of the first column, we pipe the first row through `Get-Member` and filter on the type of `NoteProperty`. We place the name of the first result into a variable so that we can reference it later.

In the fifth step, we add our data to the chart. We start by calling `$myChart.Series.Add` to create a data series, and set the `ChartType` to `Line`. We then pass our dataset through a `ForEach-Object` loop to enumerate our dataset, and add the values for the `% Processor Time` counter to the data series.

Lastly, we call `SaveImage` to save the chart object as a PNG file. The file can then be viewed, or attached to an e-mail or document to create a report.

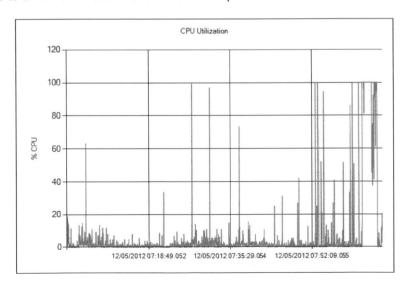

There's more...

In addition to the single data series shown here, it is possible to add multiple data series to a single graph. For example, to report on the utilization of multiple hard disk drives in a system, each disk can be added to the same graph, each with a different color line, so that their utilization can be viewed as a set.

The .NET charting object support many advanced features. For example, you can add a static line reporting the 95th percentile or other threshold. You can also use multiple axes on the same report, add legends, combine line and bar charts, create pie charts, and so on.

A good example of using PowerShell to create more advanced graphs can be found at `http://blogs.technet.com/b/richard_macdonald/archive/2009/04/28/3231887.aspx`. This blog uses .NET 3.5 for its examples, but shows how to perform many of the different charting configurations possible by using PowerShell.

Creating a server performance report

In Windows Server 2012, several performance reports are included with Performance Monitor. These reports are included as in-built Data Collector Sets. However, instead of just collecting statistics, they also generate reports showing the system configuration and performance.

Getting ready

Depending on the features installed on your server, the in-built Data Collector Sets will vary. To view the available sets, open Performance Monitor and browse to **Data Collector Sets | System**. When generated, the reports will appear in the **Reports** node, as shown in the following screenshot:

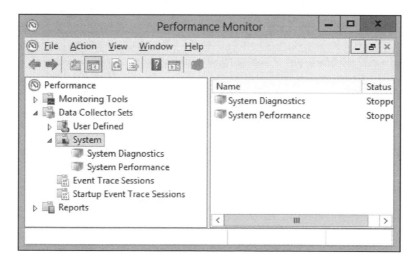

How to do it...

In this recipe, we will be executing and using the `System Diagnostics` report. Complete the following steps to generate a report and send it via e-mail:

1. Start the data collector on the local system.

    ```
    $perfReport="System\System Diagnostics"
    $dsSet = New-Object -ComObject Pla.DataCollectorSet
    $dsSet.Query($perfReport,$null)
    $dsSet.Start($true)
    ```

2. Wait for the data collector to finish.

    ```
    Sleep $dsSet.Duration
    ```

3. E-mail the report.

    ```
    $dsSet.Query($perfReport,$null)
    $myReport = $dsSet.LatestOutputLocation + "\report.html"
    Send-MailMessage -SmtpServer mail.corp.contoso.com `
    -From reports@contoso.com -To serveradmin@contoso.com `
    -Subject "Diagnostic performance report" -Attachments $myReport
    ```

How it works...

In the first step, we start by initiating the target Data Collector Set. First, we create a `PLA.DataCollectorSet` COM object and then query the Data Collector Set by name. In this example, we are executing the `System\System Diagnostics` data collector, but we could have executed any other available set. We then `Start` the Data Collector Set.

In the second step, we sleep until the data collector is finished. This uses the value in `$dsSet.Duration` as the maximum duration for which the collector can run, which may be more than what is necessary in all circumstances.

Lastly, we identify the `LatestOutputLocation` to find the report on the system, and then send it via e-mail. In this example, we are attaching the report to the e-mail as a file; however, we could also include the report in the contents of the e-mail. When finished, we can view the report in the Internet Explorer or any other web browser.

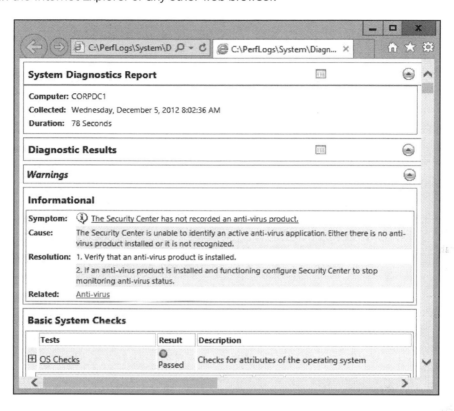

11

Inventorying Servers with PowerShell

This chapter covers the following topics:

- ▶ Inventorying hardware with PowerShell
- ▶ Inventorying the installed software
- ▶ Inventorying system configuration
- ▶ Reporting on system security
- ▶ Creating a change report
- ▶ Exporting a configuration report to Word

Introduction

This chapter explains how to inventory the hardware and software configurations of Windows 8 Servers and create a detailed inventory and configuration report. Additionally, this chapter will cover methods to track configuration changes over time, export the configuration report via Word. This chapter should cover everything necessary to create a centralized hardware and software inventory of all servers in the enterprise.

Inventorying hardware with PowerShell

Often times, a system administrator needs to identify what hardware is installed in their environment. This could be for an asset tracking project, finding available resources, or even identifying older equipment that needs to be retired. Most hardware information on a system is stored in WMI and can be accessed via in-built PowerShell functions or via WMI queries.

In this recipe, we will review the various methods for gathering inventory information from our local system. In addition to collecting from the local system, these methods can be expanded to include remote systems.

How to do it...

We can review the various methods for gathering inventory information as follows:

1. Gather disk information from the local system.

   ```
   $TargetSystem="."

   $myCim = New-CimSession -ComputerName $TargetSystem

   Get-Disk -CimSession $myCim
   ```

   When executed, the results will be displayed similar to the following screenshot:

   ```
   PS C:\> Get-Disk

   Number Friendly Name                              Operationa Total Size Partition
                                                     lStatus               Style
   ------ -------------                              ---------- ---------- ---------
   0      VMware, VMware Virtual S SCSI Disk De... Online          60 GB MBR
   1      VMware, VMware Virtual S SCSI Disk De... Online          60 GB MBR
   ```

2. Review the contents of the `Get-Disk` function.

   ```
   Get-Content Function:Get-Disk
   ```

   When executed, the contents of the function will be displayed as shown in the following screenshot:

   ```
   PS C:\> get-content function:get-disk

       [CmdletBinding(DefaultParameterSetName='ByNumber',
   PositionalBinding=$false)]
       [OutputType([Microsoft.Management.Infrastructure.CimInstance])]
   [OutputType('Microsoft.Management.Infrastructure.CimInstance#ROOT/Microsoft/Win
   dows/Storage/MSFT_Disk')]
   ```

3. Retrieve results using WMI.

   ```
   Get-WmiObject -Class MSFT_DISK `
   -Namespace ROOT\Microsoft\Windows\Storage
   ```

When executed, the results will be displayed similar to the following screenshot:

```
PS C:\> Get-WmiObject -Class MSFT_DISK -Namespace ROOT\Microsoft\Windows\Storage


__GENUS          : 2
__CLASS          : MSFT_Disk
__SUPERCLASS     :
__DYNASTY        : MSFT_Disk
__RELPATH        : MSFT_Disk.ObjectId="SCSI\\DISK&VEN_VMWARE_&PROD_VMWARE_VIR
                   TUAL_S\\5&22BE343F&0&000000"
__PROPERTY_COUNT : 31
```

How it works...

We start by gathering the disk information from the local system. First, we call `New-CimSession` to create a CIM connection to the target system, in this case we are connecting to the local system, so we can use "`.`" instead of a system name. Next, we call the in-built PowerShell function `Get-Disk` to return the disk information. By default, PowerShell only returns a subset of information; more can be returned by piping the output through a `Select-Object` statement and choosing which columns to return.

In the second step, we review the contents of the `Get-Disk` function to learn how it works. Because this command is a function, we can use `Get-Content` to view the contents of the function. This will return the full content of the script, but in this case we are only interested in the `OutputType`. In this line, we see that the function retrieves its content from WMI at the `ROOT\Microsoft\Windows\Storage\MSFT_Disk` namespace and class.

Finally, we query WMI directly using the namespace and class previously identified. To perform this we use `Get-WmiObject` to search WMI directly. We use the `-Namespace` switch to connect to the `ROOT\Microsoft\Windows\Storage` namespace. We use the `-Class` switch to return all objects in the `MSFT_Disk` class. This information is the same as previously returned, confirming the location is the same.

There's more...

In addition to the disk values shown here, there are several additional PowerShell commands and WMI locations to report hardware inventory. Only a few of these inventory types have been converted to in-built PowerShell functions, the remainder needs to be queried directly against WMI. Examples of additional counters are as follows:

- Logical disk

  `Get-Disk -CimSession $myCim`

- Physical disk

  `Get-PhysicalDisk -CimSession $myCim`

- Network adapters

  `Get-NetAdapter -CimSession $myCim`

- ▸ System enclosure

  ```
  Get-WmiObject -ComputerName $TargetSystem `
  -Class Win32_SystemEnclosure
  ```

- ▸ Computer system

  ```
  Get-WmiObject -ComputerName $TargetSystem `
  -Class Win32_ComputerSystemProduct
  ```

- ▸ Processor

  ```
  Get-WmiObject -ComputerName $TargetSystem -Class Win32_Processor
  ```

- ▸ Physical Memory

  ```
  Get-WmiObject -ComputerName $TargetSystem -Class Win32_
  PhysicalMemory
  ```

- ▸ CD-Rom

  ```
  Get-WmiObject -ComputerName $TargetSystem -Class Win32_CDromDrive
  ```

- ▸ Sound card

  ```
  Get-WmiObject -ComputerName $TargetSystem -Class Win32_SoundDevice
  ```

- ▸ Video card

  ```
  Get-WmiObject -ComputerName $TargetSystem `
  -Class Win32_VideoController
  ```

- ▸ BIOS

  ```
  Get-WmiObject -ComputerName $TargetSystem -Class Win32_BIOS
  ```

Inventorying the installed software

In addition to inventorying a system's hardware, it is often necessary to inventory the installed software. There are two primary methods to query the installed software: using the `Microsoft Installer`, and the `Uninstall` registry key. These two locations generally return the same information, however as we will see there are different uses for each.

How to do it...

Complete the following to review the installed software:

1. Get installed features.

   ```
   Get-WindowsFeature | Where-Object Install`State -EQ "Installed"
   ```

2. Return software inventory via MSI.

```
Get-WmiObject -Class Win32_Product
```

3. Open event viewer and review the system event logs. Note the multiple `Event ID 1035` messages as shown in the following screenshot:

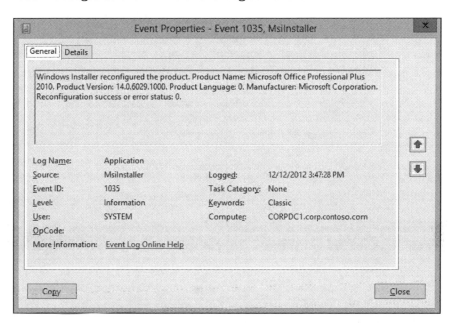

4. Return inventory via a registry.

```
$HKLM = 2147483650
(([wmiclass]"root\default:stdregprov").EnumKey($HKLM, `
"Software\Microsoft\Windows\CurrentVersion\Uninstall")).sNames
```

5. Return installed patches.

```
Get-WmiObject -Class Win32_QuickFixEngineering
```

How it works...

We start by using `Get-WindowsFeature` to list the features installed in our Windows 2012 Server. This command returns all of the installed features and roles on the current server. If you are unfamiliar with a system, this is a great method to know what Windows services include.

In the second step, we use WMI to query the `Win32_Product` class. This class interacts with the MSI packages on your system and returns a list of all packages currently installed. However, this command should be used with caution as it also causes the MSI packages to be reconfigured, or reset to their default configurations. If we open `Event Viewer` and review the `Application`, log on your system after executing this task, we will notice a large number of `Event ID 1035`.

In the fourth step, we use WMI to query the registry and return a list of applications. We start by defining the variable `$HKLM` and assigning the value `2147483650` which is used by WMI to reference the `HKey_Local_Machine` registry hive. We then query the results from the `Software\Microsoft\Windows\CurrentVersion\Uninstall` key. This returns information used by the `Programs` control panel icon. Often times this list will be different from the previous list because not all applications are installed as MSI packages, and because not all MSI packages appear in the `Programs` list.

Lastly, we return the installed hotfixes. Most Microsoft hotfixes add an entry to the `Win32_QuickFixEngineering` WMI namespace when they are installed. This provides a quick and simple method to identify which updates are installed on a system.

Inventory system configuration

When cataloging your environment, it is also important to inventory the system configuration. To fully document your environment, information such as the network configuration, local users, and service state is necessary. This information is useful when recreating your environment in a DR scenario, or simply for a Dev/Test environment.

In this recipe, we will be returning the configuration for a basic Windows Server.

Getting ready

For this recipe we will be using a Windows Server 2012 system.

How to do it...

Perform the following to gather the system information:

1. Retrieve the network configuration

   ```
   $TargetSystem="."
   $myCim = New-CimSession -ComputerName $TargetSystem
   Get-NetIPAddress -CimSession $myCim
   Get-NetRoute -CimSession $myCim
   ```

When executed, the network information will be displayed similar to the following

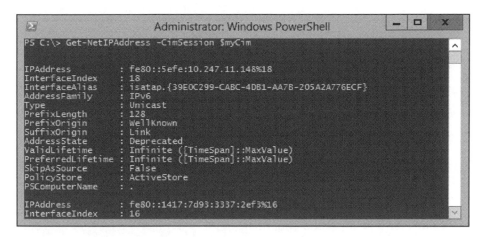

2. List the event logs.

```
Get-EventLog -List -ComputerName $TargetSystem
```

3. Display the local users and groups.

```
Get-WmiObject -ComputerName $TargetSystem `

-Query "Select * from Win32_Group where Domain='$TargetSystem'"

Get-WmiObject -ComputerName $TargetSystem `

-Query "Select * from Win32_UserAccount where
Domain='$TargetSystem'"
```

4. List the services.

```
Get-Service

Get-WmiObject -Class Win32_Service | `

Select-Object Name, Caption, StartMode, State
```

5. List the currently running processes.

```
Get-Process
```

6. Show the system's shares and printers.

```
Get-SmbShare

Get-Printer
```

7. Display the startup information.

```
Get-WmiObject -ComputerName $TargetSystem -Class Win32_
StartupCommand
```

8. Show the system time zone.

```
Get-WmiObject -ComputerName $TargetSystem -Class Win32_TimeZone
```

9. Display information about the registry.

```
Get-WmiObject -ComputerName $TargetSystem -Class Win32_Registry
```

How it works...

We start by retrieving the network configuration of the system. The first `Get-NetIPAddress` command returns the current IPv4 and IPv6 addresses assigned to the network adapters. The second `Get-NetRoute` command returns the current routing table, which helps define the network configuration around the system.

In the second step, we use `Get-EventLog` to retrieve information about the event logs. The `-List` switch returns information about the event logs, which logs exist on the system, the retention settings, and current sizes.

Next, we retrieve the local users and groups. To return this information we query WMI for the `Win32_UserAccount` and `Win32_Group` classes. We add a filter to our query to only return users and groups that belong to the local system. Without the filter, the query will return users and groups in the entire domain instead of the local system.

In the fourth step, we retrieve the status of the installed services. To return service information we can use the in-built Cmdlet `Get-Service` or query the `Win32_Service` WMI class. The WMI class provides more information for reporting, including the startup setting for the service; however, this method comes at the price of performance.

Next, in the fifth step, we return the currently running processes. On a workstation or a Dev/Test system, the process information will be very dynamic and possibly not very useful. However, on a stable system where the running processes don't change often, such as a mail server, this can help confirm changes to the running configuration of the system.

In the sixth step, we use `Get-SmbShare` and `Get-Printer` to return the shares and printers on the system. This information provides a quick snapshot of the file/print configuration that can be used for change tracking as well as security auditing.

In the seventh step, we use `Get-WmiObject` to return the contents of the `Win32_StartupCommand` WMI class. The startup commands are additional executables, in addition to services, that are executed at systems startup and when users log in.

Lastly, the `Win32_TimeZone` class returns the currently configured time zone for the system. The time zone can be useful when using scheduled tasks to execute commands at a certain time of day. And the `Win32_Registry` class returns the current and maximum sizes of the system.

There's more...

In addition to the basic configuration information shown here, additional applications can be included as well. Built-in features such as IIS and Active Directory can also be inventoried. Additional Microsoft and third-party applications such as Exchange or reporting applications can also be included.

Reporting on system security

In newer versions of Windows, Microsoft has added the Action Center. This area reports on key security and maintenance aspects of your system and quickly alerts Administrators to errors.

In Server 2012, there are five categories tracked in the Action Center:

- **Network Access Protection**: This controls network access in secure environments
    - Service name `napagent`

- **Smart Screen**: This controls how unknown applications are handled on the system
    - It is stored in `HKLM:\SOFTWARE\Microsoft\Windows\CurrentVersion\Explorer`

- **User Account Control**: This controls how elevated permissions are handled on the system
    - It is stored in `HKLM:\Software\Microsoft\Windows\CurrentVersion\Policies\System`

- **Windows Activation**: It activates Windows with Microsoft
    - It is Stored in the **WMI** `SoftwareLicensingProduct` key

- **Windows Update**: It provides patching and updates
    - It is stored in `HKLM:\SOFTWARE\Microsoft\Windows\CurrentVersion\WindowsUpdate\Auto Update`

In this recipe, we will be reporting on the security status of the system as viewed by the Action Center.

Getting ready

For this recipe we will be using a Windows Server 2012 system.

How to do it...

1. Retrieve the user's account control settings.

```
$secSettings = Get-ItemProperty -Path `
HKLM:\Software\Microsoft\Windows\CurrentVersion\Policies\System
```

2. Report on the UAC values.

```
IF($secSettings.PromptOnSecureDesktop -eq 1)
{
    IF($secSettings.ConsentPromptBehaviorAdmin -eq 2)
    {
        Write-Host "4: Always notify me"
    } Else {
        Write-Host "3: Notify me only when apps try to make
changes to my computer (default)"
    }
} Else {
    IF($secSettings.ConsentPromptBehaviorAdmin -eq 5)
    {
        Write-Host "2: Notify me only when apps try to make
changes to my computer (do not dim my desktop)"
    } Else {
        Write-Host "1: Never notify me"
    }
}
```

When executed, the results will be displayed similar to the following screenshot:

3. Retrieve the smart screen settings.

```
$ssSettings = Get-ItemProperty -Path `
HKLM:\SOFTWARE\Microsoft\Windows\CurrentVersion\Explorer
```

4. Return the smart screen value.

```
$ssSettings.SmartScreenEnabled
```

When executed, the results will be returned as shown in the following screenshot:

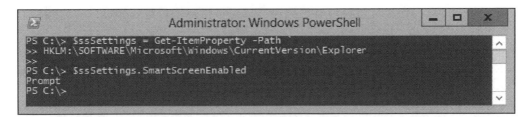

5. Retrieve the Network Access Protection settings.

```
Get-Service napagent
```

6. Retrieve the Windows Update settings.

```
$auValue = 0

$auLocSettings = Get-ItemProperty `
-Path "HKLM:\SOFTWARE\Microsoft\Windows\CurrentVersion\
WindowsUpdate\Auto Update"

$auGpoSettings = Get-ItemProperty `
-Path "HKLM:\SOFTWARE\Policies\Microsoft\Windows\WindowsUpdate\AU"

IF($auGpoSettings) {
    $auValue = $auGpoSettings.AUOptions
} Else {
    $auValue = $auLocSettings.AUOptions
}
```

7. Return the Windows update values.

```
IF($auValue -eq 4) {
    Write-Host "4: Install updates automatically (recommended)"
}

IF($auValue -eq 3) {
    Write-Host "3: Download updates but let me choose whether to
install them"
}
```

```
IF($auValue -eq 2) {
    Write-Host "2: Check for updates but let me choose whether to
download and install them"
}
IF($auValue -eq 1) {
    Write-Host "1: Never check for updates (not recommended)"
}
```

When completed, the results will be displayed similar to the following screenshot:

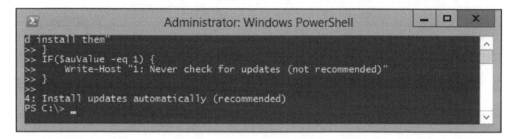

8. Retrieve the Windows activation status.

    ```
    $licResult = Get-WmiObject `
    -Query "Select * FROM SoftwareLicensingProduct WHERE LicenseStatus
    = 1"
    $licResult.Name
    ```

    When executed, the licensed products will be returned as shown in the following screenshot:

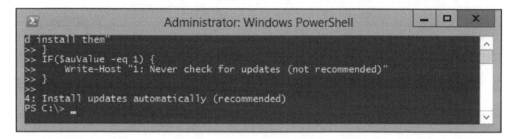

How it works...

We start by retrieving the values for **User Account Control**. These values are stored in two registry keys named PromptOnSecureDesktop and ConsentPromptBehaviorAdmin under the HKLM\Software\Microsoft\Windows\CurrentVersion\Policies\System key. These two keys work together to define the UAC slider visible in the control panel. The results are returned with the appropriate value and description.

We can review these settings by opening the **Action Center** on a Server 2012 system. In the **Action Center**, under **Security** and **User Account Control**, click on **Change settings** to view the current settings as shown in the following screenshot:

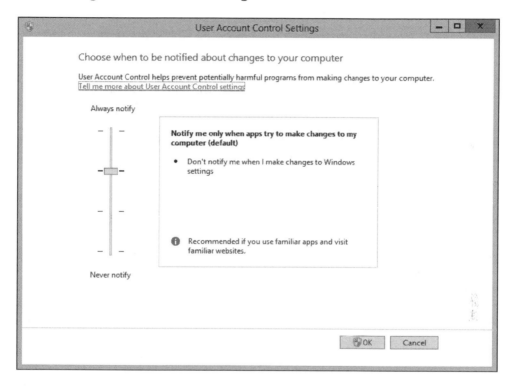

In the third and fourth steps, we retrieve the **SmartScreen** settings. This setting is stored in the registry value SmartScreenEnabled in the HKLM\Software\Microsoft\Windows\CurrentVersion\Explorer key. This value will be one of three values: Off, Prompt, or RequireAdmin.

We can also view these settings by opening the **Action Center**. In the **Action Center**, under **Security** and **Windows SmartScreen**, click on **Change settings** to see the screen shown as follows:

In the fifth step, we retrieve our **Network Access Protection** settings. The **Action Center** only reports on the state of the NAP client agent, so our script uses Get-Service to query the state of the napagent service.

Next, we retrieve our Windows update settings. These settings can be stored in two different registry locations depending on if the settings are configured locally (HKLM:\SOFTWARE\Microsoft\Windows\CurrentVersion\WindowsUpdate\Auto Update) or via a Group Policy (HKLM:\SOFTWARE\Policies\Microsoft\Windows\WindowsUpdate\AU). It is possible for both these locations to contain values, in which case the Group Policy setting takes precedence. The registry value AUOptions returns a number 1 to 4 detailing the current setting. The value is then returned to the PowerShell console.

Lastly, we retrieve the status of Windows activation. The Windows activation status is stored in WMI under the SoftwareLicensingProduct key. Here we query the key for any product with a LicenseStatus of 1 and it returns the name.

Creating a change report

With computers, the only thing that is consistent is change. A change can be as simple as installing a hotfix or as major as upgrading the operating system. Regardless of the cause or severity, tracking the changes made to your environment is often the key to resolving problems and retaining a secure and stable environment.

In this example, we will be reporting on changes to the network configuration of our system. This sample process can be expanded to include the installed hardware and software, system configuration, and security settings as well.

Getting ready

For this recipe, we will be using a Windows Server 2012 system.

How to do it...

Perform the following to create a change report:

1. Create a custom PSObject to store our configuration.

   ```
   $myComp=@{}
   ```

2. Collect the network information, and add it to the PSObject.

   ```
   $ipAddresses = Get-NetIPAddress | `
   Select-Object  InterfaceIndex, InterfaceAlias, IPAddress,
   PrefixLength
   $myComp.IPaddr = $ipAddresses
   ```

3. Save the PSObject to a file.

   ```
   Export-Clixml -InputObject $myComp -Path "c:\temp\myComp.clixml"
   ```

4. Change the network settings to simulate a configuration change.

5. Create a new PSObject to store our new configuration.

   ```
   $myComp=@{}
   ```

6. Collect the updated network information, and add to our PSObject.

   ```
   $myComp.IPaddr = Get-NetIPAddress | `
   Select-Object  InterfaceIndex, InterfaceAlias, IPAddress,
   PrefixLength
   ```

7. Load the original PSObject.

   ```
   $oldComp = Import-Clixml "c:\temp\myComp.clixml"
   ```

8. Export and import the new `PSObject` to ensure the objects are of the same type.

```
Export-Clixml -InputObject $myComp -Path "c:\temp\myComp.clixml"

$myComp = Import-Clixml "c:\temp\myComp.clixml"
```

9. Compare objects.

```
$keys = $myComp.GetEnumerator()

$keys | ForEach-Object {

Write-Host $_.Name

Compare-Object $oldComp.($_.Name) $myComp.($_.Name)}
```

How it works...

We start by creating an empty custom PowerShell object. There are multiple different methods to create custom PowerShell objects, however most methods require the object to be defined at the beginning. By simply creating an empty object we are provided with the flexibility to add attributes and variables as needed in the future.

In the second step, we query the local system for information. We use the `Get-NetIPAddress` command to query the local network adapters. We use `Select-Object` to filter the results for the information we are interested in and place the results in the variable `$ipAddresses`. Next, we extend our custom PowerShell object with a new attribute composed of our IP information.

In the third step, we save our custom PowerShell object to a file. The command `Export-CliXml` exports PowerShell objects and saves them to XML files. These files can then be retrieved at a later time and accessed as PowerShell objects. At this point, we can close our PowerShell session and reboot the computer. Because the custom object is saved to a file, the values will be consistent after a few minutes or a few years (assuming the file isn't deleted).

In the fourth step, we change the local network information. This step is optional and can be performed manually or via PowerShell. The purpose for this step is to create configuration changes to be reported later.

In the fifth and sixth steps, we repeat our first two steps to gather and catalog the new network information.

In the seventh step, we use `Import-CliXml` to read into PowerShell our previous custom object, this time into an object named `$oldComp`. At this point, we have two custom PowerShell objects in memory: `$oldComp` and `$myComp`.

Lastly, we compare our custom objects. The PowerShell command `Compare-Object` performs the comparison for us and returns a list of the information that has changed. Additionally, it returns both the old and new values for visual comparison.

There's more...

By using a custom PowerShell object, we can easily expand it to include additional information. In this case we can add additional attributes to the $myComp object and then automatically compare the current and old configurations. The change report can then be viewed for an individual system, stored in a central database, or scheduled, and e-mailed on a weekly basis.

Exporting a configuration report to Word

Once we have identified all of the information about a system, it can be helpful to create a system information report. This report can take many forms, however often the most generally accepted form is using Microsoft Word. Once created, the configuration can be e-mailed, stored electronically, or printed and stored physically with the system.

In this recipe, we will create the framework for a Microsoft Word inventory report. In this situation, we will only be reporting on the network configuration, however it can be easily expanded to include the hardware, software, configuration, and security information.

Getting ready

For this recipe, we will be using a Windows Server 2012 system with Microsoft Word installed.

How to do it...

Perform the following to create a configuration report in Word:

1. Create our Word object.

```
Function New-WordDoc
{
    $oWord = New-Object -Com Word.Application
    Set-Variable -Name oDoc -Value $oWord.Documents.Add() -Scope
Global
    $oWord.Visible = $true
    Return $oWord
}
$oWord = New-WordDoc
```

2. Insert a title.

```
Function Insert-WordTitle ($text)
{
    $objSelection = $oWord.Selection
    $objSelection.Style = "Title"
    $objSelection.TypeText($text)
    $oWord.Selection.EndKey(6) > $null
    $objSelection.TypeParagraph()
}
Insert-WordTitle  $env:COMPUTERNAME
```

3. Insert a table of contents.

```
Function Insert-TOC
{
    $objSelection = $oWord.Selection
    $range = $objSelection.Range
    $toc = $oDoc.TablesOfContents.Add($range)
    $oWord.Selection.EndKey(6) > $Null
    $objSelection.TypeParagraph()
}
Insert-TOC
```

4. Insert headers.

```
Function Insert-WordH1 ($text)
{
    $objSelection = $oWord.Selection
    $objSelection.Style = "Heading 1"
    $objSelection.TypeText($text)
    $oWord.Selection.EndKey(6) > $null
    $objSelection.TypeParagraph()
}
Function Insert-WordH2 ($text)
{
    $objSelection = $oWord.Selection
    $objSelection.Style = "Heading 2"
    $objSelection.TypeText($text)
    $oWord.Selection.EndKey(6) > $null
    $objSelection.TypeParagraph()
}
Insert-WordH1 "Network Information"
Insert-WordH2 "IP Addresses"
```

5. Collect the inventory data.

```
$myComp=@{}
$IPAddresses = Get-NetIPAddress | `
Select-Object InterfaceIndex, InterfaceAlias, IPAddress,
PrefixLength
$myComp.IPaddr = $IPAddresses
```

6. Insert a table to hold the information.

```
Function Insert-WordTable ([System.Array]$text){
    $headers = $text | Get-Member -MemberType NoteProperty | `
    Select-Object Name

    $numCols = $headers.count
    $numRows = $text.count
    IF($numCols -gt 0){
        $oTable = $oDoc.Tables.Add($oWord.Application.Selection.
Range, $numRows + 1, $numCols)
        $oTable.Style = "Light Shading - Accent 1"
        $oTable.Columns.AutoFit()

        $i=1
        $headers | `
        ForEach-Object{
            $oTable.cell(1,$i).Range.Text = $_.Name; $i++;
        }

        For($row=2; $row -lt $numRows+2; $row++){
            For($col=1; $col -lt $numCols+1; $col++){
                $oTable.Cell($row,$col).Range.Text=$text[$row-2].
($headers[$col-1].Name)
            }
        }
        $oWord.Selection.EndKey(6) > $Null
    }
}
Insert-WordTable $myComp.IPaddr
```

7. Update the table of contents.

```
$oDoc.Fields | ForEach-Object{ $_.Update() }
```

How it works...

We start by creating our Microsoft Word object. To start, we create a reference to the COM object `Word.Application`. Next, we use `Set-Variable` to add a new document to our Word object. Here we specify the object to be global so that it can be referenced by other functions within our script. Next, set `$oWord.Visible` to `$true` so that our Word object is visible and then return a reference to the object.

 We didn't need to make the Word object visible at this step. Instead we could have kept it hidden and automatically save the file when finished.

In the second step, we set up our document. We identify the computer name by calling `$env:COMPUTERNAME` and pass it to our function which adds the computer name as the title of the document. This function begins at the cursor's current location and configures it to use the `Title` font style. The document title is added and finally a carriage return is sent to close out the paragraph.

Next, we create a function `Insert-TOC` to insert a table of contents. At this point the TOC will be empty, but it is put in place so that it can be updated later. The function starts at the cursor's current location and creates a `Range` to place Word fields and reference objects. The empty TOC is added and the range is closed by sending a carriage return.

In the fourth step, we begin with our Headers. Here, we are using the in-built styles `Heading 1` and `Heading 2` to signify our sections. These functions operate the same as our `Title` function, except the style name is changed. The headers styles provide the necessary fonts to segment the different sections, as well as markers for the table of contents to include later. We add two headers: `Network Information` as `Heading 1` to show general network information, and `IP Addresses` as `Heading 2` to show specific IP information.

In the fifth step, we collect our networking information. We start by creating an empty custom PowerShell object named `$myComp`. We then use the `Get-NetIPAddress` function to query the system for the local IP addresses. We filter the results for the attributes we are interested in and place the results in a variable. Lastly, we add our results into a new attribute of our PowerShell object.

In the sixth step, we write our values to Word using the `Insert-WordTable` function. The function starts by identifying the column header names. The number of rows and columns are identified and a new table is added to the document. First the column headers are written, and then each row/column combination is iterated through, with values from the array placed in the boxes. Lastly, the table is exited.

Lastly, we cycle through all of the fields in the document and execute the `Update` command. This command updates the table of contents to include all of the `Heading 1` and `Heading 2` objects in the document.

At this point, the document can be reviewed, printed, or saved for later review. An example report is shown in the following screenshot:

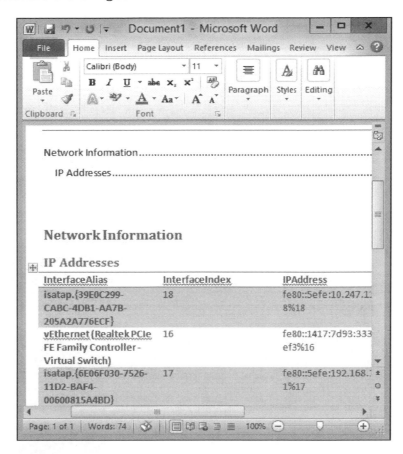

See also

For more information on using PowerShell to create Word documents, see the following links:

- http://blogs.technet.com/b/heyscriptingguy/archive/2008/11/11/
  how-can-i-create-a-microsoft-word-document-from-wmi-
  information.aspx
- http://blogs.technet.com/b/heyscriptingguy/archive/2012/06/13/
  use-powershell-to-create-a-word-table-that-shows-fonts.aspx

12

Server Backup

This chapter covers the following recipes:

- ▶ Configuring backup policies
- ▶ Initiating backups manually
- ▶ Restoring files
- ▶ Restoring Windows system state
- ▶ Restoring application data
- ▶ Creating a daily backup report

Introduction

Windows Server 2012 provides a powerful and flexible backup toolset. The backup can be configured to protect the full server, specific volumes, folders or files, and the system state. Once backups are completed, we can recover files, volumes, applications, or even the entire server.

This chapter covers setting up and scheduling backups on a Windows server. This will include on-demand backups, restoring files and Windows components, and standardizing the configuration among systems.

Configuring backup policies

A backup policy defines what is backed up in a system and when is it backed up. Instead of defining what you want to back-up every time you execute the backup process, the policy allows an Administrator to define what is being retained, and the process happens automatically.

There are normally two primary goals for creating system backups: operational recovery and disaster recovery. Operational recovery is used to recover individual files, folders, or programs in case of accidental deletion or recover of an older version. Disaster recovery (DR) is used to recover an entire system in case of loss of the system. For DR purposes, it is generally suggested to backup the entire system, and use exclusions to keep from backing up certain files.

Windows Server Backup provides capabilities for both types of backups and restores. In this recipe, we will perform a DR-level backup of our system that allows for recovery of the entire system as well as individual components.

Getting ready

For this recipe, we will be working with a newly installed Windows Server 2012 system with two hard disks: `C:\` and `E:\`. We will configure the backup policy to protect the `C:\` drive system state, allow for bare metal recovery, and store the backup files on the `E:\` drive.

How to do it...

Carry out the following steps in order to configure a backup policy:

1. Install Windows Server Backup feature using the following command:

   ```
   Add-WindowsFeature Windows-Server-Backup -IncludeManagementTools
   ```

2. Create a backup policy:

   ```
   $myPol = New-WBPolicy
   ```

3. Add the backup sources.

   ```
   $myPol | Add-WBBareMetalRecovery
   $myPol | Add-WBSystemState
   $sourceVol = Get-WBVolume C:
   Add-WBVolume -Policy $myPol -Volume $sourceVol
   ```

   When executed, the results will be returned to the screen, as shown in the following screenshot:

```
PS C:\> Add-WBVolume -Policy $myPol -Volume $sourceVol


VolumeLabel :
MountPath   : C:
MountPoint  : \\?\Volume{067e56dd-566b-11e2-93ef-806e6f6e6963}
FileSystem  : NTFS
Property    : Critical, ValidSource, IsOnDiskWithCriticalVolume
FreeSpace   : 32745406464
TotalSpace  : 42947575808


PS C:\>
```

4. Define the backup target.

```
$targetVol = New-WBBackupTarget -Volume (Get-WBVolume E:)
Add-WBBackupTarget -Policy $myPol -Target $targetVol
```

When executed, confirmation of the target will be returned, as shown in the following screenshot:

5. Define the schedule.

```
Set-WBSchedule -Policy $myPol -Schedule ("12/17/2012 9:00:00 PM")
```

6. Save the policy.

```
Set-WBPolicy -Policy $myPol
```

How it works...

We start by calling `Add-WindowsFeature` to install the `Windows Server Backup` feature. This feature is not included in the default Windows Server configuration and needs to be installed as an additional component, or added in an answer file when the server is installed. The installation of this component does not require a reboot, and can be done without interrupting the normal service of the server.

In the second step, we create and configure our backup policy. We start by calling `New-WBPolicy` to create a blank backup policy and assign it to the variable `$myPol`.

Next, in steps 3 and 4, we add our backup sources. In this instance, we are adding three backup sources:

- ▶ `Add-WBBareMetalRecovery`: This allows for recovery of the system in case of a total system failure. This feature allows you to restore the system to dissimilar hardware or into a virtual environment.

- ▶ `Add-WBSystemState`: This feature backs up the registry, user database, and other system components.

- ▶ `Add-WBBackupTarget`: This feature backs up all files on the `C:\` drive.

In step 5, we define the backup schedule. Here we use `Set-WBSchedule` to define the schedule to back up the system once per day at 9 P.M., starting on December 17th. If desired, multiple schedules can be defined with this command.

Lastly, we use `Set-WBPolicy` to save the policy to the server.

 There can only be one backup policy for a server. If additional policies are created, they overwrite the existing policy.

There's more...

By default, Windows Server Backup includes several files and locations to be excluded during backup. The default set contains information normally not needed for a restore (such as the page file, memory dumps, temporary files, and downloaded but not installed updates). A full list of excluded files and directories can be found at `HKEY_LOCAL_MACHINE\SYSTEM\CurrentControlSet\Control\BackupRestore\FilesNotToBackup`.

Additional exceptions can be added to this list in the form of `[Drive] [Path]\FileName [/s]`.

See also

> ▸ For more information about the PowerShell Cmdlets for Windows Backup, see `http://technet.microsoft.com/en-us/library/jj902428.aspx`

Initiating backups manually

Once a backup policy is defined, the backups will occur automatically according the defined schedule. However, there are occasions when an on-demand or one-off backup is necessary—for instance before performing system maintenance or installing new software.

In this recipe, we will show how to perform an on-demand backup using the existing backup policy outside of the predefined schedule. Additionally, we will create a one-off backup policy to back-up the files and folders in `C:\InetPub` and store them on the `E:\` drive.

Getting ready

For this recipe, we will be using a system configured for backups similar to the previous recipe *Configuring backup policies*.

How to do it...

1. Initiate the default backup policy.

   ```
   Get-WBPolicy | Start-WBBackup
   ```

2. Monitor the backup using `Get-WBSummary` command:

   ```
   Get-WBSummay
   ```

   When executed, the status is displayed, as shown in the following screenshot:

   ```
   PS C:\> Get-WBSummary

   NextBackupTime                : 12/19/2012 8:00:00 PM
   NumberOfVersions              : 5
   LastSuccessfulBackupTime      : 12/19/2012 12:01:44 PM
   LastSuccessfulBackupTargetPath  : \\?\Volume{ec1948a9-29ad-4a99-814(
   LastSuccessfulBackupTargetLabel : Server2 2012_12_18 14:48 DISK_02
   LastBackupTime                : 12/19/2012 12:04:20 PM
   LastBackupTarget              : E:
   DetailedMessage               :
   LastBackupResultHR            : 2155348327
   LastBackupResultDetailedHR    : 0
   CurrentOperationStatus        : BackupInProgress
   ```

3. Perform a one-off backup of `C:\InetPub` using the following command:

   ```
   $myPol = New-WBPolicy

   $mySpec = New-WBFileSpec -FileSpec "C:\InetPub"

   Add-WBFileSpec -Policy $myPol -FileSpec $mySpec

   $targetVol = New-WBBackupTarget -Volume (Get-WBVolume E:)

   Add-WBBackupTarget -Policy $myPol -Target $targetVol

   Start-WBBackup -Policy $myPol
   ```

   When executed, the backup will begin, as shown in the following screenshot:

   ```
   Administrator: Windows PowerShell                             _ □ X

   PS C:\> Start-WBBackup -Policy $myPol
   WARNING: If you are creating a backup of volumes hosting virtual hard disk
   (VHD) files, the VHD files will be automatically excluded from the backup if
   they are mounted at the time the backup is created. To back up the contents of
   the VHD files, either back up the virtual volumes separately or dismount the
   VHD files before every backup operation.
   Initializing the list of items to be backed up...
   Creating a shadow copy of the volumes in the backup...
   Updating the backup for deleted items...
   Updating the backup for deleted items...
   Updating the backup for deleted items...
   Updating the backup for deleted items...
   Updating the backup for deleted items...
   Updating the backup for deleted items...
   ```

How it works...

We start by calling `Get-WBPolicy` to query the system for the current backup policy. We then pipe the current backup policy into the `Start-WBBackup` command to initiate an on-demand backup. This uses the predefined backup policies and simply starts the backup outside of the normal backup schedule.

In the second step, we use `Get-WBSummary` to view the status of the active backup. The main item of interest at this point is the `CurrentOperationStatus`, which reports that the backup is in progress.

In the third step, we perform a one-off backup of the `C:\InetPub` folder. This is useful when making changes to a specific application or folder structure and you wish to back-up the effected files before making changes. This process is similar to configuring the system backup policy; however, instead of backing up the entire system or volume, we are backing up only a single folder. Additionally, in this case, we do not save our policy; instead, we call `Start-WBBackup` to start our temporary policy immediately.

There's more...

In addition to using `Get-WBSummary` to view the backup status, you can also review the backup logs at `C:\Windows\Logs\WindowsServerBackup`. Each activity creates two log files in this directory: one for successes and one for failures. These files can be viewed in a text editor or can be parsed using PowerShell to identify the status of the backup environment.

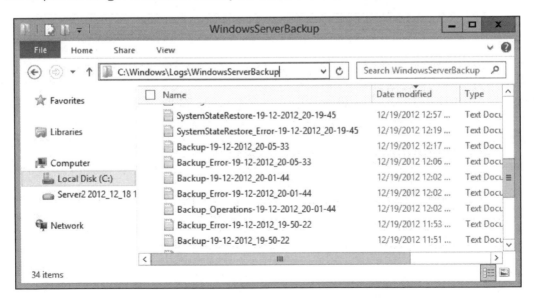

Restoring files

Once backed up, individual files or folders can be recovered as part of an operation recovery. If a file is deleted or overwritten, it can be restored from a prior backup to recover a file or roll back changes to an earlier version of a file.

In this recipe, we will perform recoveries of individual files and folders.

Getting ready

For this recipe, we will be using a server configured for backups similar to the *Configuring backup policies* recipe that has successfully completed at least one backup.

How to do it...

1. Identify the backup set.

   ```
   Get-WBBackupSet
   ```

   When executed, the available backup sets will be displayed, as shown in the following screenshot:

   ```
   $myBackup = Get-WBBackupSet | `
   Where-Object VersionId -eq 03/03/2013-19:31
   ```

2. Perform a single file recovery.

```
Start-WBFileRecovery -BackupSet $myBackup `
-SourcePath c:\temp\perfcounter.csv
```

3. Recover a folder.

```
Start-WBFileRecovery -BackupSet $myBackup `
-SourcePath c:\inetpub\ -Recursive -TargetPath c:\
```

When executed, the recovery process will begin, as shown in the following screenshot:

How it works...

We start by identifying the backup set from which we want to restore the files. First, we execute Get-WBBackupSet to list all available backups on the computer. Next, we filter based on the VersionId of the backups and place a reference to the source backup into the $myBackup variable.

Next, we perform a single file recovery. This recovery identifies a single file in the backup set and restores it to the original file location.

Next, we perform a folder recovery. In this case, we include the −Recursive switch, which instructs the backup to restore the folder and all of its subfolders from the backup source. Additionally, we use the −TargetPath switch to define where the restored files should be placed. In the case of a folder recovery, the target should be the parent folder. In case of a redirected restore, or a restore to a different location, the target will be the destination for the recovered files.

There's more...

Windows Backup can restore files using various methods. To define the restoration type, add the –Option switch with one of the following settings:

- ▸ SkipIfExists: This setting will only restore files that have been moved or deleted
- ▸ CreateCopyIfExists: This is a default setting. If the file exists, this setting will rename the restored file
- ▸ OverwriteIfExists: If the file exists, this setting will overwrite it with the restored file

Restoring Windows system state

The Windows system state contains the components necessary to recover the individual system without data or applications. Server access, file shares, Active Directory, Certificate Services, Clustering, Registry, DHCP, and IIS are a few components that are included in the system state backup. When recovering an entire server for DR or testing, the system state is a key component to the recovery process.

Getting ready

For this recipe, we will be using a server configured for backups, similar to the *Configuring backup policies* recipe, and that has successfully completed at least one system state backup.

How to do it...

1. Identify the backup set.

    ```
    Get-WBBackupSet
    $myBackup = Get-WBBackupSet | `
    Where-Object VersionId -eq 03/03/2013-19:31
    ```

2. Initiate the system state restore.

    ```
    Start-WBSystemStateRecovery -BackupSet $myBackup
    ```

When executed, the system state will restore as follows:

```
PS C:\> Start-WBSystemStateRecovery -BackupSet $myBackup

Warning
Start system state recovery to original location ?
[Y] Yes  [N] No  [S] Suspend  [?] Help (default is "Y"): y
Initializing.
System state recovery failed to complete.
WARNING: A computer restart is required to complete the system state recovery
operation.

Warning
Restart the computer?
[Y] Yes  [N] No  [S] Suspend  [?] Help (default is "Y"):
```

3. Select Y to reboot the system.

How it works...

We start by identifying the backup set that we want to restore from. First, we execute Get-WBBackupSet to list all available backups on the computer. Next, we filter based on the VersionId of the backups and place a reference to the source backup into the $myBackup variable.

Next, we use Start-WBSystemStateRecovery to initiate the restoration process. This process will restore the registry and files associated with the system state, and overwrite the current configuration. When finished, if the system does not automatically reboot, restart the system.

There's more...

This same process is used to perform an Active Directory (AD) restore on a domain controller. To perform an AD restore, the system needs to first be rebooted into the Directory Services Restore mode. Then, the above process can be followed with the -AuthoritativeSysvolRecovery switch included.

Restoring application data

Many applications register with the Windows Backup service. These applications can then be backed up and restored independently of the rest of the system. Active Directory, Registry, and Hyper-V are examples of some of the in-built services that support this feature. Additional applications by Microsoft and third-party vendors can also utilize this feature.

Depending on the applications installed when backups occur, different applications will be available for restore. In this recipe, we will restore the system's Registry.

Getting ready

For this recipe, we will be using a system configured similar to the first recipe, *Configuring backup policies,* and that has had at least one full system backup.

How to do it...

1. Identify the backup set.

    ```
    Get-WBBackupSet
    $myBackup = Get-WBBackupSet | `
    Where-Object VersionId -eq 03/03/2013-19:31
    ```

2. Determine the application.

    ```
    $myApp = $myBackup.Application | `
    Where-Object Identifier -eq Registry
    ```

3. Start the recovery.

    ```
    Start-WBApplicationRecovery -BackupSet $myBackup `
    -ApplicationInBackup $myApp
    ```

How it works...

We start by identifying the backup set that we want to restore from. First, we execute `Get-WBBackupSet` to list all available backups on the computer. Next, we filter based on the `VersionId` of the backups and place a reference to the source backup into the `$myBackup` variable. Note, here, the applications available in the backup are for restore.

Next, we search our backup object and list the available applications. In this case, we are filtering based on the `Registry` application. We then place a reference to the application into the `$myApp` variable.

Lastly, we start the application recovery. Depending on the application being restored, the application may need to be stopped for the restore, or the system may need to be rebooted.

There's more...

Multiple applications register with Windows Server Backup automatically. On a newly installed system, only the Registry will be available for recovery as an application, but additional Windows features can register additional applications. Additional features include, Active Directory, Hyper-V, and so on.

Creating a daily backup report

When performing backups of a system, one of the most critical components is reporting on the success or failure of the backups. With backup reports, you can prove that the backups are performing properly, resolve problems, identify recurring issues, and determine if the sizing and performance is sufficient for your environment.

In this recipe, we will create a basic backup report that will be sent to an Administrator every day. The report will capture the basic success and failure status for backups of a server.

Getting ready

For this recipe, we will be using a system configured similar to the first recipe, *Configuring backup policies*.

How to do it...

1. Define the report.

   ```
   $now = Get-Date
   $startTime = $now.AddDays(-2)
   $myReport = "Backup Report for $Env:COMPUTERNAME on $now`n"
   ```

2. Query the backup sets.

   ```
   $myReport += "`tBackup Sets"
   $myReport += Get-WBBackupSet | `
   Where-Object BackupTime -gt $startTime | Out-String
   Get-WBBackupSet | where BackupTime -gt $startTime | Out-String
   ```

3. Create an array of interesting alert IDs.

   ```
   $myReport += "`tEvent Log Messages"
   $myArray = 1, 4, 5, 8, 9, 14, 17, 18, 19, 20, 21, 22, 49, 50, 52,
   100, 224, 227, 517, 518, 521, 527, 528, 544, 545, 546, 561, 564,
   612
   ```

4. Search the Windows event logs for events.

   ```
   $myReport += Get-WinEvent -LogName "Microsoft-Windows-Backup" | `
   Where-Object {$_.TimeCreated -ge $startTime} | `
   Where-Object {$myArray -contains $_.ID} | `
   Format-Table TimeCreated, LevelDisplayName, ID, Message | Out-
   String
   ```

5. Search the backup logs for errors.

```
$myReport += "`tWBS error logs"
$myLogs = Get-ChildItem C:\Windows\Logs\WindowsServerBackup\
*.log | `
Where-Object LastWriteTime -gt $startTime
$myReport += $myLogs | Select-String "^Error" | Out-String
```

6. Send the e-mail.

```
Send-MailMessage -From BackupAdmin@contoso.com `
-To Admin@contoso.com -SmtpServer mail.corp.contoso.com `
-Body $myReport `
-Subject "Backup Report for $Env:COMPUTERNAME on $now"
```

7. Save and schedule the script using the task scheduler.

```
# Define the action to be executed
$taskAction = New-ScheduledTaskAction -Execute `
"%SystemRoot%\system32\WindowsPowerShell\v1.0\powershell.exe" `
-Argument "C:\scripts\dailyBackup.ps1"


# Define the execution schedule
$taskTrigger = New-ScheduledTaskTrigger -Daily -At 5am


# Define the user account to execute the script
$taskUser = "Corp\ScriptAdmin"
$taskPassword = 'P@$$w0rd'


# Name the task and register
$taskName = "Daily Backup Report"
Register-ScheduledTask -TaskName $taskName -Action $taskAction `
-Trigger $taskTrigger -User $taskUser -Password $taskPassword
```

How it works...

We start by determining that we are looking for information on backups from the last two days and placing the date and time into the variable `$startTime`. Next, we create a `$myReport` variable that will hold the contents of the report. We begin the report with information about the system and the report time.

In the second step, we list the available backup sets during our report window. We call `Get-WBBackupSet` and filter based on the `BackupTime` attribute to only return backups from the last two days. We then pipe the contents through `Out-String` to convert the `BackupSet` object to text, and then append this information to `$myReport`.

Next, we create an array of alert IDs. These are alert IDs that most frequently report on the success or failure of the backup and restore processes. These alert IDs include backups starting, backups ending, restores, and common errors that occur during backups and restores.

In the fourth step, we query the `Microsoft-Windows-Backup` event log. The log is filtered based on the date of the alert and on the event IDs in our array.

In the fifth step, we search the backup log files for errors. We start by getting a list of all of the log files in `C:\Windows\Logs\WindowsServerBackup` that have been updated in the last two days. Next, we pipe each log through `Select-String` to search for the word `Error` at the beginning of a line in the log files. The returned information is then included in our e-mail text.

In the sixth step, we e-mail our report using `Send-MailMessage`. Once we confirm the script is working properly, we can save it as a file and schedule it using Windows Task Scheduler.

Index

production network, Hyper-V 136
PSDrive 99
public key 104

R

Redundant Array of Independent Disks
    (RAID) 186
Remote Installation Services (RIS) 182
RemoteSigned execution policy 10
Remove-Job 45
RemovePrinterConnection method 268
restricted execution policy 10

S

SDDL
    about 264
    URL 265
security
    managing, on PowerShell scripts 8, 9
Security Definition Description Language. *See*
    SDDL
server
    testing 277-280
server backup
    about 335
    application data, restoring 344, 345
    backup policies, configuring 335-337
    backups, initiating manually 338-340
    daily backup report, creating 346, 348
    files, restoring 341, 342
    Windows system states, restoring 343, 344
Server Message Block (SMB) 196
Server Name Indicators (SNI) 109
server performance report
    creating 309, 310
sessions
    recording, with transcripts 32
SetAccessRuleProtection command 178
SetDefaultPrinter method 268
Set-DhcpServerv4OptionValue command 76
settings, $ErrorActionPreferece variable
    continue 49
    inquire 49
    SilentlyContinue 49
    stop 48

Set-WebBinding 108
Smart Screen 321
soft quotas 190
sorting 38
SSL encryption
    IIS, configuring for 100
Standalone root CA 82
Standalone subordinate CA 82
StartSynchronizationForCategoryOnly()
    method 229
static networking
    configuring 60-63
storage pools
    about 186
    configuring 186-188
    reporting 188, 189
superuser report
    creating 92, 93
    e-mailing 93, 94
SysPrep
    URL 150
system configuration
    inventorying 318
system security
    Network Access Protection 321
    reporting 321-326
    Smart Screen 321
    User Account Control 321
    Windows Activation 321
    Windows Update 321

T

TCP/IP 60
TCP/IP Offload Engine (TOE) 204
Test-Connection command 278
Test-PhoneNumber function 28
three-tier website
    configuring 120, 121
    content, promoting 121-123
troubleshooting packs
    using 280, 281
troubleshooting servers
    Best Practices Analyzer, using 282, 284
    event logs, forwarding to central log server
        288-294

Thank you for buying
Windows Server 2012 Automation with PowerShell Cookbook

About Packt Publishing

Packt, pronounced 'packed', published its first book "*Mastering phpMyAdmin for Effective MySQL Management*" in April 2004 and subsequently continued to specialize in publishing highly focused books on specific technologies and solutions.

Our books and publications share the experiences of your fellow IT professionals in adapting and customizing today's systems, applications, and frameworks. Our solution-based books give you the knowledge and power to customize the software and technologies you're using to get the job done. Packt books are more specific and less general than the IT books you have seen in the past. Our unique business model allows us to bring you more focused information, giving you more of what you need to know, and less of what you don't.

Packt is a modern, yet unique publishing company, which focuses on producing quality, cutting-edge books for communities of developers, administrators, and newbies alike. For more information, please visit our website: www.PacktPub.com.

About Packt Enterprise

In 2010, Packt launched two new brands, Packt Enterprise and Packt Open Source, in order to continue its focus on specialization. This book is part of the Packt Enterprise brand, home to books published on enterprise software – software created by major vendors, including (but not limited to) IBM, Microsoft and Oracle, often for use in other corporations. Its titles will offer information relevant to a range of users of this software, including administrators, developers, architects, and end users.

Writing for Packt

We welcome all inquiries from people who are interested in authoring. Book proposals should be sent to author@packtpub.com. If your book idea is still at an early stage and you would like to discuss it first before writing a formal book proposal, contact us; one of our commissioning editors will get in touch with you.

We're not just looking for published authors; if you have strong technical skills but no writing experience, our experienced editors can help you develop a writing career, or simply get some additional reward for your expertise.

**Microsoft Windows
PowerShell 3.0 First Look**

Microsoft Windows PowerShell 3.0 First Look

ISBN: 978-1-849686-44-0   Paperback: 200 pages

A quick succinct guide to the new and exciting features in PowerShell 3.0

1. Explore and experience the new features found in PowerShell 3.0

2. Understand the changes to the language and the reasons why they were implemented

3. Discover new cmdlets and modules available in Windows 8 and Server 8

**Windows Server 2012
Hyper-V Cookbook**

Windows Server 2012 Hyper-V Cookbook

ISBN: 978-1-849684-42-2   Paperback: 304 pages

Over 50 simple but incredibly effective recipes for mastering the administration of Windows Server Hyper-V

1. Take advantage of numerous Hyper-V best practices for administrators

2. Get to grips with migrating virtual machines between servers and old Hyper-V versions, automating tasks with PowerShell, providing a High Availability and Disaster Recovery environment, and much more

3. A practical Cookbook bursting with essential recipes

Please check **www.PacktPub.com** for information on our titles

[PACKT] enterprise
PUBLISHING professional expertise distilled

**SQL Server 2012 with
PowerShell V3 Cookbook**

Increase your productivity as a DBA, developer, or IT Pro,
by using PowerShell with SQL Server to simplify database
management and automate repetitive, mundane tasks

Donabel Santos [PACKT] enterprise

SQL Server 2012 with
PowerShell V3 Cookbook

ISBN: 978-1-849686-46-4   Paperback: 634 pages

Increase your productivity as a DBA, developer, or IT
Pro, by using PowerShell with SQL Server to simplify
database management and automate repetitive,
mundane tasks

1. Provides over a hundred practical recipes that
   utilize PowerShell to automate, integrate and
   simplify SQL Server tasks

2. Offers easy to follow, step-by-step guide to getting
   the most out of SQL Server and PowerShell

3. Covers numerous guidelines, tips, and
   explanations on how and when to use PowerShell
   cmdlets, WMI, SMO, .NET classes or other
   components

enterprise
professional expertise distilled

**Oracle Database and
PowerShell How-To**

Utilize the power of Microsoft's powerful scripting engine to
automate database tasks with Oracle from PowerShell.

Geoffrey Hudik [PACKT]

Instant Oracle Database and
PowerShell How-to [Instant]

ISBN: 978-1-849688-58-1   Paperback: 80 pages

Utilize the power of Microsoft's powerful scripting engine
to automate database tasks with Orcale from PowerShell

1. Learn something new in an Instant! A short, fast,
   focused guide delivering immediate results.

2. Load Oracle Data Access components and
   connect to Oracle databases

3. Retrieve, format, filter, and export data

4. Execute database procedures and modify
   database objects

Please check **www.PacktPub.com** for information on our titles

Made in the USA
San Bernardino, CA
14 February 2017